SURVEY OF
UNITED STATES
INTERNATIONAL FINANCE
1949

PREPARED BY GARDNER PATTERSON

DIRECTOR, INTERNATIONAL FINANCE SECTION

T0314123

PRINCETON UNIVERSITY PRESS

PREFACE

THIS document is an experiment. It is hoped it will prove of value, both as a source of reasonably current information and as a reference, not only to students but also to persons in the United States and abroad who are more immediately involved in or affected by some aspects of the international financial affairs of the United States. Preparation of surveys for future years will depend upon whether these hopes prove justified.

The purpose of this survey is to bring together in summary form the more important information on the policies and activities of the United States in the general area of international finance during 1949. It attempts only to be orderly, accurate, and discriminating reporting. Except for the concluding chapter and an occasional footnote, no judgments or assessments of the policies or affairs have been included. Since it is almost entirely an historical record, a source could have been given for nearly every statement but such documentation was considered unnecessary, and in general only those sources have been cited which have been drawn upon very extensively.

This is a survey and no subject is treated exhaustively. No attempt has been made to build up a complete bibliography; however, an effort has been made to cite at the appropriate places certain selected sources, especially official documents, which it is hoped will at least provide useful leads to further study for those who may wish more detailed information and analysis on the various subjects treated.

In many places it has been necessary to state that "data are not available," by which is meant either that at the time of writing the data have not been collected or are not yet in the public domain, or that in the time permitted for preparing this survey they have not been located.

In general this document covers only the calendar year 1949, but an effort has been made to provide a minimum of background information on the various subjects treated. In some instances developments during 1950 which were particularly significant in the sense of qualifying or completing actions taken in 1949 have been covered, but usually only in a very summary fashion; it is planned to treat them more carefully and completely in the following survey, if such a survey proves worthwhile. In a few special cases information which became available after going to press and which appears importantly to qualify material in the text has been inserted in brief form in brackets.

A word of warning should be added regarding the statistical data in this survey. Most statistics on international financial transactions are estimates and so are not only subject to considerable error but are frequently revised. It has been the practice in preparing the present study to include the latest estimates available at the time of correcting the galley proofs. Nonetheless, there will be further revisions of many of the statistics. Readers who have need for later estimates are therefore advised to consult the current numbers of the various periodicals cited as sources, especially the issues of the *Survey of Current Business* after May 1950, and of the quarterly *Foreign Transactions of the U.S. Government* dated after March 1950. It is planned that any future issues of this survey will append revised data which have become available in the meantime.

In addition to the cooperation of members of the Department of Economics and Social Institutions of Princeton University considerable assistance has been given by Miss Laura S. Turnbull, Curator of the Benjamin Strong Collection of International Finance, and Miss Dorothea Collins, Librarian of the Pliny Fisk Library of Economics and Finance, of the Princeton University Library. Several persons outside the University have been kind enough to check certain parts of the study for accuracy.

Mr. Jack N. Behrman and Mrs. Mary B. Fernholz have rendered extensive help but responsibility for presentation and accuracy is borne by the undersigned.

GARDNER PATTERSON, *Director*
INTERNATIONAL FINANCE SECTION

Princeton University
May 1950

CONTENTS

LIST OF TABLES

LIST OF TABLES

INTRODUCTION

THE United States has reached primacy in the international economic and financial affairs of the world. The unprecedented distortion and disruption in the world economy, the fundamental causes and appropriate remedies of which are subjects of much dispute, have been clearly reflected in this country's policies and activities since the recent war. The broad dimensions of the post-war disequilibrium in world trade and finance, as they affect and are affected by the United States, were recorded in its current account surpluses of $7.8 billion in 1946, $11.3 billion in 1947 and $6.3 billion in 1948. These huge export surpluses in part reflected the higher prices after the war, but they were primarily the result of a more than two-fold expansion in the *volume* of our merchandise exports over 1936–38, whereas the *volume* of merchandise imports of the United States in the first three years after the war was only slightly greater than in the pre-war period and smaller in relation to our national income. An important contribution to the export surplus also was the large net income on investments (and to a lesser extent transportation) received by the United States, reflecting our position as an international creditor.[1] The character of the present international disequilibrium is shown not only by large shifts in the sources of United States imports and the huge increase in total United States exports but also by the fact that the latter reflected a major shift in sources of world supply; despite the unprecedented

---

[1] For statistical details on our balance of payments during these years, see Chapter VII and especially Table XXVI. It should be recorded here that, although the total quantity of United States imports in 1946–48 exceeded 1936–38, this total hides the important fact that imports from Europe and Asia were less in the recent period than in the former but were more than compensated for by expanded imports from the Western Hemisphere.

peacetime volume of exports by the United States, the total volume of imports by the rest of the world from all sources in the years 1946–48 was smaller than before the war.

Since the war social and political considerations have played a new and impressive role in our foreign economic policies and activities, which frequently were designed to meet particular problems as they arose, and a myriad of official programs developed involving the participation of many agencies.[2] During the twenties and thirties, the United States Government was an almost negligible direct factor in our exports and imports, but in each of the post-war years it has played a dominant role, weighting the balance of payments heavily with its official unilateral transfers and loans. For the three and a half years from July 1, 1945 through 1948, *net* utilized foreign grants and credits of the United States Government totalled approximately $19 billion (excluding its subscriptions to the International Monetary Fund and Bank), with slightly more than half in the form of gifts. This amount was equal to more than one-third of our total exports of goods and services during these years. Some three-fourths of this total aid was rendered to Europe and nearly one-fifth to Asia. In large part this was in recognition that the needs of much of the world, especially Europe and the Far East, for goods and services (both for consumption and investment) were greatly in excess of the amounts which could be earned by these countries without adjustments which the United States regarded as involving socially and politically unacceptable hardships and repercussions.

Immediately after the war ended, official gifts were cut dras-

[2] In 1945 Congress established the National Advisory Council on International Monetary and Financial Problems and directed it to coordinate the foreign monetary, financial and exchange policies and operations of all agencies of the Government, as well as the policies and operations of the United States representatives in the International Bank and International Monetary Fund (Public Law 171, 79th Congress, Section 4). The original members of the National Advisory Council were the Secretaries of Treasury, State, and Commerce, the Chairman of the Board of Governors of the Federal Reserve System, and the Chairman of the Board of Directors of the Export-Import Bank. Later the Administrator of the Economic Cooperation Administration was added.

The reader wishing detailed official statements of United States policy on many international financial questions is referred to the *Semi Annual Report to the President and to the Congress* of the National Advisory Council. These documents have been heavily relied upon in this survey.

tically; the general policy of the United States Government during the first two post-war years with respect to grants was to limit them to relief supplies and to those nations whose international reserves were of negligible amounts. Thus, the bulk of such aid was given via the United Nations Relief and Rehabilitation Administration to certain of our former allies (supplemented in 1947 by direct post-UNRRA aid) and via the armed forces as part of their responsibilities for preventing "disease and unrest" in the occupied and former enemy countries. It was official policy, however, to encourage private gifts; such remittances from the United States since the war have been at a rate approximately three and one-half times that recorded during the pre-war years 1936–38, but the absolute amounts were relatively small.

The loan policy of the Government in the years immediately following the war was that the International Bank should be the principal agency for making foreign loans which could not be provided from private sources—except for the very special case of Britain which, it was argued, warranted separate treatment, and except for certain property credits by which large amounts of lend-lease supplies and military surplus property were transferred. Until the International Bank began making loans, it was provided that the Export-Import Bank should meet some of the more urgent reconstruction needs abroad of nations deemed not eligible for relief grants because they still possessed sizeable international reserves. The Government did encourage expanded private loans; the net amount of such credits, which had been negative in the years 1931–43, expanded rapidly after the war but were neither in the form, nor of the dimensions, necessary to finance any but a small portion of the imports by the rest of the world from the United States.

During the two years after the war, it was expected that, except for these grants and loans, the rest of the world could meet their requirements for imports from the United States by their exports to it and by liquidating their gold and dollar balances. By mid-1947, however, as the official grant programs were beginning to taper off and the official loans and credits which had previously been extended were nearly all utilized, many foreign nations were liquidating their gold and dollar reserves at an alarming rate. (The drain on the rest of the world's reserves in their transactions with the United States was $4.5 billion in 1947.) It thereafter became apparent that the post-war disequilibrium in world trade was much more deep-rooted and intractible than had been thought. Many of the problems were seen to be beyond the scope of the International Monetary Fund and Bank (which were making relatively large disbursements in 1947 in the face of problems and conditions quite different from those with which they were created to deal) and the then existing United States institutions and programs. Europe at least was regarded as in immediate danger of suffering grave economic, social, and political disaster. Therefore, the United States in mid-1947 reconsidered its entire foreign aid program.

The new approach was outlined in June 1947 by Secretary of State Marshall: Attention was still to be concentrated on Europe. The Government believed that continued large-scale assistance for several years was necessary if a serious set-back in European recovery was to be avoided. The emphasis was shifted from loans to grants as respects those nations which had previously been forced to rely in large measure on their own reserves. Finally, the principle was introduced that United States help would be effective only if the European countries were able to co-operate among themselves in general programs of self-help and mutual aid.

Nearly ten months were required to develop and obtain Congressional approval for the new European Recovery Program. In the meantime, early in 1947 large-scale military and economic assistance had been authorized for Greece and Turkey in support of the Truman Doctrine to "contain" communism in that area, and in view of what was regarded as the desperate position of some of the countries—especially Austria, France, and Italy—a special Interim-Aid Program was launched later in the year. The Foreign Economic Assistance Act was finally approved by Congress in April 1948, outlining the European Recovery Program. It also provided for continuance of military assistance to Greece and Turkey and for additional contributions to various international relief organizations. A special title of the law authorized military and economic assistance to China, but this was conceived of as at best a holding operation and not a recovery program such as was being undertaken in Europe. The foreign aid appropriation legislation also continued and expanded the previous programs of civilian relief to the occupied countries.

With the expanded American aid program in Western Europe the International Monetary Fund and Bank, with United States approval, for all practical purposes withdrew from that area but not from the rest of the world; their dollar disbursements in 1948 were thus only about one-half the 1947 amounts. This action represented an attempt to strike a balance between what were considered the exigencies of the current situation and a policy of preserving the assets of these institutions for the purposes for which they were created. While the reserves of most countries were below the amounts judged necessary for a return to currency convertibility and multilateral trade (a continuing long-term objective of American policy), the United States did not yet feel it should adopt a policy designed specifically to replenish these reserves.[3]

During the first three post-war years, the United States recognized that the existing pattern of exchange rates was not satisfactory for many countries, but it apparently did not press or urge any extensive revaluations in view of the difficulties of establishing rates which could be maintained under the then existing conditions, partly on the grounds that exports by foreign nations were not being seriously retarded because of the fixed (over-valued) rates and a devaluation might aggravate the internal inflation in many of these countries. By mid-1948 there was growing evidence, however, of a belief that the time might be approaching when extensive devaluations would be appropriate, and by that time the U.S. Government also thought the Fund should make greater efforts to eliminate multiple currency practices. The policy continued to be one of favoring stable over fluctuating rates. With respect to gold, American policy was consistently one of keeping its dollar price fixed and preserving it as an international means of payment.

The United States commercial policy during the three first post-war years was consistently one of favoring a reduction of trade barriers and a return to multilateral trade. To this end the United States played a dominant role in the development of

---

[3] Secretary of the Treasury Snyder in early 1948 did foresee a time when direct United States loans for this purpose might be desirable.

the International Trade Organization Charter. It encouraged and actively participated in the General Agreement on Tariffs and Trade in 1947, which resulted in substantial reductions in United States tariffs. But this liberal trade policy received at least a temporary setback in 1948 when Congress extended the Reciprocal Trade Agreements Act for only one year instead of the usual three and inserted the protectionist "peril points" clause.

As a prelude to the survey of 1949 affairs, a summary of the 1948 transactions would show the following: Total official aid during 1948 was less than in 1947 but the bulk of it was in the form of gifts rather than loans and the rate of assistance was expanding rapidly as the year ended. Liquidation of gold and dollar assets by foreign countries in their transactions with the United States, while still large in 1948, were only 20 percent of the previous year. Private investment from the United States, paced by the petroleum industry, reached in 1948 the highest level since 1929, and private remittances were the largest of any year since 1919. The value of current exports from the United States during 1948 was 15 percent less than in 1947 and imports were nearly one-fifth larger in value, but for the year the current account surplus was still some $6.3 billion.

By the beginning of 1949 the United States was still a long way from having achieved international equilibrium or its frequently professed goal of a world of freely convertible currencies and multilateral trade.

I · GIFTS

INTRODUCTION

NET United States Government gifts and other miscellaneous uni- [7] lateral transfers abroad totalled nearly $5.1 billion in 1949 and financed 32 percent of total United States exports of goods and services.[1] Net private gifts totalled more than one half billion dollars and financed another 3.5 percent of our exports. While private gifts were the lowest of any year since the end of the war, both the amount of official unilateral transfers and the percentage of exports financed by them were at a peacetime peak as Government foreign aid programs, gifts and loans combined, reached a new high and the shift begun in 1948 from loans to grants was accelerated. Several of the more important official gift programs were, however, declining rapidly during the last half of the year, and only two, the military defense assistance program and the program for aid to refugees in the Middle East, gave promise at year's end of expanding in 1950.

Unilateral transfers from the United States have been of much greater importance—both relatively and absolutely—in financing our exports since the recent war than they were after the first world war or during the years immediately preceding the last war. It is also to be noted that private remittances accounted for most of the gifts in the inter-war years, while the United States Government has been the source of nearly 85 percent of the total in the past four years.

The European Recovery Program (ERP) was by far the most

[1] Unless otherwise specified, statistics on aid rendered or "utilized" under official gift programs represent shipments where procurement is by a United States Government agency and cash payments when other methods of procurement are used. During 1949 two-thirds of total gross aid rendered by the Government under both its gift and loan programs was in the form of cash and one-third in goods and services.

I. GIFTS

TABLE I

Net United States Gifts and Other Unilateral Transfers, 1919–1949

	TOTAL		United States	
Period	As percentage of exports of goods and services	In millions of dollars	Government (In millions	Private of dollars)
1919–21 (average)	8	743	104	639
1936–38 (average)	5	191	22	169
1946	19	2877	2279	598
1947	12	2380	1812	568
1948	26	4409	3761	648
1949ᵖ	35	5623	5085	538
Annual Rate				
First quarter	33	5680	5092	588
Second quarter	37	6524	5960	564
Third quarter	38	5504	5072	432
Fourth quarterᵖ	33	4784	4216	568

p. Preliminary.
Sources: Pre-war and 1946–1948 data: *The Balance of International Payments of the United States 1946–48*, U.S. Department of Commerce, Washington, D.C., 1950, pp. 193, 194, 275. 1949 data: *Survey of Current Business*, U.S. Department of Commerce, Washington, D.C., March 1950, p. 4.

important channel of our official aid to foreign areas during 1949, accounting for over 70 percent of total gross gifts; second place was held by the Occupied Areas Program, accounting for another 17 percent. Other important programs were Philippine rehabilitation, military assistance to Greece and Turkey, military and economic aid to China, economic aid to Korea, and the various refugee and children's relief programs. The major policy issues during the year arose in connection with the European Recovery Program, the Mutual Defense Assistance Program, and the question of aid to China and Korea.

A. EUROPEAN RECOVERY PROGRAM

Legislative Issues and Changes

In February 1949, the Administration asked Congress for authority and funds to carry on the European Recovery Program for another year. The success of the Marshall Plan in combatting communism and strengthening democratic political organizations was repeatedly underlined. Extensive data were presented showing that the process of physical recuperation from the effects

8

of the war was nearly completed and that inflationary forces were rapidly being brought under control. It was argued, further, that continued financial aid was necessary if Western European nations were to become self-supporting at an acceptable standard of living by 1952 and that this in turn required basic and complicated structural changes and expansion in domestic production and international trade. Mr. Paul G. Hoffman and his advisers outlined to Congress the following major goals the Economic Cooperation Administration (ECA) would pursue in Europe in 1949: (1) expand production, (2) end the inflation, (3) increase exports through lower prices, increased productivity, and better marketing techniques, (4) reduce dollar imports and develop non-dollar sources of supply, (5) expand and free intra-European trade, and (6) coordinate national investment programs.[2]

ECA in 1948 had received $4 billion in cash appropriations, plus $1 billion to be provided out of public debt transactions for the specific purpose of making loans and investment guaranties to the ERP nations. This $5 billion was to cover the fifteen months ending June 30, 1949. The law provided, however, that if the President deemed it necessary he could order the expenditure of the whole $5 billion during the year ending April 2, 1949; at Administrator Hoffman's request, the President so ordered on November 26, 1948. At the end of 1948 over $4 billion had been obligated, and it was anticipated that the entire $5 billion would be committed by the first of April.

The Administration asked Congress in February to authorize appropriations of $1150 million for the period April-June 1949 and $4280 million, plus $150 million in forward contracting authorizations,[3] for the year July 1949–June 1950. This amount was approximately $500 million less than the total which had been asked by the European national governments. The Administration's request was based, in most cases, on November 1948 prices and

---

[2] For details on the 1948 progress and future problems as then seen, see A Report on Recovery Progress and United States Aid, Economic Cooperation Administration, Washington, D.C., February 1949, and Hearings before the Committee on Foreign Relations, U.S. Senate, 81st Cong., 1st Sess., on S. 833 and Hearings before Committee on Foreign Affairs, House of Representatives, 81st Cong. 1st Sess. on H.R. 2362.

[3] This $150 million was to authorize the purchase of goods and services by participating countries on which disbursements would not be made and for which appropriations would not be requested until 1951 or later.

was calculated to be the minimum necessary to (a) increase European industrial production in 1949–1950 by 5 to 10 percent over 1948–49, (b) permit some increase in agricultural production, (c) permit nations to devote about 20 percent of their gross national product to capital formation, (d) permit a slight increase in consumption standards—the goal as regards food was an over-all per capita average of 2700 calories daily, and (e) maintain imports at the same general level and provide for a 25 percent increase in exports, as compared with 1948–49.

It was stated that the general procedure used to determine the amount of the request for funds was to have each nation prepare a recovery program designed to provide for viability by 1952 and draw up a balance of payments based on such a program. Later, these programs and the balances of payments were successively reviewed, and usually reduced by four different agencies: ECA country missions, the Organization for European Economic Cooperation (OEEC), Mr. Harriman's group in Paris, and ECA-Washington. The remaining deficits in the balance of payments served as the basis for requests for funds from Congress. As will be noted later, a different procedure and approach was followed in determining the requests for funds for fiscal year 1950–51.

In the 1949 request for funds, Administration spokesmen urged that they be left free to determine in each case whether the aid should be extended as a grant or as a loan and not be required, as they had under the 1948 Act, to provide a specified amount on a loan basis. They argued that while there were a few countries which properly should receive aid in the form of loans, the total amount should certainly be much less than the $1 billion earmarked in the 1948 Act. They pointed out that the European nations as a group were already carrying very heavy fixed dollar obligations and estimated that in late 1948 the payments of interest and amortization on such obligations absorbed about one-eighth of the area's current dollar earnings and that on the basis of existing obligations these charges would be nearly doubled in the years immediately following the end of the recovery program.[4] It was maintained that, if these nations contracted additional fixed

[4] The following are the supporting figures on the estimated external debt of ERP countries to the Western Hemisphere as of the end of 1948 and on the 1952 charges:

dollar debt in substantial amounts, their recovery in 1952 would be seriously prejudiced, and they would be in no position when ERP ended to attract private capital. Secretary Snyder also made the point that a large debt would intensify the international reprecussions of an economic recession in the United States or abroad.

The law extending the ECA Act was signed by the President on April 19 and authorized the appropriation of the requested $5430 million, with none of the funds earmarked for loans.[5] The law was passed, however, only after moves in the Senate (arising largely from general efforts to reduce Government expenditures and so to avoid new taxes or a deficit) to reduce the amount first by 15 percent and then by 10 percent were defeated and after amendments in the House to reduce it by 10 percent and 7 percent also failed to be approved. The Reconstruction Finance Corporation was authorized to advance $1 billion to ECA pending appropriations.

The President requested appropriations on April 22 of $5272.2 million,[6] reducing his earlier estimates because of price declines

	1948 Debt[a]	1952 Charges		
		Interest	Amortization	Total
		(in millions of dollars)		
U.S. Government	8222.2	156.1	219.8	375.9
Other U.S. Dollar[b]	977.8	32.2	29.8	62.0
Other Western Hemisphere[c]	2289.6	45.4	94.8	140.2
Total	11489.6	233.7	344.4	578.1

a. Excludes German and all World War I indebtedness.
b. International Bank and private holders of dollar bonds. For most part private foreign obligations are not included.
c. Principally Canada and Argentina.
Source: *Hearings before the Committee on Foreign Affairs, House of Representatives, 81st Cong., 1st Sess., on H.R. 2362*, Part II, pp. 834–8. For a detailed discussion of fixed charge debts owed by all foreign nations to the United States Government, see Ryan, F. W., "Servicing Foreign Credits of the U.S. Government," *Survey of Current Business*, November 1949, pp. 14–17.

[5] The law contained no contract authorizations, but, in addition to the $5430 appropriation authorization, ECA was empowered to borrow $150 million from the Treasury for the purpose of extending investment guaranties (see page 77), less any amount previously allocated for that purpose. This amount was not limited for use within the fiscal year 1949–50.

[6] $1074 million for the period April 3–June 30, 1949 and $4198.2 million for fiscal year 1949–50.

in the United States. Congress, following long discussion on various aspects of the recession in the United States and much bickering over the provision of funds to continue the Joint House-Senate ERP "Watch Dog" Committee, finally agreed on September 29[7] to appropriate $4702.4 million in cash—an amount which resulted from several cuts and some partial restorations. In addition it earmarked $150 million for loans, with funds to be provided out of public debt transactions[8] (Table II). Thus the total funds for the twelve months ending June 1950 were almost 25 percent less than the first ECA appropriation, which had been obligated in twelve months.

TABLE II
ECA Appropriations and Loan Authorizations, 1949
(in millions of dollars)

Appropriations: April–June 1949	1074.0
July 1949–June 1950	3628.4
	4702.4
Loan Authorization: July 1949–June 1950	150.0
Total	4852.4

Source: Foreign Aid Appropriation Act, 1950.

During the hearings and debate there was also much discussion regarding the shipping restrictions in the original Act. While the Administration said it was prepared to "live with" the clause requiring that at least 50 percent of the ECA-financed cargoes go in United States bottoms if available at market rates, it requested that the law make clear whether market rates meant world rates or the higher United States rates. It strongly opposed any further restrictions such as were included in the so-called Bland Bill (H.R. 1340). The law as passed, however, reflected the desire

[7] Because of the long delay in the appropriation, the ECA was authorized by Congressional joint resolutions during the summer to obligate funds at the fiscal year 1948–49 rate, with amounts so disbursed being deductible from funds finally appropriated.

[8] Loans under this authority are handled for ECA by the Export-Import Bank, and funds are obtained by ECA issuing notes for purchase by the Treasury. In addition to the above amounts the 1949 enabling legislation authorized ECA to borrow $150 million from the Treasury for the purpose of extending investment guaranties less any amount allocated for that purpose prior to April 3, 1949. This amount was not limited to fiscal year 1950.

of Congress to give even greater special assistance and protection to the shipping industry. It not only specified that "market rate" for shipments in United States vessels meant the market rates for United States ships and not world rates but also required that ECA endeavor to get a fair and reasonable participation by American ships by geographic areas and further that the 50 percent rule be applied separately for bulk, liner, and tanker vessels.[9]

Congress also discussed at length the ECA request for deleting the 1948 provision requiring that 25 percent of all wheat exports financed by ECA on a grant basis be shipped in the form of flour. The Administration stated that this provision had cost ECA about $8 million in 1948 and that, since there were in 1949 adequate milling facilities in Europe and no shortage of grain for feed purposes in the United States (the by-products from milling are an important source of animal feed), there was no longer any justification for continuing this restriction. In the Bill as passed this requirement was not eliminated but was reduced to 12½ percent.

Among other important changes in the basic law was the insertion by Congress of a clause placing on ECA the general responsibility of taking a positive and forceful approach in assisting American small businesses to participate in the program. It was specifically required to provide them with information as to goods which would be purchased in the United States and to inform prospective foreign buyers of commodities and services produced by small business concerns in the United States.[1]

There was serious debate on the provisions in the original Act providing that ECA should facilitate the transfer of strategic materials to the United States and encourage the increased production of such goods. Mr. Hoffman said that, while ECA had been able to accomplish a little along these lines in 1948, nothing much could be done unless additional dollars were provided and authority granted to make long-term contracts and so provide as-

---

[9] However, the legislation gave ECA permission to require counterpart fund deposits on the basis of world and not United States shipping rates; ECA's request for authority to waive the requirement of counterpart funds for the value of technical assistance provided was also granted.

[1] Suggestions that small business should get a fixed percentage of total ECA-financed purchases were turned down because it would involve the actual placing of orders by ECA and would mean additional work and because it raised the bogey of state trading.

sured markets for potential investors. ECA apparently wanted to be relieved of stockpiling responsibilities, but Congress decided otherwise. Thus the 1949 law reemphasized ECA's obligation to make use of its bargaining power to increase production of such materials and authorized it, with the approval of and within the appropriations available to the Bureau of Federal Supply (now Federal Supply Service), to enter into long-term contracts of up to twenty years for the purchase of such goods.

Finally, and by no means of least importance, Congress inserted into the general objectives and purposes section of the law the statement that it was " . . . the policy of the people of the United States to encourage the unification of Europe. . . . " This declaration of purpose, which strengthened and made more explicit a goal implied in the preamble of the original Act, was followed (as is discussed at some length in Chapter V) by important changes in ECA policy for Europe.

A series of very restrictive amendments, offered during the Congressional debate on the enabling measure, were either defeated or eliminated on points of order. They are worth noting, however, because there was considerable support for each of them and because they may again become major issues. They included amendments to (1) require that $2 billion of the total foreign aid appropriation be used to buy United States farm surpluses, (2) deny aid to any country using ECA funds directly or indirectly to acquire or operate any industry as a nationalized industry, (3) forbid the use of counterpart funds to reduce national debts, (4) withhold aid from any country discriminating against American businessmen, and (5) earmark $50 million for aid to Spain.

It is important to note that in 1949 Congress still insisted, despite no little pressure from many segments of the economy for special considerations and the protection afforded to United States shipping and agriculture, that the ERP was designed to promote the recovery of Europe and not to support the United States economy or certain parts of it.[2]

[2] In addition to the exceptions noted above, it should be mentioned that minor concessions were made to the marine insurance industry; also, Senator Brewster of Maine, a state which, like Europe, finds tourism an increasing source of revenue, got approval for prohibiting the use of ECA funds to advertise foreign travel or goods in the United States.

The ECA European Programs[3]

It is not within the scope of this survey to examine the economic recovery of Western Europe during 1949. It will have to suffice merely to point out that accomplishments during the year in many fields were impressive and that the rescue operations phase of the ECA program seemed to have been successfully concluded. Estimated total output of goods and services in 1949 exceeded pre-war by about 5 percent and was some 25 percent above 1947. Industrial production for the area as a whole was estimated at some 15 percent above 1938, while agricultural production was less than 5 percent below pre-war. Productivity increased during the year, with output per man per year, excluding Germany, being estimated at 10 percent above pre-war. Although inflationary pressures were still strong, in most of the countries prices were relatively stable. Unemployment was generally low (Germany, Italy and Belgium being the only important exceptions), and there were but few strikes. Something like 20 percent of gross national product was being used for investment. While average per capita consumption of consumers' goods and services was still some 10 percent below 1938 (the population of the area was some 20 million larger than in 1938), it did increase during the year, and at year's end it was estimated the average daily calory consumption was 2800. While it was generally recognized that this impressive record was made possible by United States aid and that further improvement or even maintenance depended on future aid, it did appear that several of the goals, set for the year by ECA as noted above, were met.[4]

Intra-Western European trade was at about pre-war volume in 1949 as compared with only two-thirds of that level in 1947, and there was also a striking reduction or reversal in the net debtor or creditor position of several countries in such trade.[5]

[3] ECA activities in China and Korea are discussed separately below.

[4] For details and analysis of European economic recovery see especially *European Recovery Programme, Second Report*, Organization for European Economic Cooperation, Paris, February 1950 and the excellent quarterly bulletins and annual report by the U.N. Economic Commission for Europe, Geneva.

[5] This leveling off of intra-European balances was of very great importance, as OEEC pointed out in its second report cited above, since the

Trade with Eastern Europe increased slightly during the year, but its volume was still less than 40 percent of 1938.

Primarily because of rising exports, the area's current accounts with all the world except the United States and Canada were in approximate balance for 1949, but there was a dollar deficit on current account with North America which it was estimated would be $3.4 billion for the year ending July 1, 1950. While this was appreciably less than the $6.4 billion and $4.4 billion deficits in 1947 and 1948, this reduction was due entirely to reductions in imports, with the value of exports to the United States and Canada being somewhat less than in 1948.[6]

The persistent and large imbalance with the dollar area was proving more intractible than many had anticipated, and during the year this problem became the primary concern of ECA's policy makers. Their chief efforts were directed toward "integrating" the European economy, which it was thought was a necessary step to closing the "dollar gap" at acceptable import levels. This "integration" policy is discussed at length in Chapter V. In addition they favored exchange depreciation (see page 114) and encouraged many direct methods for expanding dollar exports (see page 154). ECA activities with respect to stockpiling and investment guaranties are discussed on pages 166 and 77 respectively. In this section attention will be given to those ECA activities and policies regarding the allocation of funds, commodities supplied, purchases from the United States, technical assistance, industrial projects, and counterpart funds.

i. GEOGRAPHIC ALLOCATION OF AID

ECA is a financing and not a procurement organization. The normal financing procedure is to make periodic "allotments" to each participating country. (Through 1949 the funds provided

---

pre-war pattern of intra-European surpluses and deficits rested in large part on overseas invisible income and large trade with Eastern Europe and the Far East, both of which have been greatly reduced.

[6] The dollar deficit of Western Europe is larger than its current account deficit with North America since for the former not only must capital transactions be taken into account but also gold and dollars are used for some settlements with certain other countries and also the position of associated monetary areas should be included. Thus, the total gold and dollar deficit in 1947 was over $8 billion, in 1948 about $5.5 billion, and for the year ending July 1, 1950 was estimated at slightly below $4.5 billion.

by Congress were allocated among the various ERP nations primarily on the basis of recommendations by OEEC.) On the basis of these allotments each country submits to ECA in Washington and to the ECA mission in its own country an application for "procurement authorizations" to cover the goods and services it wants financed. ECA examines these requests on the basis of "needs, availabilities, and other pertinent considerations."[7] On receipt of approved authorizations from ECA the participating country makes sub-authorizations to its importers, who usually then work through normal commercial trade channels.[8]

During 1949, ECA allocated $3.6 billion of its funds among the various European recipient nations and issued procurement authorizations of $4 billion. Actual shipments of ECA-financed goods, including ocean freight paid by ECA,[9] were estimated at more than $3.9 billion. The total value of aid rendered during the year, including services, was about $4.1 billion, of which $3.7 billion was on a grant basis and the balance on a loan basis. From ECA's beginning in April 1948 through 1949 the totals were approximately $8.5 billion of funds allocated, $8.0 billion of procurement authorizations issued, and nearly $6.0 billion of actual shipments; total aid rendered, including services, slightly exceeded $6 billion.

ECA extends aid on three bases: direct grants, loans, and "conditional grants," these accounting for $4.3, $0.9, and $0.8 billion

[7] *A Report on Recovery Progress and United States Aid, op. cit.,* p. 105. No more precise statement as to the criteria used by ECA or data on the extent of refusals to approve requests was found.

[8] Actual purchases under these authorizations may be financed in several ways: (a) the country involved may make dollars available to importers and be reimbursed by ECA; (b) ECA may issue a letter of commitment to a United States bank obligating ECA to reimburse the bank for payments by it against a procurement authorization; (c) ECA may issue a letter of commitment to a supplier; (d) ECA may permit the recipient country to draw drafts against ECA's account at the United States Treasury; or (e) ECA may pay directly to a United States Government agency procuring commodities for a foreign government. (For further details see *Ibid.,* pp. 104–108.)

[9] ECA practice has been to pay freight charges on cargoes originating in the United States if carried in United States or third country bottoms where the customs of the trade call for dollar payments. Only occasionally has ECA paid freight charges on off-shore purchased cargoes and then only if carried by United States flag vessels.

respectively of the aid rendered from April 1948 through 1949. "Conditional grants" represent aid extended to a country on condition that it in turn grant assistance to other participating countries in the form of "drawing rights" under the Intra-European Payments Scheme (see Chapter V). To obtain the effective distribution of ECA assistance among the various countries it is, therefore, necessary to subtract drawing rights extended from the aid received from ECA and to add drawing rights received. When this is done it is seen (Table III) that, from the beginning of the ECA program in April 1948 through December 1949, the United Kingdom was the largest recipient of aid and France was a close second, together accounting for over half the total. It is also to be noted that, for this period, Belgium-Luxembourg broke even whereas Sweden gave more than it received, but it was planned that this deficiency would be made up before the termination of the program.[1] It is, of course, probable that a country benefits by exchanging a European export surplus for United States dollars; there is, however, no means of calculating such "gains."

ii. COMMODITIES SUPPLIED

ECA finances a wide variety of goods. However, a very large share of the funds have been spent on food, feed and fertilizer, and fuel. Nearly three-fourths of the value of the goods shipped in 1948, excluding freight which is not allocated in the available data, were in these categories. As European agricultural output and coal production recovered and as Poland began exporting large quantities of coal to Western European countries, shipments of these items fell off; nevertheless, they still accounted for slightly over one-half of the shipments during 1949. The percentage of raw materials and semi-finished products (cotton being by all odds the most important single commodity in this category) rose from 23 percent of the total in 1948 to 34 percent in 1949, also reflecting the recovery in Western Europe (Table IV).

[1] Through 1949 Belgium-Luxembourg, Sweden, and Turkey had extended respectively $62, $15 and $14 million more aid under the Intra-European Payments Scheme than the United States had provided in the form of conditional aid. These deficiencies would be made up before the end of the ECA program.

TABLE III
Aid Received and Provided Under European Recovery Program, 1948 and 1949
(in millions of dollars)

| | 1948 | 1949 | | | | | |
| | Net Aid Received(+) or Provided(−) | Net Aid Received(+) or Provided(−) | Aid received from the United States | | | Aid under Intra-European Payments Plan | |
			Total	Direct and Conditional[a] Grant Basis	Credit Basis	Received from Other Participants	Provided to Other Participants
Total	+1873	+4160	4160	3735	425	809	809
France	+504	+1072	852	807	45	254	33
United Kingdom	+692	+929	1107	1027	81	48	226
Netherlands-Indonesia	+142	+440	352	254	98	102	15
Germany	+113	+392	491	491	0	46[b]	145
Italy	+155	+378	418	389	0	0	40
Austria	+100	+294	202	202	0	93	1
Greece	+64	+259	129	129	0	130	0
Norway	+42	+134	66	43	23	72	5
Denmark	+41	+123	108	94	14	19	4
Ireland	0	+67	67	3	64	0	0
Turkey	0	+33	30	10	20	27	24
Trieste	+6	+9	9	9	0	0	0
Portugal	0	+5	0	0	0	5	0
Iceland	+2	+2	5	5	*	0	4
Sweden	−8	+1	38	38	0	7	44
Belgium-Luxembourg	+13	−12	253	202	51	4	268
Unallocated	+8	+33	33	33	0	0	0

a. Conditional grants not sufficient to cover aid provided by Turkey, Sweden, and Belgium-Luxembourg.
b. Includes $3.5 million extended by Iceland to Germany outside Intra-European Payments Plan.
* Less than $500,000.
Source: *Survey of Current Business*, April 1950, p. 21.
Note: The data on aid "received" from the United States for the two years exceeded by $60 million the published ECA data on "shipments." The difference is due to the inclusion in the above table of (1) "unallocated" which includes both dollars and $21 million of counterpart funds used for certain ECA administrative expenses, and (2) costs of certain technical assistance supplied by ECA and postal subsidy payments on relief parcels.

TABLE IV

ECA-Financed Shipments, by Major Commodity Groups, 1948 and 1949

Commodities	1948			1949				
	Second & Third Quarter	Fourth Quarter	Year	First Quarter	Second Quarter	Third Quarter	Fourth Quarter	Year
	(in percentages)							
Food, Feed & Fertilizer[a]	56.4	48.2	51.8	46.7	35.5	32.4	37.2	37.9
Fuel	25.4	18.8	21.7	11.3	15.7	14.5	11.3	13.4
Raw Materials & Semi-Finished Products	17.7	26.5	22.6	31.4	35.5	35.9	34.4	34.3
Machinery & Vehicles	0.5	6.1	3.7	10.1	12.6	16.2	16.0	13.6
Miscellaneous	—	0.4	0.2	0.5	0.7	1.0	1.1	0.8
Total Commodities	100.0	100.0	100.0	100.0	100.0	100.0	100.0	100.0
	(in millions of dollars)							
Total Commodities	817	1053	1870	910	1093	886	752	3641
Ocean Freight[b]	103	81	184	83	102	60	34	279
Grand Total	920	1134	2054	993	1195	946	786	3920

a. Including tobacco.

b. Includes very small amounts for technical services in some quarters.

Source: Compiled from data in the *Second, Third, Fourth, Fifth* and *Sixth Report to Congress*, Economic Cooperation Administration, Washington, D.C., February 1949–January 1950, pp. 150 f, pp. 144 f, pp. 114 f, pp. 116 f, and pp. 120 f, respectively; and the *Nineteenth Report to the Public Advisory Board*, Economic Cooperation Administration, Washington, D.C., January 1950, p. 44. The reader is referred to these documents for a detailed commodity breakdown.

Note: For 1949, data are ECA expenditures supplemented by movement reports; for 1948, data are "reported shipments." Actual movements exceed these data on shipments because of a lag in receipt of shipping documents.

20

iii. PURCHASES IN THE UNITED STATES

In 1949, as domestic supplies of many commodities became relatively abundant at the current prices, ECA placed increasing emphasis on " . . . using surplus domestic stocks wherever they are needed to meet the requirements of the European countries."[2] During 1948 some 54 percent of the value of all commodity shipments financed by ECA were purchased in the United States, while the percentage was 70 percent for 1949 (Table V). The proportion for purchases in the United States was even higher in the case of food and agricultural items, being nearly 61 percent in 1948 and 78 percent in 1949. For certain important agricultural commodities (coarse grains, cotton, and tobacco), purchases have been for all practical purposes restricted to the United States.

TABLE V

ECA-Financed Shipments, by Commodity Groups and Area of Origin, 1948 and 1949

(in percentages)

Area of Origin	Total		Agricultural Commodities		Industrial Commodities	
	1948	1949	1948	1949	1948	1949
United States	53.5	70.0	60.7	78.0	43.4	61.3
Canada	24.4	11.5	28.3	9.8	19.1	13.3
Latin America	7.7	8.9	6.7	10.1	8.9	7.5
Participating Countries	8.7	4.4	3.1	0.7	16.7	8.5
Other	5.7	5.2	1.2	1.4	11.9	9.4
Total	100.0	100.0	100.0	100.0	100.0	100.0
Total by Value (millions of dollars)	1870	3641	1086	1914	784	1727

Sources: *Third Report to Congress,* Economic Cooperation Administration, Washington, D.C., May 1949, pp. 144–145 and *Nineteenth Report for the Public Advisory Board,* Economic Cooperation Administration, Washington, D.C., January 1950, p. 46. The reader is referred to these documents for a detailed commodity breakdown.

In accordance with the Economic Cooperation Act, whenever the Secretary of Agriculture determines that agricultural commodities are in surplus relative to the needs of the domestic economy, ECA fills requests for such commodities by the participating

[2] *Sixth Report to Congress,* Economic Cooperation Administration, Washington, D.C., January 1950, p. 56.

countries only from United States sources, including stocks acquired by the Government under its agricultural price-support programs. From its beginning in 1948 through 1949 ECA had issued procurement authorizations for over $2.3 billion of commodities so declared in surplus. To encourage further purchases of certain surplus agricultural products in the United States, the Act also authorizes the Secretary of Agriculture, out of funds provided in Section 32 of the Agricultural Adjustment Act, to pay up to 50 percent of their cost or market price, whichever is lower. Such subsidy payments were made in 1948 and 1949 on flaxseed, dried and frozen eggs, peanuts, dried fruits, citrus fruits, pears and tobacco.[3]

Canada has been the most important beneficiary of offshore purchases, these being largely for bread grains and non-ferrous metals and products. Latin America was the second, providing mostly petroleum products and sugar. The participating countries themselves have benefitted from offshore purchases of fuel and edible fats and oils, but their share of total purchases fell following the establishment of the Intra-European Payments Scheme in late 1948 (see page 136). Purchases financed by ECA in the rest of the world have been relatively unimportant and were chiefly for petroleum products.[4]

The requirement in the law that at least 12.5 percent of the authorized purchases of wheat and flour after April 2, 1949 be in the form of flour (see page 13) was apparently met with a minimum of difficulties; the actual percentage through December was 15.3 percent. Some difficulties did arise, however, in connection with the requirement that at least 50 percent of ECA-financed shipments from the United States (whether liner, bulk, or tanker cargo) be in American flag vessels (see page 12). ECA records showed that in the second quarter of 1949 only some 46 percent of the *liner* cargo had been in United States vessels, although more than the required 50 percent of bulk and tanker

[3] From April 1948 through June 30, 1949 these subsidy payments totalled $27 million. During the same period similar subsidy payments totalling $4 million were made in connection with purchases by the Army of civilian supplies for occupied areas.

[4] It is to be noted that many of the offshore purchases of petroleum, sugar, and mining products were from sources in which American direct investments were important.

shipments had been in United States bottoms. As a result, in October ECA notified OEEC that new procedures would be put into effect to enforce the shipping provisions, and shortly thereafter seven countries were requested to reimburse ECA for the cost of some 170 thousand tons of cargo carried in foreign flag liners in excess of the maximum permitted quotas.[5] For the period April–September 1949, 56.9 percent of *all* cargoes from the United States were in United States bottoms.

iv. TECHNICAL ASSISTANCE PROGRAM

Although ECA gave considerable publicity during the year to its technical assistance program, especially the visits of European groups to study United States industrial and agricultural methods, it had authorized dollar expenditures for such purposes of only $4.4 million from April 1948 through November 30, 1949, and actual expenditures totalled only $2.5 million.[6] Some attention was given this problem in 1948, but it was not until after President Truman's Point Four declaration in his January 1949 inaugural address that a Technical Assistance Division was created by ECA. ECA consults with the Interdepartmental Committee on Scientific and Cultural Cooperation on the selection of projects to be undertaken; all projects must have the full support of the participating government. ECA efforts through 1949 were directed primarily to activities in Europe which would show appreciable results by 1952 and so differ in both location and emphasis from the regular Point Four Program of the Government.

The ECA technical assistance program has concentrated on helping to increase European industrial productivity and to improve public administration. Most of the expenditures have been for employing United States experts. The distribution of dollars authorized and spent by the end of November 1949 among fields of activity and type of assistance is shown in Table VI.

One country, Greece, had received 77 percent of the total authorizations; the United Kingdom was second with under 10

[5] There was some dispute as to the accuracy or completeness of the ECA records, with the foreign nations insisting that they had lived up to the regulations (see *New York Times,* November 26, 1949), but reimbursement was finally made to ECA.

[6] Recipient governments met the local currency cost of such programs, but data on these costs are not available.

TABLE VI
ECA Technical Assistance Program, through November 30, 1949
(in thousands of dollars)

	Authorizations	Expenditures
Field of Activity		
Industrial Productivity	2137	1205
Public Administration	970	544
Transportation and Communications	458	313
Agricultural Productivity	418	217
Manpower Utilization	240	132
Market Research and Analysis	126	70
Development of Overseas Territories	54	17
Tourism	21	11
Total	4428	2509
Type of Assistance		
U.S. Experts	3654	2213
Foreign Experts	710	268
Technical Materials	41	0
Basic Surveys	13	18
Special Services of U.S. Agencies	10	10
Total	4428	2509

Source: *Nineteenth Report for the Public Advisory Board,* Economic Cooperation Administration, Washington, D.C., January 18, 1950, p. 48.

percent, followed by Turkey and Italy, who had each received slightly more than 3 percent of the total. The balance was divided among eight other recipient nations and OEEC. When it is remembered that United States technical assistance to Greece had been developing since 1947 and that ECA had a keen interest in its own technical assistance program, the above very modest record of expenditures indicates that the technical assistance part of the Administration's Point Four Program, if and when approved by Congress, would probably be slow in getting under way.

V. INDUSTRIAL PROJECTS PROGRAM

An important part of ECA's program has been the financing of industrial projects, and through it some influence has been exercised on the pattern of industrial production in Europe.[7] To facilitate the screening and analysis of large-scale investments,

[7] These projects are not tied or even necessarily related to that part of ECA aid given on a loan rather than a grant basis.

ECA in November 1948 established a procedure whereby an applicant country requesting ECA assistance for $1 million or more for an industrial undertaking was required to present an economic justification for each project and to submit a detailed statement setting forth: the materials needed, where they were to be procured, the source of funds, and the results expected in terms of productivity, costs, employment, and marketability of product. These requests are considered in turn by the ECA country mission and Mr. Harriman's office in Paris, with final approval or denial being the responsibility of the Projects Committee in ECA-Washington.[8] ECA has reported that projects approved by it must have one or more of the following objectives: (1) increased output, (2) reduced dollar imports, (3) increased productivity, (4) better utilization of available manpower, (5) improvement of quality of product.

A question of great importance here is the extent to which ECA conditions its approval of individual projects on their being appropriate to an economically unified Europe. It has stated that it takes into consideration the competitive ability of the firm concerned on the assumption of a liberalization of trading conditions within Europe, but a Congressional staff group has concluded that as regards the iron and steel industry—whose modernization and expansion accounted for nearly half of the approved projects through 1949—ECA approvals have been dominated by "short run political considerations," are resulting in " . . . the establishment of an industrial pattern which is much closer to the prewar normal than to the hoped-for objective of a new and unified Europe . . . " and are retarding "the attainment of that objective."[1]

[8] In some cases ECA also refers them to OEEC for an opinion.
[1] See *Senate Document No. 142*, 81st Cong., 2nd Sess., March 3, 1950, pp. 3–8, for their arguments. It may also be noted that in November 1949 the Economic Commission for Europe (ECE) released a study indicating that Europe's plans called for a yearly production of over 70 million tons of crude steel by 1953, while the maximum amount which it could expect to market, including exports, was some 62 million tons of basic steel products expressed in crude steel equivalents. (*European Steel Trends in the Setting of the World Market*, Economic Commission for Europe, Geneva, U.N. Pubs. 1949. II. E. 2.) From the data available no conclusions can be drawn as to whether the specific productive facilities being financed by ECA would be regarded as probably excess by ECE.

By the end of 1949 ECA approval had been given for projects estimated to cost the equivalent of $1440 million (Table VII), of which $337 million were to be financed with ECA dollars and the balance with local currencies, drawing rights, free dollars, or dollars borrowed from the International Bank or the Export-Import Bank. ECA dollars were to be used only for purchasing equipment in the United States.

The United Kingdom, the Netherlands, France, and Italy had prepared elaborate programs since the war for expanding their petroleum refining and producing capacities. The problem of aiding (or even permitting) this expansion was a particularly delicate one for ECA in view of the basic nature of the industry in the United States, the large foreign investments of the American oil companies, and the fact that it was an important branch of our foreign trade. ECA accepted the plans of Europe, both to import larger proportions of crude and to draw relatively less oil from the western hemisphere, as a necessary concomitant of an integrated program designed to decrease Europe's dependence on the United States for extraordinary aid, and on occasion it defended Europe's plans from critics in the American oil industry. Nonetheless ECA made it clear that a luxuriant growth of oil refineries in Europe would not meet with its approval. Extensive studies were made on this problem in 1949. ECA questioned whether the planned expansion in output in non-European producing areas could be sold without continued currency controls and other trade barriers and concluded that some of the European refining program was in high-cost, small refineries " . . . which could compete with imports only if the countries concerned resorted to tariffs, quotas, or other trade barriers."[2] Through 1949 it had approved no crude production or refinery expansion outside Europe and only oil refining projects within Europe which it regarded as a basic minimum and directly essential to European recovery. There was some evidence that ECA had encouraged American companies to build refineries in Europe. This has been interpreted as a move to insure that Europe continue to take at least some of its crude oil from American companies,[3] but it can also be interpreted as an attempt to get United States companies

[2] *Sixth Report to Congress,* Economic Cooperation Administration, *op. cit.* p. 44.

[3] *The Economist,* May 14, 1949, p. 901.

TABLE VII

Value of Industrial Projects Approved, as of December 31, 1949,
by Type and by Country
(in millions of dollars)

| | Projects Approved | | ECA Procurement |
	Total Cost	ECA Cost	Authorizations Issued*
Type of Project			
Raw Materials Extraction	*222.9*	*27.6*	*17.5*
Coal Mining	52.7	11.0	8.0
Iron and Nickel Mining	45.2	12.6	7.4
Potash Mining	125.0	4.0	2.1
Manufacturing	*944.8*	*221.2*	*130.8*
Iron and Steel	697.8	167.4	92.8
Petroleum Refining	160.9	23.8	12.2
Automotive Products	43.7	14.6	14.6
Other	42.4	15.4	11.2
Transportation, Communication and Utilities	*267.6*	*87.2*	*39.1*
Power Facilities	110.7	61.8	28.5
Roads and Air Transport Facilities	77.8	18.0	6.4
Communication Equipment	60.0	1.3	0
Waterways, Harbors and Railroads and Equipment	19.1	6.1	4.2
Engineering and Technical Services	*4.8*	*0.7*	*0.7*
Total	*1440.1*	*336.7*	*188.1*
Country			
France	507.2	110.1	45.6
United Kingdom	402.2	45.9	29.7
Italy	201.4	82.1	61.2
Turkey	148.7	29.7	21.0
Austria	43.0	19.9	16.0
Norway	29.0	5.0	2.5
Netherlands	68.0	26.9	3.4
Belgium	20.6	7.3	6.9
Greece	10.5	4.7	0
Denmark	9.5	5.1	1.8
Total	1440.1	336.7	188.1

* *Excluding ocean transportation expenses.*
Source: *Nineteenth Report for the Public Advisory Board,* Economic Cooperation Administration, Washington, D.C., January 18, 1950, p. 47.
Note: The data do not include Technical Assistance Projects, Strategic Materials Projects, unless submitted under the Industrial Projects procedure, and Counterpart Fund Projects. These are discussed elsewhere in this study.

to cooperate in reducing the dollar costs to Europe of its oil imports. By the end of the year, the question of United States petroleum exports had become a very acute one (see pages 132–133), and it appeared probable that the problem of petroleum in all its aspects would be critically studied by Congress in 1950.

vi. COUNTERPART FUNDS

By terms of the Economic Cooperation Act and of the bilateral agreements between ECA and the participating countries, each of the latter is required to deposit in a special account amounts of its own currency—called counterpart funds—commensurate with the dollar cost of the ECA-financed goods and services received by it on a grant basis.[4] Five percent of such deposits are allocated for the use of the United States in the country, and 95 percent are to be used in the participating country for purposes agreed to by that country and ECA.

Joint control over these funds has given the American authorities some influence in the internal economic affairs of the European countries. The stated broad policy of ECA with respect to the 95 percent has been to use (or not use) them first to promote or maintain internal monetary and financial stability and, second, to promote production, reconstruction, and rehabilitation, and third, for miscellaneous other purposes.[5] Since the goods financed by ECA are, in most instances, sold for local currency, an immobilizing of the counterpart funds is anti-inflationary (or deflationary). A similar effect is achieved when the funds are used to retire public debt held by the central bank. To the extent that they are used for internal investment or other expenditures, this counter-inflationary effect is lost, in whole or in part,

[4] Deposits of counterpart funds are not required for aid received in the form of loans or, except for Germany, conditional aid. Deposits are required for drawing rights utilized under the Intra-European Payments Scheme (see page 136). Deposits are made at "agreed upon conversion rates" which are the par values agreed to by the International Monetary Fund where they exist or, otherwise, rates agreed upon by the participating country and ECA.

[5] The advice of the National Advisory Council on International Monetary and Financial Problems (NAC) is requested by ECA on policy matters regarding the use of these funds. For details on the counterpart funds program of ECA see its quarterly *Report to Congress* and its monthly *Local Currency Counterpart Funds*. These documents are the sources of the statistical data in this section.

but such a use does give ECA some control over the direction of investment in the recipient countries.[6]

ECA has, as a matter of policy in countries suffering inflation, attempted to condition its consent for release of these funds on the local government's undertaking what ECA officials considered to be appropriate fiscal and monetary policies. Application of this principle is obviously a delicate task, and from press reports it appears that political considerations on occasion, for example in the case of France and Greece, dictated a release of funds in advance of the country's completing what were regarded by ECA as desirable monetary and fiscal reforms.

An effort had been made in Congress early in the year to amend the Economic Cooperation Act so as to prohibit the use of counterpart funds to retire internal debt. This move was directed at the United Kingdom, since some members of Congress thought such use of the counterpart funds served to strengthen the financial position and aid the nationalization policies of the Labor Government. On November 1 and December 1, 1949 ECA did not make its usual monthly releases of sterling counterpart funds for debt retirement. This was interpreted by the press as an effort to placate Congressional opposition in anticipation of the request for funds for the third year of ECA.[7]

In 1948 a total of the equivalent of $1.1 billion of counterpart funds were deposited in the special accounts for use in the recipient country; withdrawals, other than for debt retirement,

---

[6] While it would be possible for a recipient nation to adopt investment, monetary, and fiscal policies offsetting the use of counterpart funds, it would seem unlikely that such action would be taken, since it would not only be in direct violation of the spirit at least of the bilateral agreements but it could also conceivably lead to withdrawal of ECA assistance. The counterpart funds are certain to be a powerful control instrument only when the country concerned has a large budgetary deficit and is unwilling or unable to increase its rate of borrowing. See McLeod, A. N., "Local Currency Proceeds of an Import Surplus," *Staff Papers*, International Monetary Fund, February 1950 for a detailed discussion of the policy implications in the use of these funds. For the views of OEEC the reader is referred to its *Second Report, op. cit.*, pp. 62–63.

[7] It is to be noted that since approval of both nations is required the unwillingness of the British authorities to agree to a use other than debt retirement will have much the same effect as if they were used for this purpose, since, in the absence of an agreement, they must simply be immobilized.

totalled only $226.4 million. Thus, if one may assume that the deposits were in fact at least approximately matched by receipts from sales of ECA-financed goods, the administration of these funds did have important counter-inflationary effects. During 1949 the equivalent of $3.0 billion (after adjustment)[8] were deposited for use by the recipient countries; withdrawals, other than for debt retirement, totalled $1.4 billion. In other words, in 1948 when inflation was considered a major deterrent to European economic recovery, approximately 80 percent of the counterpart fund deposits were used to combat inflation. But in 1949, as inflationary pressures eased and unemployment increased, more and more attention was placed on using the funds to finance internal investments, and only slightly over 50 percent of the deposits were frozen or used for debt retirement.[9] Of the funds withdrawn for expenditures within the country the largest part went to finance investment in public utilities, coal mining, and agriculture.[1] Some was spent directly for relief. Only very small amounts were spent to promote manufacturing.

As noted above, 5 percent of the counterpart fund deposits are reserved for the use of the United States in the country. Through 1949 less than one third of these deposits had been spent; they went largely to purchase or develop the production of strategic and critical materials (see pages 166 and 167) and to cover ECA local currency administrative expenses.

Table VIII shows the status of the counterpart fund accounts for the entire period April 1948–December 31, 1949.

[8] The dollar equivalent of these deposits at the conversion rates in effect at the time of deposit was computed at $3.5 billion. In order to make these deposit figures comparable with withdrawals after the September 1949 devaluations, the ECA has adjusted the deposit figures to reflect the conversion rate in effect at the time of withdrawal, and the balances remaining in the accounts at the end of 1949 were adjusted to the devalued rates. (See footnote (b) to Table VIII for further details.)

[9] In addition to the above-described counterpart funds, Italy, France, and Austria were also required to make similar deposits for aid received under the Post-UNRRA Aid Program (P.L. 84) and the Interim Aid Program (P.L. 389). These had been substantially all used by the end of 1948, the bulk of them for internal rehabilitation purposes, especially of communications and public utilities.

[1] It may be, as OEEC has pointed out, that some of these *particular* investments could not otherwise have been made since funds for these specific purposes may not have been available in the private capital market and such investments may also have been outside the scope of central bank activities.

I. GIFTS

TABLE VIII
Status of Local Currency Counterpart Accounts,
As of December 31, 1949
(in millions of dollar equivalents)

Total Deposits[a]		*4341.6*[b]
Deposits for Use by Recipient Country		4145.8[b]
Withdrawals for		
Debt Retirement	1068.7	
Promotion of Agriculture and Extractive Industries	411.8	
Promotion of Manufacturing	121.1	
Promotion of Transportation, Communication and Utilities	666.0	
Other Promotion of Production	110.1	
Construction of Public Buildings and Housing Facilities	*130.8*	
Special Relief Projects	57.6	
Other	157.4	
	2723.5	
Deposits for Use by United States		195.8[b]
Withdrawals for[c]		
ECA Administration	11.9	
Deficiency Materials[d]	36.3	
Information Projects	3.2	
Other	12.1	
	63.5	

a. Deposits are made in local currency at conversion rates which are the par values agreed to by the International Monetary Fund; where no such par values exist the rates used are mutually agreed upon by ECA and the participating country concerned.

b. These deposit figures are "adjusted" to provide comparability between deposits and withdrawals. The dollar equivalent of withdrawals made prior to the September devaluations have been computed at the average rates at which deposits were made. Withdrawals after the devaluations have been computed at the conversion rates in effect at the time of withdrawal which were different from the rates at which some of the deposits were made. ECA has therefore adjusted the deposit figures so as to express their dollar equivalents " . . . in terms of the rates in effect at the time the funds were withdrawn or at the current rate for balances remaining in the accounts." The unadjusted deposit figures were $4850.7 million for total deposits, $4608.2 million for deposits for use by recipient countries, and $242.5 million for deposits for use by the United States.

c. In addition the equivalent of $11.7 million was transferred in 1949 to the U.S. Treasury for use by other agencies of the Government in the participating countries.

d. An additional $14.5 million had been committed for deficiency materials but not yet spent.

Sources: *Local Currency Counterpart Funds*, December 31, 1949 and April 1950, Economic Cooperation Administration, Washington, D.C., 1950; *Seventh Report to Congress*, Economic Cooperation Administration, Washington, D.C., May 1950, p. 146 f.

B. MILITARY ASSISTANCE

Since the war the United States has been involved in several collective military defense arrangements.   Under a series of laws and authorities,[2] the Government had rendered extensive military assistance to foreign countries between V-J Day and the early summer of 1949; the *procurement* cost of combat material alone exceeded $2 billion.[3]   The year 1949 saw the replacement of sporadic and piecemeal assistance by an enlarged, coordinated, and long-term program of foreign military aid.   While the program was shaped in 1949 and promised to be an important element in United States international financial transactions in the future, actual expenditures were small during the year.

The post-war political background for joint defense arrangements began in December 1947 with the Treaty of Rio de Janeiro, which was ratified by the President after it had been approved with only one dissenting vote in the Senate.   In March 1948, the governments of Belgium, France, Luxembourg, the Netherlands, and the United Kingdom, with the encouragement of the American Government, signed the Brussels Treaty.   In June 1948, the Senate adopted by a large majority the famous Vandenberg Resolution; on the basis of this expression by the Senate, the Executive branch began exploratory talks on mutual defense with Canada and the signers of the Brussels Treaty.   The conclusion was reached that a defense treaty for the whole North Atlantic area was desirable and, further, that this should be supplemented by a program of mutual military aid.[4]

North Atlantic Defense

The North Atlantic Treaty was signed on April 4 in Washington and was overwhelmingly approved by the Senate on July 21st.

[2] The more important were: Surplus Property Act of 1944, Greek-Turkish Aid Act of 1947, Greek-Turkish Assistance Act of 1948, China Naval Assistance Act of 1946, China Aid Act of 1948, Republic of Philippines Military Assistance Act of 1946, and the plenary powers of the President.

[3] For a detailed but reportedly incomplete statement of such military assistance, see report prepared by the Department of State and included in *Hearings before Committee on Foreign Affairs, House of Representatives, 81st Cong., 1st Sess., on H.R. 5748 and H.R. 5895*, pp. 31–34.

[4] See *Senate Document No. 48*, 81st Cong., 1st Sess., for background detail on the North Atlantic Treaty.

This twenty-year collective alliance with Canada and ten Western European countries declares that an armed attack against one shall be considered an attack against all; each member country commits itself to take such action as it considers necessary, including the use of armed force, to restore and maintain the security of the North Atlantic area. The signatories agree "by means of continuous and effective self-help and mutual aid" to maintain and develop their individual and collective capacity to resist armed attack; to implement this undertaking provisions are made in the treaty for establishing a defense council, which in turn will establish a defense committee.

During the Congressional Hearings and debate on the treaty, the Administration insisted that although the treaty and the prospective proposals for military assistance were related they were different things. While it was admitted that the treaty bound the United States to the general proposal of mutual aid, it was maintained that it did not commit those who voted for it to support the specific assistance program being prepared by the Administration or any particular kind of implementation program.[5]

The President signed the instruments of ratification of the Treaty on July 25th and on the same day sent a special message to Congress asking for an appropriation of $1400 million for the fiscal year 1950 for a consolidated military aid program to Western European and other nations whose security was important to the United States.[6] To insure an integrated program, it was planned that the President would delegate the broad responsibility for its administration to the Secretary of State. He in turn would collaborate closely with the Secretary of Defense; ECA would also help

[5] Although most of the debate and discussion surrounding the measure made it clear that it was directed against Russia, Senator Vandenberg in the Senate debate made the point that it applied to all potential aggressors —Germany included—and was, therefore, a powerful and well-nigh indispensable aid to maximum German recovery and, *consequently*, European recovery, because it permitted greater production latitudes than Germany's neighbors would otherwise tolerate.

[6] In the course of preparation of the program formal and informal requests for aid had been received from various foreign countries. It was planned that this aid would be on a grant basis. An additional 50 million for interim continuation of military aid to Greece and Turkey had previously been requested in the foreign economic aid program.

formulate policies.[7] A large part of actual operations in the United States would be handled by the Department of Defense, and both ECA and the Department of Defense would be represented in the overseas operations.

Although the State Department had previously published data on how it planned to distribute the aid, the original proposed legislation gave the President authority to grant military aid on terms he deemed appropriate to any foreign country whose increased ability to defend itself was important to American national interests. This broad authority aroused much concern and opposition, and in the middle of the House Hearings a new bill was introduced which specifically designated the countries which were to receive aid: North Atlantic Pact countries $1,160,-990,000; Greece and Turkey $211,370,000 (plus $45 million included in pending legislation for foreign economic aid); Iran, Korea, and the Philippines $27,640,000.

In justifying the program the Administration advanced several arguments.[8] Much attention was placed on its economic justification, with the contention that insecurity and fear of aggression were exceptionally great handicaps to continued economic recovery in Europe. It was stated that only when this fear was removed would the people of Europe work, save, and invest in the required amounts. It was also argued that this was a continuation of a program to assure peace and security in the world (of which ERP, the Atlantic Treaty, Greek-Turkish aid, activities in UN, and post-war relief were major examples) and that any sign of weakness or irresolution in extending military aid would prejudice the gains made to date.

On military grounds, it was maintained, the requested aid was the minimum needed by recipient nations to guard adequately against internal subversion. It was admitted that the aid was not sufficient to permit foreign nations to meet an armed attack, but it was argued that this aid plus the treaty might be enough

---

[7] In mid-November a Mutual Defense Assistance Office was established in the Department of State.

[8] The reader is referred to the *Joint Hearings before the Committee on Foreign Relations and the Committee on Armed Services, U.S. Senate, 81st Cong., 1st Sess., on S. 2388* and *Hearings before Committee on Foreign Affairs, House of Representatives, 81st Cong., 1st Sess., on H.R. 5748 and H.R. 5895* for details on much of what follows.

to prevent an attack. General Bradley testified that the strategy back of the program was to deter a potential aggressor for our own protection. Secretary Acheson went somewhat further. He testified that the strategy was also to keep the European-Atlantic shore open long enough to permit our coming to Europe's aid if she were attacked.

In the Hearings on the bill much concern was expressed as to the effect of increased military expenditures on European economic recovery. The Administration argued that it would strengthen rather than impair economic recovery for the reasons stated above. It was also stated that increased military production in Europe would not impinge on its economic recovery. On closer questioning, Secretary Acheson admitted that any armament expenditure might be thought of as an economic burden but added that the amounts envisaged in this program were consistent with the economic plans worked out by ECA and the participating countries. Since emphasis was on modernizing and coordinating Europe's armed forces rather than enlarging them, it was hoped there would be no serious inflationary consequences.[9]

A matter of much more serious concern to Congress was whether the measure would insure the rapid integration of Western Europe's military efforts. Considerable reference was made to those parts of the Atlantic Treaty which related to mutual aid and collective capacity to resist armed attack. The majority of Congress insisted that the assistance program must be so drawn and executed as to assure military unity, coordination, and integration. In the Hearings, the Administration attempted to meet these views by stating that much progress was being made in Western Europe's military coordination, more was anticipated, but that the United States could not dictate on such matters and must not press for too rapid action. They also argued that Congress must not delay approval of aid until they were satisfied that integration was satisfactory for it then might be too late and that such delay would in any case be a serious blow to European morale.

Congress was not completely convinced by the Administra-

[9] On November 18, it was announced that a "Defense Financial and Economic Committee" under the North Atlantic Treaty had been established to advise and guide the North Atlantic Council on financial and economic aspects of defense measures. (For details see *Department of State Bulletin,* November 28, 1949, p. 819.)

tion's arguments, and, in an effort to get prompt action on integrated defense arrangements, the House originally passed a measure cutting in half the Administration's request for aid to the Pact countries. The Senate version, which was finally approved by both houses on October 6 as the Mutual Defense Assistance Act of 1949, authorized the appropriation for Atlantic Pact countries of $500 million, plus contract authorizations of $500 million. But it specified that no assistance was to be provided until appropriate bilateral agreements had been signed between the United States and each of the recipient nations and that not more than $100 million were to be available until after the President had approved the recommendations for an integrated defense of the North Atlantic area to be made by the Council and the Defense Committee to be established under the North Atlantic Treaty. Congress also specified in the law that American aid was to be granted on the principle of self help and mutual assistance and that provisions to this effect were to be included in the bilateral agreements.

Congressional concern over possible delays in the coordination of defense arrangements appears to have been well-founded. On December 1, the North Atlantic Defense Committee, with Secretary Johnson as Chairman, announced in Paris that an integrated defense plan had been approved, but the North Atlantic Defense Council did not give its approval until January 6, 1950. Although the bilateral agreements with most of the Western European nations raised few difficulties, the British raised serious objections to the United States draft. According to press reports, they insisted the agreement should give clear priority to domestic economic recovery over the mutual aid phase of the program (thus evidencing more concern over the economic consequences than had been shown by the Administration spokesmen before the Congressional committees), and they objected to the American suggestion that the United States be consulted before any domestically produced military equipment be shipped outside the North Atlantic area. There was also some uneasiness in Britain over making commitments to maintain United States bases in England in the event of war. The United States acceded to most of the British objections, but the agreements with the North Atlantic nations were not signed until January 27, 1950; on that day President Truman was finally able to approve the integrated defense plans.

As a result of the delays in signing the bilateral agreements noted above, no goods were shipped under this legislation in 1949 (the press reported some $50 million had been spent in the United States for assembling and reconditioning equipment for shipment). It was reported at year's end that officials were confident the entire amount provided for the North Atlantic area at least would be either spent or allocated before June 30, 1950, but the first shipments to that area did not take place until mid-March.

China Defense

Another point of compromise between the Administration and Congress had to do with China. The Administration in its plans provided no funds for aid to China and argued that it saw no effective way of rendering assistance to China. Earlier in the year, a proposal had been made by some members of Congress that $1.5 billion in military and economic aid be provided the Nationalist Government in China but was dropped following Administration opposition. Congressional interest in aiding China was still strong, however. Secretary Acheson finally said that, while he was in no position to justify a request for aid to China, if Congress wished, it might prove useful to give the President some funds to be used at his discretion in the Far Eastern area. Thereafter, a $75 million emergency fund for the President was written into the law. He could spend it, confidentially if he so wished, in the "general area" of China, and the assistance could be in any form which would contribute to realizing the policies and purposes of the legislation.[1] Congress also added a section expressing itself as favoring the creation by the Far Eastern countries of a joint organization " . . . to establish a program of self-help and mutual cooperation designed to develop their economic and social well-being, to safeguard basic rights and liberties and to protect their security and independence."[2]

None of the $75 million was spent during 1949 (in May 1950 it appeared most of it would be used to provide military equip-

---

[1] The Administration interpreted this to mean it need not be spent on military aid.

[2] Mutual Defense Assistance Act of 1949 (Public Law 329, 81st Cong., 1st Sess.). The act did not specify United States participation in such an organization, but it was pointed out in the House-Senate Committee Conference Report that this omission did not prejudice the question of participation.

ment to the Indo-Chinese states), but China did utilize $45 million of the funds provided for military assistance under the China Aid Act of 1948 as amended (see pages 44–5), leaving some $9 million still unspent.   The rate of utilization declined during the year, and on January 5, 1950 President Truman announced the United States would extend no further military aid or advice to the Chinese forces.

Other

Neither the Senate nor House altered, or spent much time discussing, the requested aid to Greece, Turkey, Iran, the Philippines and Korea.   During 1949, however, the United States provided military assistance to Greece and Turkey to an amount of $172 million from funds provided under the Greek-Turkish Assistance Act of 1948 as amended.   Disbursements under this program declined steadily throughout the year.[3]

The Mutual Defense Assistance Act of 1949 was finally passed by a two-to-one majority and was signed by the President on October 6.[4]   Appropriations and contract authorizations were included in the Second Supplemental Appropriation Act, passed on the day Congress adjourned, providing the following amounts for the period ending June 30, 1950:[5]

North Atlantic Pact Countries	
Contract Authorization	$500,000,000
Cash Appropriation	500,000,000
	$1,000,000,000
Greece and Turkey	211,370,000
Iran, Korea, and Philippines	27,640,000
"General Area" of China	75,000,000
	$1,314,010,000

[3] Disbursements totalled $349 million in 1948, but some non-military aid to Greece was included.

Congress did, however, insert in the law a restrictive shipping clause similar to that added to ECA legislation (see page 12).

To forestall accusations that the United States was fostering the building of a foreign armament industry Congress also inserted a section providing that none of the funds should be used for any capital expansion or maintenance abroad except for the provision of machine tools.

[4] Congressional delays and debate quickly ceased after the President announced there had been an atomic explosion in Russia.

[5] North Atlantic aid includes nothing for Canada, Portugal or Ireland,

Adding the $45 million for military aid to Greece and Turkey included in the Foreign Economic Aid Appropriation Act, the total provision for direct foreign military aid for the fiscal year 1950 was $1,359,010,000.

The Administration was frank in admitting that this was only the beginning and that future appropriations would also be required. It was reluctant to state how long or how large this program might ultimately be but hoped the first year's appropriations would be the largest. Only Secretary Johnson was rash enough to suggest a time limit—he thought such assistance might be necessary, in decreasing amounts, for five or six years.

C. OCCUPIED AREAS PROGRAM

The United States began providing civilian relief supplies to occupied countries when its forces landed in North Africa in November 1942 and continued the practice, whenever necessary, in both friendly and enemy countries throughout the rest of the war as a matter of military precaution against "disease and unrest."[6] In the period following the war, non-military agencies (including UNRRA) took over this responsibility in most countries, but the military continued to meet the problem in areas formally occupied by it. As the cold war developed, relief feeding and economic reconstruction in occupied countries became a fixed part of American foreign policy, with large special appropriations being granted to the Army for Government and Relief in Occupied Areas (GARIOA). By the end of 1949, except for Japan and the Ryukyus, responsibility had for the most part been turned over to civilian agencies, and the aid programs for "occupied areas" were very similar in type and purpose to those for our former allies.

---

which countries had not requested financial aid. In addition to these direct grants, The Mutual Defense Assistance Act permits any nations which have joined the United States in collective defense and regional arrangements to buy military goods from the United States for cash. It also specified that excess United States military equipment shipped under the program could not exceed in value $450 million, based on original cost, and that only the amount spent to put such equipment into usable condition would be charged against the above appropriations.

[6] During the war period $813 million were spent for this purpose by the Army and Navy.

From mid-1945 to the end of 1948, $3.2 billion had been spent by the armed forces, distributed as shown in Table IX.

TABLE IX

Civilian Supplies Furnished Occupied Areas by the Military, 1946–1948
(in millions of dollars)

	Fiscal Year 1946	Fiscal Year 1947	Fiscal Year 1948	Jul–Dec. 1948	Total
Germany	155	273	626	379	1433
Austria	50	35	9	*	94
Italy	231	13	0	0	244
Unclassified Europe	158	0	0	0	158
Japan	96	292	436	202	1026
Ryukyus	15	11	6	4	36
Korea	2	43	101	43	189
Philippines	28	0	0	0	28
Other #	9	0	3	0	12
Total	744	667	1181	628	3220

* Less than $500,000.

\# Indonesia $4 million and various Pacific Islands $5 million in fiscal year 1946 and Trieste $3 million in fiscal year 1948.

Source: Compiled from data in *Foreign Transactions of the U.S. Government,* Department of Commerce, Washington, D.C. October 1949, Appendix Table 3.

Note: In addition to this aid Germany had, from the end of the war through 1948, also received from the United States $118 million of ERP assistance and $3.6 million from the UNRRA in the form of grants, plus $126 million of various loans—mostly surplus property and cotton credits. Japan and her possessions had received no other grants from the United States but had utilized $216 million of various credits—mostly short-term cotton credits extended by the Department of Agriculture. Austria had also received from the United States grants of $328 million through ECA, UNRRA and under the Post-UNRRA and Interim Aid Programs, plus $19 million of various loans. Italy had received grants of $828 million from the same sources and $318 million of loans. Other assistance to Korea and the Philippines is discussed below.

During the war and the first three years after its end, civilian goods supplied were largely foodstuffs and were limited to amounts called for under the Hague Convention of 1907 requiring the victor to furnish minimum supplies and relief necessary to insure "public order and safety" in occupied areas.[7] The Administration had come to the conclusion by early 1948 that, if

[7] After the first world war Congress appropriated $100 million for European relief but specified that none of it was to be used for former enemy nations; the American Society of Friends was the principal provider of post-war relief supplies to Germany and Austria.

United States aid remained at this minimum level, dependence on grants would be indefinitely prolonged and that it was therefore necessary to stimulate economic recovery in these areas.[8] The program in that year evolved from one of relief to one of relief and recovery, and the Army divided its occupied areas' appropriation of $1.3 billion for fiscal year 1949 into two sections, $1.2 billion for GARIOA and $150 million for ERIOA (Economic Rehabilitation in Occupied Areas); the latter was for economic rehabilitation in Japan, the Ryukyus, and Korea. In that year Congress also provided that ECA funds could be spent for economic recovery purposes in the other occupied countries—Germany, Austria, and Trieste.

During 1948 and 1949 United States policy in western Germany and Japan changed from one primarily of preventing their resurgence as menaces to peace to one designed to revive them economically, politically, and socially (and in the case of Germany of "integrating" its economy with those of the other Western European countries), while at the same time taking precautions to prevent their becoming militarily dangerous. In addition to the political considerations arising out of United States differences with Russia and the belief that only by such a policy would it be possible in the foreseeable future to eliminate large and continuing relief expenditures, this shift in policy with respect to Germany was prompted by the conviction that the recovery of the rest of Western Europe required a prosperous Germany.

In early 1949, with our armies still occupying Germany, Japan, and the Ryukyus,[9] the Administration requested $1 billion for the fiscal year 1950, and stated that it planned to spend $877 million for civilian relief supplies in Germany, Japan, and the Ryukyus and $123 million for raw and semi-finished materials needed for "economic rehabilitation" in Japan and the Ryukyus. Approximately 70 percent of the total amount requested was for the purchase and

[8] In mid-1948 industrial production in Germany was estimated at only 47 percent of the 1936 level and in Japan at 55 percent of the 1930–34 average.

[9] The Army was also formally occupying Austria and Trieste, but ECA has since its beginning been responsible for the aid programs to these two countries. The Army continues as the operating agency in many important respects. ECA took over responsibility in Korea on January 1, 1949 (see pages 47–48).

41

transportation of agricultural commodities. The relationship between this program and United States agricultural policy was discussed at length in Congress, it being recognized that this was an important outlet for surplus agricultural commodities. The discussion was not concerned with inconsistencies in our foreign trade and farm policies but centered around possible ways of using funds appropriated to handle farm surpluses to reduce the cost of the occupation feeding. The possibility of including Germany and Japan in the International Wheat Agreement was explored but abandoned. Congress also investigated the possibility of using for GARIOA purchases the funds provided in Section 32 of the Agricultural Adjustment Act for export subsidies on agricultural commodities. The Secretary of Agriculture reported, however, that these funds could not be so definitely earmarked since they were to subsidize commodities according to the needs of United States farmers and not those of the occupied countries, and that many of the commodities being subsidized were not in the import programs for the occupied countries.[1]

There was no serious questioning in Congress of the need for, or purposes of, the program and, while the amount was subjected to the summer's economy drive, Congress finally provided $912.5 million on October 6 for the year ending June 30, 1950.[2] The President was authorized, with respect to Germany, to transfer funds, personnel, and functions from the Army to civilian agencies. During the latter part of 1949 officials of the new Federal Republic of Germany were invited to participate directly in OEEC, and responsibility for all United States economic aid to Germany was transferred from the Army to ECA.

During the year 1949, $928 million of civilian supplies and services were provided from the occupied areas appropriation, as compared with $1.3 billion in 1948. Germany utilized $431 million of GARIOA funds, as against $808 million in 1948. How-

[1] For details of the Occupied Areas Program in 1948 and 1949 and discussions of the changes in United States policy regarding these areas, the reader is referred to *Hearings before the Subcommittee of the Committee on Appropriations, House of Representatives, 81st Cong., 1st Sess., on the Foreign Aid Appropriation Bill for 1950*, pp. 809–969.

[2] Legally both Germany and Japan are required to pay for the supplies furnished by the occupying forces; it is conceivable that these debts may be an issue at the time when the peace treaties are drafted.

ever, grants to Germany by ECA *and* the Army in 1949 totalled $921 millon and were only four million less than the previous year. Japan and the Ryukyus received $440 million of supplies under the GARIOA and ERIOA programs, which was ten percent greater than in 1948. Some $57 million of the 1949 total went to Korea (see pages 47 ff), and about one hundred thousand dollars were spent in Austria.

In his January 9, 1950 Budget Message, President Truman said that the costs of our aid programs in Germany beginning in July 1950 would be met from European Recovery Program funds. Army-administered aid to occupied areas would, he reported, thereafter be limited for all practical purposes to Japan and the Ryukyu Islands. He requested only $320 million for these two areas for fiscal year 1950–51, as compared with $485 million estimated to be provided in fiscal year 1949–50, but as regards the future he said only that this would " . . . bring us nearer to termination of this program."[3]

D. CHINA AID PROGRAM

The question of our aid programs in China and Korea was among the more bitterly debated issues between the Administration and certain members of Congress during 1949. There was some sentiment in Congress not only for very large assistance—economic and military—to Nationalist China but also for a single and inclusive aid program for the Far East similar in approach to that taken by the United States in Western Europe. Both of these were resisted by the Executive branch. Following a dispute over the Administration's Korean Aid Program, a law was passed in February 1950 providing for continued aid of only token importance to China; respects were paid to those urging

[3] The Budget Message of the President, January 9, 1950. Drastic internal economic and political changes in Germany and Japan followed the shift in United States policy regarding the future role of these two countries. For official details the reader is referred, in addition to the *Hearings* cited above, to: *Germany, 1947–1949: The Story in Documents,* Department of State, Washington, D.C., March 1950, Publication 3556; *Weekly Information Bulletin,* Office of Military Government for Germany (U.S.), now *Information Bulletin* (monthly), Office of the United States High Commissioner for Germany; Department of State, *Far Eastern Series,* Nos. 8, 11, 15, 17, 19, 20, 22, 25, 26, 27, and the *Department of State Bulletin.*

an integrated Far East program by including aid to Korea in the same law. At this time the Administration stated it was not contemplating a Marshall Plan for the Far East but was studying the possibility of extending additional economic assistance to Southeast Asia.

From the end of the war through 1948 China had received various types of financial assistance from the United States Government to an amount of $1644 million, most of which was in the form of outright grants.[4] By 1948 the Executive branch questioned seriously whether further aid could either arrest the trend toward economic chaos in China or give the Nationalists facilities with which successfully to resist the Communists.

The China Aid Act of 1948[5] had authorized a limited program

[4] $723.9 million of lend-lease supplies were given in the fiscal year 1946; the remaining $119.6 of the $500 million Treasury Stabilization Fund aid of 1942 was also utilized in the fiscal year 1946 (this aid had originally been granted, at China's insistence, without specifications as to payment or non-payment). In the period from July 1945 to June 1947 the United States had contributed $362.9 million to UNRRA relief for China, and in fiscal 1948 $41.2 million of assistance had been provided under the United States Post-UNRRA Aid Program (P.L. 84). In 1948 $72 million in military assistance and $95.9 million in civilian economic assistance were granted under the China Aid Act of 1948. (ECA reported the civilian shipments at $119.7 million.) Total credits, as distinct from grants, extended to China during this period from the end of the war through 1948 totalled $227 million and included $59 million by the Office of Foreign Liquidation Commissioner (OFLC); $20 million by the Army in form of surplus property credits; $16 million by the Maritime Commission; $82 million by the Export-Import Bank; and $50 million in a lend-lease credit. (Source: *Foreign Transactions of the U.S. Government*, Department of Commerce, Washington, D.C., October 1949, appendix Tables 3 and 7.)

In its *United States Relations with China*, Far Eastern Series No. 30, August, 1949, pp. 1042–1053, the State Department estimates this aid at approximately $2.0 billion. The differences are due primarily to the facts that (a) the State Department includes total aid authorized by Congress under the China Aid Act of 1948 while the Commerce Department includes only aid "utilized"; (b) State includes the original cost of 131 naval vessels transferred to China while Commerce includes nothing in the absence of data as to their value at the time of transfer; and (c) State estimates the United States share of the value of all goods delivered to China under the world-wide UNRRA program while Commerce allocates to China only the landed cost of shipments by United States Government agencies.

[5] Title IV, of the Foreign Assistance Act of 1948. Title I was the Economic Cooperation Act of 1948.

of continued economic and military assistance to China. Subequent legislation appropriated $275 million for economic aid to be administered by ECA, and in another appropriation the President was authorized to spend $125 million for military aid. As then conceived, the economic program was designed only to help retard the economic deterioration of China and to give the Nationalist Government an opportunity to initiate measures aimed at establishing more stable internal economic conditions. During calendar year 1948, $96 million of the economic aid and $72 million of the military assistance were utilized. In addition, in early 1948 China received $36 million of aid under the 1947 Post-UNRRA Aid Program.

In early 1949 the economic, political, and military situations in China were deteriorating at an accelerating rate. The Administration, in requesting funds for foreign economic assistance for fiscal year 1949–50, did not feel it could justify requests for further assistance to China. In March some fifty Senators endorsed a proposal for providing up to $1.5 billion in military and economic aid to Nationalist China, but Secretary Acheson opposed this action on the ground that it would not alter the pattern of current developments. After much discussion it was finally agreed that no new funds would be appropriated in 1949 for economic aid to China. But in the legislation extending the ECA Act a provision was included whereby the balance of the 1948 appropriation of $275 million, which had not been obligated on April 2 or which was subsequently released from obligation, was to be available to the President for use through February 15, 1950 " . . . for assistance in areas in China which he may deem to be not under Communist domination, to be furnished in such manner and on such terms and conditions as he may determine."[6]

Shortly thereafter the Communists made great sweeps across China and soon controlled the important ports which had been receiving ECA-financed supplies. Some shipments had to be diverted to Japan and Korea, and many procurement authoriza-

[6] Public Law 47, 81st Congress. Public Law 327, 81st Congress, earmarked $4 million of the unexpended funds for use over an indefinite period for aiding Chinese students in the United States. These funds were subsequently transferred by ECA to the State Department and $300 thousand were spent in 1949.

tions were cancelled. Shipments had virtually ceased by the end of the summer. In August 1949 the Administration formally declared, in the face of bitter criticism of its Far Eastern policies by friends of China in Congress, that additional aid to Nationalist China at that time would be of no avail.[7]

For the entire year the reported value of economic aid extended was only about $64 million (including $2 million of counterpart funds used for additional assistance to China), largely rice, petroleum products, raw cotton, and fertilizers.[8] At the end of 1949 over $100 million of the $275 million appropriated in 1948 for economic aid to China were unspent. On February 14, 1950, following the Congressional dispute over aid to Korea (see below), the spending authority which was scheduled to stop on February 15 was extended to June 30, 1950. It was estimated that probably no more than $10 million would be spent in China (Formosa) during this extension period, and in May it appeared a larger portion of it would be diverted to granting economic aid to Southeast Asia. (During 1949 the Chinese Government also used $2.0 million of Export-Import Bank loans authorized in 1945 and 1946; at the end of the year there were over $15 million of these loan authorizations still undisbursed.) The question of aid to China under the military defense assistance program, as noted above, was also an issue during the year between the Administration and some members of Congress and, while $45 million of the 1948 appropriation were utilized during the year, President Truman announced on January 5, 1950 that no further military aid or advice was to be given the Chinese forces.

It thus appeared at year's end that aid to China, which had totalled over $3.1 billion[9] since July 1, 1940, would in the foreseeable future be of no significance in the international financial affairs of the United States.

[7] The reader is referred to *United States Relations with China, op. cit.,* for a detailed history of United States aid to China since 1940.
[8] The inflation in China rendered the counterpart funds practically worthless and special arrangements were made to meet the local currency requirements of ECA. The quarterly *Report to Congress,* Economic Cooperation Administration, will provide the reader with details on many of ECA's problems and activities in China.
[9] This is a Commerce Department figure. The State Department estimate is some $3.5 billion—see second paragraph of footnote 4 on page 44 for explanation of differences.

E. KOREAN AID PROGRAM

Since the war the United States has felt it has special responsibilities for and interest in South Korea. In December 1943 the United States, United Kingdom, and China declared at Cairo that an independent Korea would be established after the war; Russia joined in this agreement in the Potsdam declaration of July 1945. For the purposes of accepting the surrender of the Japanese troops, however, a division was made at the 38° parallel. Korea has remained divided ever since, with Russia occupying the north and the United States the south. For two years the United States unsuccessfully negotiated with the Russians to establish a unified nation; in September 1947 the United States submitted the matter to the United Nations General Assembly, which appointed a Temporary Commission to conduct elections and establish a national government. The Republic of Korea was inaugurated on August 15, 1948 in South Korea only, after Russia refused to permit the north to participate. The United States recognized the Republic on January 1, 1949 and by June had withdrawn all troops but a military training mission of some 500 men.[1]

Legislative Issues

At the end of the war the southern part of Korea, as a former Japanese possession, was occupied by the United States and received relief supplies from it under the Government and Relief in Occupied Areas (GARIOA) program.[2] On January 1, 1949, when recognition was granted, an Executive Order of the Presi-

[1] On August 25, 1948 an election was held in North Korea and the People's Republic was established on September 9 and was recognized by Russia.

[2] For the period from liberation to the end of 1948 Korea had received GARIOA aid totalling $188 million. In addition the Foreign Liquidation Commissioner had extended a $25 million surplus property credit which was utilized in 1947; during 1948 the United States made an occupation payment of $24 million and had turned over as a gift some $40 million of miscellaneous military and naval equipment; and through UNRRA the United States had granted $546 thousand of aid in 1946 and 1947. (Source: *Foreign Transactions of the U.S. Government, op. cit.,* October 1949 and *Hearings before Committee on Foreign Affairs, House of Representatives, 81st Cong., 1st Sess., on H.R. 5330,* p. 57.)

dent assigned to ECA responsibility for administering economic aid to Korea. Goods already under procurement by the Army were to be shipped, and any unobligated funds out of the Army's allocation to Korea from its fiscal year 1948–49 GARIOA appropriation were to be transferred to ECA to be used during the first six months of 1949. $29.9 million were so transferred during 1949.

On June 7, 1949 President Truman requested Congress to pass a Korean Aid bill envisaging a three year program of economic recovery to be administered by ECA; for the first year, July 1949–June 1950, Congress was requested to authorize the appropriation of $150 million. The Administration supported its aid program by arguing that Korea was an important "testing ground" in the cold war and that the survival and economic progress of the Republic would have a great influence on the people throughout Asia. Representatives Judd and Vorys, champions of aid to China and bitter critics of the Administration policy of withdrawing support from the Nationalist Government in China, led the opposition to the program and the concept. They argued that there was little justification for establishing or supporting democratic governments in Korea (and the Philippines) and then allowing China to be "taken over by the Communists." They believed that this fragmentary approach was doomed to failure and that the only solution was to combine military assistance with an overall plan for the Far East similar to the approach taken in Western Europe under the European Recovery Program.[3]

As a result of this opposition, the authorizing legislation was still pending in the House when Congress adjourned, although it had passed the Senate in October. Joint Resolutions of June 30 and August 1, however, had authorized expenditures at the 1948–49 rate against anticipated appropriations, and two stopgap appropriations of $30 million each were granted in the Third Deficiency Appropriation Act and the Second Supplementary Appro-

[3] The possibility of extending aid by a loan rather than a grant was suggested in the *Hearings*, but the Administration maintained Korean recovery would be most seriously delayed by the imposition, under foreseeable conditions, of a dollar service obligation. For an official discussion of the Korean Aid Program see *Hearings before the Committee on Foreign Affairs, House of Representatives, 81st Cong., 1st Sess., on H.R. 5330.*

priation Act of October 10 and October 28. These $60 million were to cover the period through February 15, 1950.

When the new Congress met in early January 1950 the Administration pressed for House approval of its program and agreed to reduce the appropriation authorizations for the rest of the fiscal year to $60 million in addition to the $60 million already appropriated. During the discussions Secretary Acheson announced that the United States would not extend military help to the Chinese Nationalists in Formosa. Congressional pique over this decision resulted, apparently to the surprise of many Congressmen as well as the Executive branch, in the Korean Aid bill being defeated in the House by one vote. This was the first outright defeat for the Administration in a major foreign policy measure since before the war, and President Truman asked for a "speedy rectification." A new bill was then reported by the House Foreign Affairs Committee which altered the original proposal in several respects, the more important being that it (a) included a provision that the unexpended appropriation for economic aid to China provided in the China Aid Act of 1948 would be available until June 30, 1950, (b) changed the name of the measure from Korean Aid Act to Far Eastern Economic Assistance Act of 1950, (c) specified that the commitment to aid Korea was limited to the period ending June 30, 1950 (the Administration later made it clear it intended to press for continued aid to Korea after this date), and (d) required that aid to Korea be immediately terminated in the event any member of the Communist party or the party in control of the North Korea Government were included in the Government of South Korea. This gesture, feeble as it was, to provide for assistance to China and for an "integrated" Far Eastern program, won many Congressional supporters. In this form the measure was approved in early February.

Aid Extended

During the first six months of 1949 the ECA program for Korea was essentially the same as the Army's GARIOA program, i.e., to provide goods needed to prevent disease and unrest and the minimum supplies necessary to repair and maintain essential transportation and industrial equipment. During the rest of the year in-

creasing attention was given to investment designed to increase
Korean production, especially coal, electricity, and cement.[4] Emphasis was also placed on increasing trade with Japan. ECA
found that a serious deterrent to recovery was the internal inflation, and in the summer a special mission was sent to Korea to
assist the Korean authorities in reorganizing the banking and
monetary system.[5] Efforts were also directed to reducing the government's large deficit which was primarily responsible for the
serious inflation.

United States Government-financed goods and services
supplied Korea during 1949 totalled $86 million, of which $6 million represented counterpart funds used for additional assistance
to Korea and $57 million were goods paid for out of the Army
GARIOA appropriation, for which procurement had been initiated by the Army in 1948. The bulk of this aid was in the form
of food and agricultural commodities, but shipments of industrial
commodities were increasing at year's end.

The need for military assistance was also recognized, and
Korea was scheduled to share with Iran and the Philippines $27.6
million made available in the Mutual Defense Assistance Act (see
pages 38–39). Data are not yet available as to how much of this
was allocated to Korea, but the bilateral agreement was not signed
until January 26, 1950, and no goods were shipped during 1949.

F. PHILIPPINE REHABILITATION PROGRAM

Another important grant program of the United States during
1949 was that originated in the Philippine Rehabilitation Act of
1946,[6] by which Congress, in the words of a State Department

---

[4] By the end of 1949 ECA had approved a program for expanding
power facilities estimated to cost the equivalent of $17.3 million, of which
$6.3 million was to be in ECA dollars. Specific procurement authoriza-
tions, however, had not been issued. See the quarterly *Report to Congress*,
Economic Cooperation Administration for details of ECA program and
policies for Korea.

[5] The absence of properly managed banking and credit facilities also
delayed the collection of counterpart funds; details on these accounts are
not available.

[6] During the first two years following the end of the war the Philippines
received $28.3 millions of grant aid from the United States Army, $7.7
million from the United States through UNRRA, and $61 million under
the Rehabilitation Act. Since mid-1947 all grants to the Philippines by the

official, " . . . recognized the deep moral obligation of this Government to help rehabilitate the war-devastated Philippine economy, . . . " since at the time the destruction occurred the Philippine Islands were American territory and the Philippine people were fighting as American nationals. In approving this legislation it was also considered " . . . that the independence granted by the United States to the Philippines could only be placed on a firm footing if some assistance were extended to the newly formed Government in meeting the critical problems arising out of the war devastation."[7]

Private War Damage Claims

Title I of the Act authorized appropriations of $400 million to be paid for compensation of private war damage claims. Approved claims, on the basis of the pre-war values of the properties, of $500 or less were to be paid in full but not more than 75 percent of the approved value of that part of a claim in excess of $500. The program was administered by the Philippine War Damage Commission, also created in June 1946, and was slow in getting started; through 1948, $175 million had been appropriated, of which only $100 million had been utilized. Disallowances were averaging 55 percent of claims. Only a beginning had been made on payments of the portions of approved claims in excess of

United States Government have been under the Rehabilitation Act, and from mid-1947 through 1948 these totalled $188 million. In 1946–48 the Reconstruction Finance Corporation authorized a loan of $70 million, the War Assets Corporation a property credit of $1 million, the Foreign Liquidation Commissioner a surplus property credit of $6 million, and the Maritime Commission a loan of $2 million. The total $79 million of loans and credits had been utilized prior to 1949. (Source: *Foreign Transactions of the U.S. Government*, October, 1949, *op. cit.*, Appendix Tables 3 and 7.)

[7] Assistant Secretary of State Webb in a letter to the Speaker of the House, dated June 21, 1949, quoted in *House Report No. 1028 on H.R. 5535, 81st Cong., 1st Sess.*, July 13, 1949. Further to facilitate the rehabilitation of the Philippine economy and to provide for an orderly readjustment of trade relations between the two nations, there was signed at Manila on July 4, 1946 an executive agreement, based on and authorized by the Philippine Trade Act of 1946, providing for free trade between the United States and the Philippines for eight years and for a subsequent twenty-year period of declining customs preferences. This agreement entered into force in January 1947 following its proclamation by the Presidents of the two nations.

$500. The Commission had adopted the policy of paying only 30 percent of such excess valuations although it was thought that it might be able to pay another 10 percent at the time of liquidation of the program; in late 1948 the rate of payments was increasing rapidly. The Executive branch requested, and received, an appropriation of $184.8 million for fiscal year 1950, of which $20 million was to be available in fiscal year 1949, leaving approximately $40 million still to be appropriated for winding up activities in fiscal year 1951. Actual expenditures under this part of the program during 1949 totalled $165 million, and it was anticipated that the program would be completed in 1950. It was estimated in January 1950 that when the program ended the average rate of disallowances would be around 54 percent, that all approved claims under $500 would have been paid in full, and that larger claims would have received $500 plus 45 percent of the excess.

Public Reconstruction

Title III[8] of the 1946 Act authorized nine agencies of the United States Government to carry out specific programs for reconstructing public facilities and rehabilitating certain essential governmental services of the Philippine Republic. $120 million were authorized to be appropriated for roads, ports and harbors, public buildings, and public health services, to be allocated not later than June 30, 1950;[9] additional appropriations without specific limitation were authorized, as might be required, for maintaining and developing inter-island commerce, inter-island air navigation, weather information, fisheries, and coast and geodetic surveys. Authority was also included for a training program to prepare Filipino technicians to carry on the governmental services being restored, improved, and rehabilitated. The various activities of the nine agencies are coordinated under the State

[8] Title II authorized the Office of the Foreign Liquidation Commissioner to transfer as a gift up to $100 million of surplus property. These transfers, totalling $100 million, were completed by early 1948.

[9] A law passed on September 7, 1949 (Public Law 295) authorized extension of the program until June 30, 1951 to make possible completion of work on roads and port and harbor facilities and provide supervision until completion of the work already under contract. The War Damage Commission, although concentrating on private claims as noted above, is also allocated funds under Title III to make cash payments to compensate the Philippines for damage to public buildings.

Department and supervised by the United States Ambassador. Appropriations for these purposes are made to the State Department which allocates funds to the participating agencies.

Through 1948, $107.9 had already been appropriated, and $26.4 million of contract authorizations had been granted under Title III. Against this only about $50 million had actually been utilized, of which nearly half had been in the form of cash payments to compensate for damage to public buildings. In 1949 the Administration requested $20.4 million for fiscal year 1950, including $16.4 to liquidate previous contract authorizations. This amount was reduced by Congress to $17.2 million. Actual disbursements during 1949 on this part (Title III) of the program were $38 million of which $11 million were cash payments for damage to public property.

Miscellaneous Assistance

The Act also authorized appropriations of $5 million for the restoration and improvement of property of the United States. By the end of 1948, $4 million of this had been appropriated; no further request was made in 1949.

In addition to the above assistance, $12.7 million were appropriated in 1949 for constructing and equipping a hospital and to provide medical care and treatment for Philippine war veterans. Finally, the Philippines were scheduled to share with Iran and Korea some $27.6 million under the Mutual Defense Assistance Program (see pages 38–39). Discussions between United States and Philippine officials regarding specific military requirements of the Philippines took place in Manila in December, and in mid-March 1950 notes were exchanged providing for the extension of such aid; no goods were shipped under this program during 1949.[1]

Questioned about the adequacy of rehabilitation and need for future assistance, Commissioner Delgado of the Philippine War Damage Commission said in February 1949 that due to low valua-

---

[1] Although not properly labelled "aid," mention might be made here of the net cash disbursements in the Philippines by the Veterans Administration which totalled $57 million in 1949. Net cash disbursements by United States military agencies were also important in the Philippines balance of payments, having totalled $83 million during 1949, and net cash disbursements by other government agencies, excluding the Philippine War Damage Commisssion, totalled another $30 million.

tion, costs of construction now being three times what they were in 1941, and amounts of awards being considerably below current values, the work of reconstruction was far from completed and " . . . an economic crisis will undoubtedly result . . . "[2] when the payments under the rehabilitation program stop. Serious difficulties, including capital flight, appeared even sooner, however, and in late 1949, with the approval of the United States, the Philippine Government imposed new and more stringent exchange and import controls as foreign exchange reserves reached a new low of about $200 million.[3] Except for possible aid under the Point Four Program, the Government did not disclose in 1949 any plans for additional future economic assistance to the Philippines. But since they constitute something of an American show-window in the Far East it would seem very possible that additional aid would be forthcoming even though there was evidence that past aid had not been effectively utilized.

G. INTERNATIONAL REFUGEE AND CHILDREN'S RELIEF PROGRAMS

Since the war the United States has assumed a large share of the financial costs of the various international programs for assistance to refugees and children. Expenditures through 1948, excluding the UNRRA, totalled $152 million and were $104 million in 1949.[4] While it was planned that most of these relief programs would taper off rapidly in 1950, one of them, that for relief to the Palestine refugees, showed signs in late 1949 of developing into a broad economic development program for the Middle East.

International Children's Emergency Fund

The United Nations International Children's Emergency Fund (ICEF) took over in December 1946 the children's feeding program originated by UNRRA; it has since provided food, medical

---

[2] *Hearings before Subcommittee of House Committee on Appropriations, House of Representatives, 81st Cong., 1st Sess., on Department of State Appropriation Bill for 1950,* p. 452.

[3] At the time of its independence the new Republic had exchange reserves of over $600 million.

[4] During the war the War Refugee Board spent $3.4 million for assistance to refugees.

care, instruction, and training to needy children in Europe, Asia, North Africa, the Middle East, and Latin America. Support for its work has come not only from governments but also from voluntary fund-raising efforts and from certain residual assets of UNRRA. Up to the end of 1949 it had received contributions in cash and kind estimated at the equivalent of $141 million. In 1947 Congress earmarked $40 million of the appropriations for the Post-UNRRA Aid Program for ICEF, and in 1948 it appropriated another $35 million to the State Department for this purpose. It was provided that these funds were to be made available to ICEF under a matching formula of 72 percent from the United States Government and 28 percent from other governments. By the end of 1948, $42 million of this $75 million had been spent.

In 1949 Congress extended the period during which the unexpended balance of previous appropriations could be used from June 1949 to June 1950 but appropriated no additional amounts. It also specified in this law that it was the express intention of Congress that participation of the United States in ICEF should cease on June 30, 1950.[5] But on December 2, 1949 the U.N. General Assembly, with United States support, unanimously decided that ICEF should continue for at least another year and called attention to the "urgent necessity of future contributions." During 1949 United States contributions totalled $18 million, leaving $15 million of the appropriation available for 1950. In his January 3, 1950 Budget Message to Congress the President included no provision for additional appropriations for the ICEF.

International Refugee Organization

The largest contributions of the United States Government in the area of refugee relief since the war have been made to the U.N. International Refugee Organization (IRO) in support of the work which it had taken over in July 1947 from UNRRA and the Intergovernmental Committee on Refugees. Congress appropriated $71.1 million for the first year of IRO and in 1948 provided an-

[5] This statement was inserted not because of lack of sympathy with the work being done but because it was felt that if the work were to be continued it should be performed by one of the permanent U.N. agencies.

other $70.7 million.[6] In July 1949 another $70.5 million was appropriated for the 12 months ending June 30, 1950. The House subcommittee which held hearings on this measure expressed much concern over the inefficiencies of IRO and stated its opinion that the program should be completed by the end of fiscal year 1950. But if this proved impossible, it warned that " . . . there should be a sufficient surplus of funds remaining to conclude the program without additional appropriations."[7] During 1949, $71 million were transferred by the State Department to IRO, leaving an unexpended balance at the beginning of 1950 of $36 million.

IRO had been scheduled to terminate on June 30, 1950, but in October 1949 it was decided to continue the organization until March 31, 1951.[8] It was, however, planned that the budget for this extension period would be much less than it had been in 1947, 1948, and 1949. In his Budget Message of January 3, 1950 the President, despite the Congressional warning noted above, asked for an appropriation of $25 million for the fiscal year beginning July 1, 1950.

Relief for Palestine Refugees

While contributions to IRO and ICEF gave promise of tapering off quickly, it appeared in 1949 that a new program originating as relief to Arab refugees in Palestine might expand into a broad program of economic development in the Middle East and might call for large expenditures by the United States over a long period. As an aftermath of the Israeli-Arab hostilities in Palestine, an acute Arab refugee problem was created in the Middle East. With these refugees then estimated to number 500 thousand, the U.N. General Assembly, with American support, appealed to its member nations in November 1948 for $32 million in contributions to provide food, shelter, and clothing for a nine months' period. On January 27, 1949 President Truman asked Congress

[6] American representatives at the U.N. had agreed that the United States would meet 39.89 percent of the administrative costs and 45.75 percent of the operational budget of IRO. Because of the failure of some nations to join, the United States contributions in fiscal year 1949 were nearly 57 percent of actual expenditures.

[7] *House Report No. 386*, April 5, 1949, 81st Cong., 1st Sess., p. 10.

[8] Recognizing that a large and complex refugee problem would still remain, the General Assembly voted in December 1949 to establish by March 1951 an Office of U.N. High Commissioner for Refugees. This is now scheduled to come into being on January 1, 1951.

to authorize appropriations of $16 million as the United States share of a program which was to be administered by an emergency organization, U.N. Relief for Palestine Refugees, headed by an American.[9]   Congress, in meeting the President's request, made it clear that it did not want its approval of this special project to be regarded as constituting a precedent or an endorsement for the general proposition of the international administration of relief financed largely through United State contributions.   Congress also warned United States delegations to the United Nations to exercise extreme care not to take any action which committed Congress to provide funds for programs to which all members do not contribute under the regular U.N. budget.

In the summer of 1949 it became apparent that this was not just an emergency problem and that many of the refugees, then numbering nearly 750 thousand, would not be able to return to their former homes.   They were creating serious economic and social problems in the areas to which they had fled and had to be given an opportunity to work where they then were.   On August 23, again with United States support, a U.N. Economic Survey Mission was created, commonly referred to as the Clapp Mission after its American chief, to examine the economic situation in the area and to make recommendations for action which might remedy the economic dislocations created by the hostilities.

In an interim report[1] signed on November 6 the Mission recommended that (a) the emergency relief be continued until April 1, 1950 and thereafter be sharply curtailed and terminated by December 31, 1950, (b) a program of public works, to begin in April 1950 and extend to June 30, 1951, calculated to put the refugees to work and to improve the productivity of the area, should be organized in cooperation with the governments of the countries where the refugees were located, and (c) a new agency should be established to organize and direct the suggested programs of relief and public works.   On December 8 the U.N. General Assembly, without debate, and again with United States

[9] The United States successfully urged several private charitable, religious, and social agencies to assist in the program.   Help was also received from ICEF, the U.S. Navy, and the U.S. Public Health Service.

[1] Appendix I of *Final Report of the United Nations Economic Survey Mission for the Middle East*, Part I, United Nations, Lake Success, New York, December 28, 1949, pp. 16–17.

support, accepted the gist of these recommendations. A U.N. Relief and Works Agency for Palestine Refugees in the Near East was created,[2] and an expenditure of $54.9 million to finance the program for the period from January 1, 1950 to June 30, 1951 was approved. The General Assembly urged all members to make voluntary contributions in cash or kind. The United States representative said the Executive branch would seek from Congress the authority and funds necessary to implement its fair share of the program. On January 30, 1950 President Truman asked Congress to pass enabling legislation authorizing United States participation in this program and appropriations of $27,450,000— half the total estimated cost. At that time over fifteen of the sixteen million dollars appropriated in June for emergency relief had been spent.

In its final report, subtitled "An Approach to Economic Development in the Middle East," signed on December 18, 1949,[3] the Clapp Mission stated that the problem of refugees could not be separated from the larger problem of economic development in the Middle East, that peace and security in the area required higher standards of living which in turn required a development of the area's resources, that immediate large-scale development projects were not feasible, and that the Middle Eastern countries themselves must bear the greatest responsibility for the burden of the economic development. The Mission then specifically recommended that each Middle Eastern government establish a national Development Board to plan overall economic development programs, define and recommend individual projects, and provide for their execution with the technical and financial assistance of the international community. As the first steps in the long-run program of developing the area's basic resources, the report put forward four specific "pilot projects" concerned primarily with electrification, flood control, hydro-electric power, and agricultural experimentation. It then recommended the creation of a

[2] An Advisory Commission composed of representatives of the United States, France, Britain and Turkey was established to advise the Director of this agency, which agency was also directed to coordinate its technical assistance programs with the expanded Technical Assistance Program of the U.N. (see pages 70 ff.).

[3] *Final Report of the United Nations Economic Survey Mission for the Middle East, op. cit.*

fund of not more than $10 million by the governments (initially the United States, Britain, France and Turkey) represented on the Advisory Commission which was established by the General Assembly on December 8. This fund was to be allocated by the Advisory Commission to the Middle Eastern governments for research, experimentation, and assistance in the execution of the four pilot projects where there were no U.N. funds for this purpose.

These proposals were not officially discussed in public by the United States during 1949, but it must be presumed that the Executive branch of the American Government approved the report since the chief of the Mission was an American, whose appointment and activities had been supported by the Government.

H. TOTAL UNITED STATES GOVERNMENT GRANTS

The United States Government foreign grants by program and by area are shown in Table X. Attention is called to the fact that ECA aid extended on a credit basis is *not* included in this table.

J. MISCELLANEOUS GOVERNMENT UNILATERAL TRANSFERS

In addition to the items discussed above there were several other unilateral transfers from and to the United States Government during 1949 which cannot properly be called gifts or grants. Preliminary estimates put such payments at $132 million for 1949 and receipts at $388 million.[4]

The more important of these miscellaneous unilateral payments were the disbursements by the Veterans Administration which totalled $72 million. In addition, $24.8 million were paid to former prisoners of war, including a lump-sum payment of $22 million made in January to the Italian Government in a final settlement of obligations to former Italian prisoners of war. On October 14, Congress appropriated some $14.6 million for the purpose of paying compensation to the Swiss Government for losses and damages inflicted by the United States armed forces

[4] The receipts estimate is taken from the *Survey of Current Business*, March 1950, Table 5 on page 6. The payments estimate represents the "other transfers" in this table less payments for Palestine relief and children's relief and less Institute of Inter-American Affairs and Post-UNRRA payments which have been included in the gifts discussed above.

TABLE X
United States Government Foreign Grants, 1949
(in millions of dollars)

By Program			By Area	
European Recovery		3735	ERP Europe[e]	4338
Occupied Areas[a]		928	Other Europe	0
Korean Aid[a]		29	Latin America	4
China Aid			Middle East[d]	15
Economic	64		Far East[e]	838
Military	45	109	Other[f]	91
Philippine Rehabilitation			Total	5286
Private Claims	165			
Public Reconstruction and Rehabilitation	38	203		
Greek-Turkish Aid (Military)		172		
Military Assistance		0		
Refugee Assistance				
Refugees	71			
Palestine Relief	15	86		
Children's Relief		18		
Other[b]		6		
Total		5286		

a. $57 million of aid extended to Korea out of funds appropriated for Government and Relief in Occupied Areas for fiscal year 1948–49 are included in the Occupied Areas Program.
b. $4.1 million of technical assistance grants to the American Republics by the Institute of Inter-American Affairs; $1.9 million from the termination of the Post-UNRRA Aid Program; and $300 thousand for aid of Chinese students in the United States.
c. Includes Indonesia and Turkey.
d. Represents U.S. contributions to the U.N. for relief to Palestine refugees.
e. China, Japan, Ryukyu Islands, Philippines, Korea.
f. Represents United States contributions to the International Refugee Organization and the International Children's Emergency Fund and the termination expenditures under the Post-UNRRA Aid Program.
Source: *Foreign Transactions of the U.S. Government*, Department of Commerce, Washington, D.C., March 1950, appendix Table 4.
Note: These data cover only aid extended *on other than credit or cash* terms. In most instances these data represent shipments where goods are procured by a U.S. Government agency and cash payments by the Government where other methods of procurement are used. For a more detailed description see the explanatory notes in the cited source. These data include $27 million of counterpart funds used by the ECA for local administration costs as well as dollar costs of administration. ECA aid extended on a credit basis is *not* included here but is included in Table XII, on page 66 and in Table XV, on page 99.

on persons and property in Switzerland during the recent war; $14.4 million was actually paid to the Swiss during the year. On November 1, $5.6 million were paid by the United States Government to the Finnish Government in settlement of claims for compensation arising out of the requisition in 1941 and 1942 of fifteen Finnish vessels lying in United States ports.[5]

Other unilateral payments included $3.7 million paid to Canada and $2.1 million to France in the form of refunds on excess deposits by these countries for the cash procurement of defense goods during the war. Most of the balance of the unilateral payments probably represented various pensions and annuities paid by government agencies other than the Veterans Administration.

During the year the United States Government *received* unilateral transfers preliminarily estimated at $388 million; $228 million of this represented five percent of the local currency counterpart fund deposits by ERP recipients which were allotted to the United States Government for meeting local administration costs and for the purchase of strategic materials. Most of the remainder represented local currencies supplied the United States armies of occupation in Germany and Japan, without compensation, to meet local expenditures.[6]

Adding these miscellaneous unilateral payments to the total grants given in Table X and subtracting the above miscellaneous receipts shows that the net Government unilateral payments during 1949 contributed $5030 million to financing our export surplus.[7]

[5] There had been a difference of opinion between the Finnish shipowners and the United States agents as to the amount of compensation payable, and a suit for compensation had been filed in the United States Court of Claims but was dismissed prior to this payment. A law approved August 24, 1949 provided that all future payments by Finland on her World War I debt should be used to finance the exchange of students and of educational and technical information.

[6] *Survey of Current Business* (March 1950, p. 6) suggests that later information may substantially reduce this figure.

[7] The balance of payments on page 175 records this item at $5085 million. This minor discrepancy is apparently due to the inclusion of preliminary data in the official balance of payments estimates and/or attempts to include items in the balance of payments at the time they are assumed to have occurred rather than when they appear in the records of the Government agencies.

Note: In addition to the huge amount of cash and kind provided foreign areas by the various grant and credit programs and the miscellaneous other unilateral transfers mentioned above, and in addition to cash disbursements in connection with certain more or less commercial operations by official United States agencies,[8] the United States Government during 1949 spent very large amounts abroad for what may be called the ordinary functions of the Government. The most important here are the net expenditures by the military agencies for pay and allowances of troops, purchases of materials and supplies, installations and construction, operation of facilities, transportation, cemeterial expenses, etc. Unfortunately published data again do not permit a precise statement but it appears such expenditures in 1949 were in the neighborhood of $700 million. In addition, civilian agency disbursements for the cost of maintaining diplomatic and other official establishments abroad and contributions to the more or less regular expenses of the thirty-odd international organizations to which we belong, were probably at least $175 million. A large part of these payments are reflected in the miscellaneous services account of the balance of payments.[9]

K. PRIVATE GIFTS

Private gifts during the first two calendar years after the war were equal to approximately 30 percent of Government foreign grants, but the percentage fell to 17 percent in 1948 and to 11 percent in 1949 as private gifts tapered off and the Government's aid programs shifted from loans to grants. Apparently largely as the result of the decline in national income in the United States and the satisfying of some of the more urgent personal needs in many foreign areas following increased domestic production, private gifts from the United States in 1949 fell to an estimated $593 million as compared with slightly more than $700 million during each of the first three post-war years, as shown in Table XI.

[8] As, for example, the large purchases of tin by the Reconstruction Finance Corporation, and sugar, rice, canned beef, etc., by the Commodity Credit Corporation. Most of these purchases are for Government use, including those for the foreign aid programs, but some are commodities later resold to domestic buyers. Stockpile purchases by the Government are largely made from private domestic importers.

[9] The reader wishing to make his own estimates is referred to the "cash" sections of the statistical appendices of the Department of Commerce quarterly reports on *Foreign Transactions of the U.S. Government, op. cit.*

TABLE XI
Private Gifts, 1919–1949
(in millions of dollars)

	1919–21 (yearly average)	1922–39 (yearly average)	1946	1947	1948	1949ᵖ
Personal Remittances						
Cash	568	250	294	245	262	
Gift Parcels	n.a.	n.a.	145	205	154	593
Institutional Remittances	121	51	283	263	294	
Total	689	301	722	713	710	593

p. Preliminary.
n.a. Not available but presumed to be negligible.
Sources: The 1946–48 data are from the *Balance of International Payments of the United States, 1946–1948*, Department of Commerce, Washington, D.C., 1950, pp. 107–114. This document is also the source for much of the other information here presented on private aid. The 1949 figures on preliminary estimates are taken from the *Survey of Current Business*, March 1950, p. 6. The 1919–1939 figures are taken from *The United States in the World Economy*, Department of Commerce, Washington, D.C., 1943, p. 216. These data do not include currency transferred through the mails or aid provided by direct personal transfer. The former may have been important during 1946 and 1947.

While such gifts in the post-war period have averaged well over twice the amounts in the years 1922–1939, it is to be noted that in the first four years after the First World War, 1919–1922, private gifts totalled $2.4 billion and so in real terms were much more important than they have been since the last war. This was to be expected since such gifts are closely related not only to national income in the United States but also to the number of foreign-born residents and the recency of their arrival in the United States. It is to be anticipated that private remittances in the immediate future will continue to decline as the economies of the rest of the world recover and war-imposed privations diminish. In view of the stringent United States immigration restrictions, it must be expected that the long-term trend of private gifts also will be downward.

Private gifts from the United States since the war have fallen into three broad categories: (1) personal cash remittances, (2) personal gift parcels, and (3) institutional remittances. Prior to 1946 gift parcels were negligible. Several factors were responsible for their importance during recent years. The greatly over-valued exchange rates in many countries dictated the sending of aid in kind rather than cash, as did the acute shortage of many essential goods in the receiving countries. These transfers were encouraged by many foreign nations relaxing their import restrictions, both as regards import licenses and tariffs on such shipments. Relief in kind was further encouraged by the United States Congress which in 1947 specified that $5 million of the funds provided for the Post-UNRRA Aid Program should be available for paying ocean transportation charges on such gifts and which in 1948 inserted a clause in the Economic Cooperation Act providing that ECA funds, without limitation, can be used to cover ocean transportation costs on relief parcels sent to ERP nations. During 1949 ECA spent approximately $10 million for such freight subsidies. Exchange rate devaluations, stabilization of price levels, and increased supplies of goods in many of the countries receiving remittances appear to account for the shift in 1948 from gift parcels to cash remittances; it is presumed that this trend continued in 1949.

Private institutional gifts have been both relatively and absolutely much more important since 1945 than they were after World War I or during the inter-war period. This development arose from the growth of highly organized solicitation campaigns in the United States, the encouragement during and since the war by the United States Government of voluntary foreign aid groups, and the large movements of ethnic groups abroad which have led to the formation in the United States of associations to grant assistance to such groups. As a result, 39 percent of the total private gifts in the years 1946–1948 were sent by institutions, as compared with 18 percent during 1919–1921.

Personal remittances *received* by the United States totalled $124 million in 1946 and $145 million in 1947 but declined to $62 million in 1948 and $55 million in 1949. These receipts are thought to be mostly from Americans residing abroad and have come largely from Canada, Cuba, and Mexico.

Net private gifts from the United States during 1949 thus totalled $538 million, financed 9 percent of our current account export surplus, and, as is shown in the following chapter, exceeded net private capital outflow.

II · LOANS AND INVESTMENTS

INTRODUCTION

IN THE first three post-war years, 1946–1948, net long and short-term loans (excluding subscriptions to the International Bank and Fund) had financed 19 percent of the United States exports of goods and services. The percentage so financed in 1949 dropped to seven. Foreign loans by the United States Government were exceptionally large in the years immediately following the war. They not only far exceeded in amount the record for any other equivalent peacetime period but also were nearly five times as large as private loans. In addition to $3.4 billion of subscriptions to the International Bank and Fund, the major Government foreign credits during 1946–1948 were the $3.75 billion line of credit to the United Kingdom, $2.2 billion of Export-Import Bank loans, nearly $2.0 billion in the form of property credits resulting from the transfer of war surpluses, and $0.5 billion of ECA aid extended on a credit basis. Government credits, which had been heavily concentrated in Western Europe, had however begun to taper off rapidly in 1948 as the European Recovery Program got under way. During 1949 net foreign loans by the Government totalled less than $0.7 billion, most of which represented ECA aid which, as required by law, was extended on a credit basis, plus short-term loans representing the deposits to United States account of counterpart funds arising out of the European Recovery Program.

Net private capital movements, after being negative for all but two years in the period 1931–1945, became positive after the war and in 1948 exceeded one billion dollars, an amount which had been surpassed only in 1927 and 1928. The outflow declined sharply in 1949, however, to less than one half billion dollars.

The bulk of the post-war private capital outflow has been direct investments by American corporations out of their undistributed profits. They have been heavily concentrated in the petroleum industry, and so in the Middle East, Latin America, and Canada.

TABLE XII
Net United States Capital Outflow, 1919–1949

Period	Total		Government		Private	
	As percentage of exports of goods and services[a]	*In millions of dollars*	*Long term*	*Short term*	*Long term*	*Short term*
			(in millions of dollars)			
1919–21 (average)	14	1261	824		437	
1936–38 (average)	(−5)	−207	*		−207	
1946	21	3431[b]	3230[b]	−134	26	309
1947	23	7934[b,c]	6891[b]	73	744[c]	226
1948	11	1922[c]	1142	−245	909[c]	116
1949[p]	7	1130[c]	482	174	656[c]	−182

p. Preliminary
* Less than one million dollars.
a. In making these calculations subscriptions by the Government to the International Bank and Monetary Fund and purchases of Bank debentures by private sources have been excluded.
b. *Includes* subscriptions to International Bank and Monetary Fund of $322 million in 1946 and $3063 million in 1947.
c. *Includes* purchases of debentures sold or guaranteed by the International Bank of $243 million in 1947, $8 million in 1948, and $20 million in 1949.
Sources: Pre-war and 1946–48 data, *The Balance of International Payments of the United States, 1946–48, op. cit.*, pp. 125, 130, 131, 152, 193, 194 and 275. 1949 data, *Survey of Current Business*, March 1950, Table 6, p. 7.

During 1949 the Administration became increasingly concerned over the many undesirable aspects of maintaining a large export surplus by gifts or an elimination of the surplus by a reduction in exports. For political, as well as economic and humanitarian reasons, concern was also felt over the low levels of production in many parts of the world. Much attention was given, therefore, to ways of expanding United States imports and the flow of capital from the United States. With respect to the latter, the Administration regarded the debts already owed the United States Government as dangerously large and stated that its policy for the future was to encourage a larger flow of private direct foreign investment, which would also be more widely diversified both as to area and type of industry than it had been in the years immediately preceding.

A major aspect of this new policy was set forth in President Truman's Point Four Program, announced in his inaugural address in early January, which came to be divided into two parts—technical assistance and capital assistance. Much time and thought were given to elaborating specific proposals. Although Congress did not give its approval during the year to either part of the program and there developed considerable opposition in the business community to the major method—investment guaranties—proposed to encourage private investment, the United States was successful in getting the United Nations to approve an expanded technical assistance program along the lines suggested by the Americans. Much attention was also given, with limited success, to the signing of new tax conventions and "Treaties of Friendship, Commerce and Navigation" designed to improve the "climate" for foreign investment and, later in the year, to certain tax reforms designed to expand private investment. Despite all this, the deterrents to private investment were great, and, as the table above shows, net private long and short-term loans during the year were less than half as large as in 1948.

A. POINT FOUR

Introduction

In his inaugural address on January 20, 1949, President Truman, in the last of the four major courses of action in his program for international relations, greatly increased the emphasis on an important aspect of United States international financial policy: "Fourth, we must embark on a bold new program for making the benefits of our scientific advances and industrial progress available for the improvement and growth of underdeveloped areas." The immediate reaction of many was that this statement presaged a huge new government gift or loan program, but the Administration quickly made it clear that this was to be an intensification of things already being done, that the bulk of the financial requirements must be met from private sources, and that it was planned to be a task lasting for decades.

During the year few tangible results could be noted, much of the immediate enthusiasm had subsided, and there were many who had come to believe that the program was neither bold nor new. But a great deal of thought and work had gone into efforts to translate a general policy statement into a detailed program for facilitating economic development in underdeveloped areas which may grow into a major and continuing element in American foreign economic policy.

At the time of his inaugural address a new program did not exist. The President was, in the words of one of his high officials, simply "lighting the spark" as Secretary Marshall had done at Harvard in June 1947.[1] A week after the inaugural speech the President asked various agencies of the Government to work out a concrete program. Over five hundred persons, both in and outside the Government, worked on the problem, but specific proposals were not introduced to Congress for six months, at which time a clear distinction was drawn between technical assistance and capital assistance.

In the President's June 24th message to Congress recommending legislation to implement his Point Four, and in earlier and subsequent statements by Administration spokesmen, several justifications, in addition to the broad humanitarian aspect of helping others to help themselves, were advanced for expanded technical assistance and an increased outflow of private capital. The more important were that they would (a) help prevent underdeveloped nations from turning to "false doctrines," (b) result in stronger nations being associated with the United States in the cause of human freedom, (c) increase United States foreign trade, (d) increase production of minerals and raw materials needed by the United States, (e) increase the stability of the United States economy, (f) be effective in aiding European recovery, and (g) strengthen the United Nations. While the United States hotly denied on many occasions the Communists' claim that this program was a bald attempt to support the United States economy, it was recognized that the " . . . expansion of foreign investment will help in maintaining domestic production and employment at maximum levels. This will become even more important as emergency foreign aid diminishes."[2]

[1] Assistant Secretary of State Thorp, "Point Four," United Nations World, May 1949, p. 54.
[2] Point Four, Department of State, Economic Cooperation Series 24, Washington, D.C., January 1950, p. 55.

II. LOANS AND INVESTMENTS

Technical Assistance

The granting of technical assistance by the United States Government was not a new idea. ECA, under the 1948 legislation, had begun a limited program of technical assistance. The Institute of Inter-American Affairs (IIAA), a Government corporation, had since 1942 been extending technical aid to the Latin American countries in the field of agriculture, health, sanitation, and education.[3] The Interdepartmental Committee on Scientific and Cultural Cooperation, created in 1938, had been undertaking long-range programs for cooperative action, also in Latin America, by exchanging information and skills in many fields, agriculture being perhaps the most important but covering also such divers areas as civil aviation, fisheries, and child welfare. Under the Philippine Rehabilitation Act of 1946 the Department of State had supervised the technical training of many Philippine nationals in this country. The Army Department had been carrying out technical assistance programs in occupied areas, and the advice of American technicians had frequently preceded Export-Import Bank loans.[4] In addition to bilateral activities the United States had also participated in programs of technical assistance through its membership in various international organizations.[5]

It has been estimated that during 1948 the United States expended approximately $13 million in bilateral technical assistance programs and contributed about $2.5 million to the $7.0 million spent for such purposes by various United Nations organizations.

[3] The Institute of Inter-American Affairs received from Congress in 1949 a five year extension of life and an increase in appropriation authorization from $5 million in 1948 to $35 million for the five year period. Actual appropriations for fiscal 1950, however, were only $4.8 million and expenditures in 1949 were $4.1 million.

[4] For a detailed discussion of these activities see *Point Four, op. cit.,* especially App. D.; Donahue, R. S., " 'Point Four' and its Relation to Existing Technical Assistance Programs," *Department of State Bulletin,* February 20, 1949; Taylor, A. E., "Technological Assistance in Latin America," *Social Science,* October 1949; and the quarterly *Report to Congress,* of the ECA. For a disscussion of some activities by non-Government groups see Hutcheson, H. H., "Government and Capital in 'Point Four,' " *Foreign Policy Reports,* June 1, 1949.

[5] See United Nations Doc. E/1345, 25 May 1949 and United Nations Doc. E/CN. 1/Sub. 3/24, 4 March 1949, for a discussion of technical services rendered by the United Nations and its specialized agencies from December 1946 to early 1949.

The amount so spent in 1949 was probably greater but details are not yet available. The expanded technical assistance program of ECA is discussed on pages 23 f above.

From the time of the President's speech, the United States made it clear that the technical assistance part of Point Four, as distinct from capital assistance, was not to be just a bilateral United States program but a cooperative enterprise through the U.N. and its specialized agencies whenever practicable. The United States quickly took the initiative in encouraging new and greater efforts by U.N. and its specialized agencies.[6] On February 25, 1949 the United States Representative submitted to the Economic and Social Council a resolution asking the Secretary General to prepare a report setting forth (a) a comprehensive program for enlarging the activities of U.N. and the specialized agencies in the field of technical assistance, (b) methods of financing such a program, and (c) ways of coordinating the planning and execution of the program. As discussed below, some of the representatives of the underdeveloped countries were disappointed at the little attention paid to capital investments by the American spokesman, and some of the Eastern European countries were critical on the ground that it was a program designed to give large United States corporations ruthless rein over underdeveloped countries. Most nations, however, indicated a willingness to cooperate, and on March 4, the Economic and Social Council (ECOSOC) adopted the United States resolution with slight amendments by a vote of 15–0, with abstentions by Russia, Byleorussia, and Poland.

[6] On December 4, 1948 the General Assembly had approved Resolution 198 (III) asking the Economic and Social Council (ECOSOC) to give " . . . urgent consideration to the whole problem of the economic development of underdeveloped countries in *all* its aspects. . . . "

Following earlier resolutions by ECOSOC in March 1947, August 1947, and again in August 1948, the General Assembly on December 10, 1948 voted some $288,000 to implement during 1949 a limited program of technical assistance to underdeveloped areas in fields of activity for which no specialized agency existed. The assistance contemplated under this program was primarily to take the form of (a) international teams of experts to make exploratory surveys and to advise on economic development programs and (b) the granting of fellowships for training experts. With United States support, this allocation was increased in November 1949 to $676,000 for 1950, plus about $200,000 for an International Center for Public Administration.

In May, in response to this United States-sponsored resolution, the Secretary General of U.N. distributed a 328-page report which was largely in the form of general projects to be carried out by six of the U.N. agencies, with the character, size and location of specific projects to depend on the nature of requests received from governments desiring help. The estimated cost for the technical assistance described was $35.9 million for the first year and $50.2 million for the second year, plus the amounts that governments of recipient countries would be expected to pay as their part of the cost. These funds were to be raised in separate appeals by each agency to its members. To coordinate the planning and execution of the program the Administrative Committee on Coordination was to establish a technical assistance subcommittee consisting of a representative of each participating organization.[7]

At its Geneva meetings in July and August ECOSOC discussed this proposal at length. The United States representative raised serious objections to it. He said the program was really only six separate sets of proposals and not a finished program and, further, that the United States believed that $36 million for the first year was too ambitious. He suggested that U.N. and the specialized agencies could spend effectively no more than $25 million and that perhaps no more than $15 million would be available from member governments for financing the first year's program. He proposed that attention for the present be concentrated on the first year's program and that the 1951 program be taken up at the February 1950 session. He recommended further that, as regards contributions, the Secretary General's proposal of having each participating agency approach its membership separately should be replaced by a general conference sponsored by the U.N. and called by ECOSOC, in which all governments belonging to any participating agency would be invited to negotiate and commit funds to a common pool. It was thought that a central account would facilitate a better balance in the program and would make possible a more efficient use of the non-convertible currencies contributed.

On August 14 and 15, after long discussion, ECOSOC ap-

[7] For details see *Technical Assistance for Economic Development*, U.N. Doc. E/1327/Add. 1, May 1949.

proved, again by a 15–0 vote with three abstentions, a series of resolutions for consideration by the General Assembly. These resolutions set forth financing proposals, organizational arrangements, and general principles and policies, and incorporated the major American suggestions during the debate. No specific amounts were mentioned. All contributions were to be voluntary, could be in currency or goods and services, and were not to be tied to specific agencies, countries, or projects. It was recommended that the General Assembly authorize the Secretary General to set up a special account, to which contributions could be credited and from which transfers should be made to participating agencies.[8] The Secretary General was requested to convene a Technical Assistance Conference of all members or participating governments during or immediately after the fourth session of U.N. General Assembly to ascertain the total amount of voluntary contributions available for the first year's program and to approve the proposed proportionate allocation of contributions among the participating agencies.[9]

To insure coordination of the efforts of the various agencies, the final resolutions incorporated a United States proposal to create a Technical Assistance Board composed of representatives of the specialized agencies and the Secretary General of U.N. This Board, responsible for day-to-day operations, would review requests for assistance and would coordinate the programs of the various operating agencies by determining the manner in which different currencies, services, and materials could be most effectively utilized. A Technical Assistance Committee, composed of representatives of the governments which are members of

[8] It was proposed to allocate contributions received as follows during the first year: FAO 29 percent; U.N. 23 percent; WHO 22 percent; UNESCO 14 percent; ILO 11 percent; ICAO one percent. A small reserve fund would be retained from the contributions to provide for some flexibility.

[9] An amendment added by the U.N. General Assembly in November permitted the Secretary General to delay calling this fund-raising conference until the United States had provided the funds requested by President Truman on June 24. The American delegation estimated at that time that this meeting would probably be held in March or April 1950 and that the total of contributions might range between $20 and $23 million. In addition the countries receiving technical assistance would be expected to provide as a minimum the currency needed for local expenses.

ECOSOC, would have general policy, supervisory, and review authority over the Board.[1] The recommended principles to guide the extending of technical assistance provided that assistance would be given only in agreement with the government of the receiving country, only to or through governments, and only on the basis of requests from governments. It provided further that technical assistance was not to be a means of political interference nor to be accompanied by any considerations of a political nature.

This program, with only minor amendments, was approved unanimously by the General Assembly in November, with the Russians drawing a sharp distinction between the U.N. program and the United States Point Four Program.[2] In his final speech the American representative urged all member governments to contribute something to the special technical assistance account. No contributions had been made by the end of the year, and it was apparent none would be unless and until Congress provided for United States participation.

In the meantime, on June 24, President Truman had sent his recommendations to Congress on Point Four legislation. With regard to technical assistance he stated that much of this could be provided most effectively through the U.N. but some could also be provided directly by the United States. To inaugurate the program he recommended a first-year appropriation not to exceed $45 million,[3] including $10 million previously requested in the 1950 budget, to cover both participation in the United Nations and direct technical assistance. The Administration later sent to Congress a measure, "International Technical Cooperation Act of 1949,"[4] authorizing the President to "plan, undertake, administer, and execute technical cooperation programs." Technical co-

---

[1] The United States strongly opposed a move to establish a committee of government representatives to sit in more or less continuous session and pass judgment on each request for technical assistance on the grounds that this would be time-consuming, encourage lobbying, and inject narrow political considerations into the decisions.

[2] See *United Nations Bulletin*, November 15, pp. 576–7, and December 1, 1949, pp. 630–34, for texts of final resolutions.

[3] On October 29 Secretary Acheson said, "It cannot be a larger sum because the number of technical specialists is limited." (*Department of State Bulletin*, November 14, 1949, p. 719.)

[4] H.R. 5615, 81st Cong., 1st Sess.

operation programs were defined as meaning " . . . activities serving as a means for the international interchange of technical knowledge and skills which are designed primarily to contribute to the balanced and integrated development of the economic resources and productive capacities of economically underdeveloped areas." It was recommended that, since a number of Federal agencies would be involved, the administration of the program should be vested in the President with authority to delegate responsibility to the Secretary of State and other government officials as might be appropriate. As regards appropriation authorizations, this enabling legislation merely authorized "such sums as may be necessary."

In the House Hearings on this proposal, which began in late September, the Administration defined an underdeveloped area for these purposes as one whose per capita income was less than $100 in 1939.[5] It was estimated by the Administration that various currencies totalling the equivalent of $85.6 million would be spent during the first year of the program by U.N. and the United States together, with the aided countries providing some $28.5 million, the United States $45 million, and other U.N. members some $12.1 million. In January 1950 the State Department stated it was planned that these expenditures would be divided among areas as follows: American Republics, 37 percent; Near East, South Asia, and Africa, 48 percent; and the Far East, 15 percent. The largest tentative planned allocations were to agriculture and forestry ($19.0 million), health ($16.3 million), and education ($9.2 million). It was also planned to spend sizeable amounts on technical assistance to industry, reclamation, labor, transportation, general economic development, social security and social services, mineral resources, fisheries, housing, public administration, geologic surveys, statistics, communications, finance, and weather.[6]

The House Committee on Foreign Affairs did not complete its hearings on the proposal in 1949, and the Senate Committee did not begin its hearings. There was evidence of considerable sympathy in the House Committee for broadening the legislation to cover many of the investment aspects of the Point Four Program

[5] It has been estimated that some two-thirds of the world's population lived in such areas.

[6] For a detailed statement on the Point Four Program as seen by the State Department at the end of 1949, see *Point Four, op. cit.*

74

along the lines of Congressman Herter's proposal,[7] which was formally introduced into the hearings and which would limit technical assistance to the fields of health, sanitation, education and agriculture and this, it appears, in the form of United States missions only and not through U.N.

The Administration announced that it intended to press for Congressional approval of its proposals early in the 1950 session.[8] [See page 85 for a summary statement of Congressional action in early 1950.]

Capital Assistance

The debates on technical assistance in U.N. throughout the year were accompanied by discussions on the question of financing economic development. Many representatives of the underdeveloped countries considered the problem of financing a crucial one and argued that improved techniques alone would not significantly increase production. United States policy was to recognize the interrelationships but to deal with the two problems separately and, except for supporting the International Bank, not to provide investment funds through U.N. It took the stand that, while some expansion in international capital flow was necessary, the United States was already encouraging such movements in various ways and that, therefore, there was "little need for debate" at that time on methods of financing economic development but rather a need for specific action by the underdevelped countries to provide the internal conditions conducive to an inflow of foreign capital.[9]

In the April meetings of ECOSOC one group, headed by the Indian representative, proposed the creation of a U.N. Economic Development Administration to undertake development projects, apparently largely with funds to be supplied by the United States Government. The United States representative and the spokes-

---

[7] H.R. 6026, 81st Cong., 81st Sess. Although discussed in connection with the technical assistance proposals, this measure was more concerned with the investment aspects of the Point Four Program and so is dealt with in more detail on page 84 f.

[8] For a series of unofficial papers on various aspects of the Point Four Program, the reader is referred to the March 1950 issue of *The Annals* of the American Academy of Political and Social Sciences.

[9] *Department of State Bulletin*, August 1, 1949, p. 142.

man for the International Bank effectively opposed this proposal, but ECOSOC did request the Secretary General to prepare a report on methods of financing economic development.

Despite the pressure by the representatives of the underdeveloped countries to discuss development financing, ECOSOC in its August meetings, under United States leadership, voted to postpone full debate on this problem at least until the next session. It did, however, approve a resolution requesting the Secretary General to prepare four studies on various aspects of international investment to serve as a basis for future debates.[1] The United States voted for the resolution. In November the General Assembly recommended that ECOSOC continue to give urgent attention to the problem. A companion resolution recommended that, in the Council's work in the area of economic development, study should be given to the question of international economic and commercial policies influencing the economic development of underdeveloped areas. The United States voted for this after leading the opposition to an amendment by Poland which stated that account should be taken of the " . . . necessity of protective customs tariffs as an efficient factor in the creation and development of the national industries of under-developed countries."[2] The American representative maintained that this dealt with matters more satisfactorily covered in the International Trade Organization Charter.

While discouraging action on investment by U.N., the United States spokesmen agreed that some expansion in international capital flows was desirable. They stated the United States policy was one of promoting American foreign investment, both public and private, by supporting the Export-Import Bank and the International Bank on the one hand, and by seeking to improve the climate for private investments on the other. The latter is to be accomplished through negotiating investment treaties to insure fair and equitable treatment to foreign investments and through tax conventions to relieve the burden of double taxation. Further, they reported that the Government was studying possible

[1] In response to the request by ECOSOC mentioned in the previous paragraph, the Secretary General had already prepared the study on "Methods of Financing Economic Development in Underdeveloped Countries."

[2] *United Nations Bulletin*, January 1, 1950, p. 19.

changes in the United States tax laws designed to encourage the flow of private capital abroad and was urging Congress to pass legislation for investment guaranties.

Investment Guaranties

The United States Government had already made limited provisions for investment guaranties. In an effort to expand American private direct investments in ERP countries (during 1947 net United States direct private investment in these countries was only $43.1 million, plus $26.9 million in their dependencies), the 1948 Economic Cooperation Act authorized the Administrator to guarantee the conversion into dollars of "returns" from new investment projects which had received the approval of himself and the Government of the country concerned. As implemented by ECA, in return for an annual fee, payable in advance, of one percent of the amount of the guarantee for the ensuing year plus one-fourth percent of the difference between such amount and the maximum that might be attained during the life of the contract,[3] the investor was assured that any local currency returns from his investment, up to the amount originally invested, which could not be converted through normal channels could be sold to ECA for dollars at the exchange rate ruling at the time of conversion.[4] The 1948 Act authorized total guaranties of $300 million, of which $15 million were to be available for conversion guaranties to enterprises producing or distributing informational media "consistent with the national interests of the United States."[5] Any guaranties issued were to be deducted from

[3] All guarantee contracts must terminate not later than April 3, 1962.
[4] Guaranties are also provided covering the convertibility of receipts from the provision of capital goods and related services for projects approved by ECA where payment is not called for under the contract until after June 30, 1950.
[5] The Export-Import Bank acts as ECA's agent in the issuance and administration of the industrial guaranties. The convertibility guaranties for informational media are handled by ECA itself, and in practice have usually been issued for a period of six months and are subject to renewal. The publisher or distributor pays in advance a fee at the rate of one percent per annum of the amount of the guarantee. The policy of ECA with respect to informational projects is that the guaranties shall cover the actual dollar costs incurred plus only nominal "earnings" or "profits."

the $1 billion authorized in the Act for loans to the participating countries.

During 1948 only one guarantee to a direct industrial investor was issued, and twelve applications totalling about $5 million were pending on January 1, 1949. Apart from administrative difficulties in initiating a new program, one reason for the failure to issue more guaranties stated during the 1949 Congressional Hearings on extending the Economic Cooperation Act was that they were in direct competition with the loan fund and the foreign governments were unwilling to give their approval since such guaranties would reduce the volume of government-to-government loans.[6] A more important reason, however, was the lack of interest shown by United States investors, resulting, some have argued, from the fact that the guarantee applied only to convertibility and not to the other risks peculiar to foreign investment: in particular, risks of confiscation, destruction by riot or revolution, and government interference preventing the transaction of business for which the guarantee was issued. Other reasons advanced were that the present profitmaking possibilities in Europe were at best not appreciably greater than in the United States and that businessmen were reluctant to become so intimately involved with Government agencies. Apparently many potential investors had simply adopted a "wait and see" attitude as to political and economic developments in Europe.

In the 1949 amendments to the Economic Cooperation Act the guarantee clause was changed in several respects. Coverage was extended to "actual earnings or profits" in addition to the amount of dollars invested, and "investment" was broadened to include "related services" as well as capital goods items. ECA announced on June 24, 1949 that investors might convert, within certain time limits, up to an aggregate of 175 percent of the value of the cash or tangible property invested, plus additional profits, as determined to be reasonable by ECA, based on unique techniques and processes contributed by the investor. Expansion, development, and modernization of existing enterprises as well as new projects were made eligible. The total amount of guaranties permitted, however, was reduced to $150 million (of which

[6] In January 1949 ECA earmarked for guaranties $27.7 million of the $1 billion loan and guarantee fund.

$10 million were available for conversion guaranties for informational media each year), including those already made,[7] but these were earmarked and, therefore, not in competition with possible loans.[8]

Even with these changes, however, American investors showed little interest in the guarantee provisions. The total value of guarantee contracts executed for industrial investments through the end of 1949 was only $3.9 million, of which $3.5 million were on investments in the United Kingdom and the balance was for investments in France and Italy. Pending applications totalled $34.3 million. ECA had also issued $2.8 million of convertibility guaranties to American firms supplying informational media in Europe, the bulk of which were to cover sales in Germany. Pending applications of this type totalled $7.6 million at the end of 1949.

Through December 31, 1949, ECA had purchased foreign currencies, exclusively under the informational media contracts, to an amount equivalent to $525 thousand. It had sold $80 thousand of these currencies at an exchange loss of $11 thousand, and the devaluations of September–October resulted in a further book loss of $19 thousand. ECA had collected fees of only $26 thousand on these informational media guaranties, plus $47 thousand on industrial guaranties.[9]

Despite the unimpressive record of the ECA investment guarantee program, the Administration placed major emphasis on such guaranties in the investment part of its Point Four legislative program presented to Congress on June 24. It argued that,

[7] Any funds allocated to a guarantee and remaining after all United States liabilities had been terminated could be used for additional guaranties.

[8] The House had approved, over ECA objections, guaranties not only against inconvertibility but also against losses from the "political risks" of confiscation and seizure, destruction by riot or revolution, and government interference which prevented the planned transaction of the business. The Senate refused to go along with this broadened coverage and in the final law provision was made only for non-convertibility. ECA objections to a broadened guarantee program *within* the European Recovery Program were that it would be exceedingly difficult to administer and would not greatly increase private investment in Europe in 1949.

[9] For further details on ECA investment guaranties see the quarterly *Report to Congress*, Economic Cooperation Administration and *Foreign Transactions of the U.S. Government, op. cit.*, March 1950, pp. 15–18.

while the bulk of the capital needed by foreign nations must be provided by the underdeveloped nations themselves, some foreign assistance was necessary. It considered that Government or international institutions such as the Export-Import Bank and the International Bank could and should provide outside assistance for such basic developments as power, transportation, and communications (it was pointed out that such investment often was a necessary preliminary to private investments). But it was stated that the major reliance on outside aid must be on an enlarged flow of private capital since that was potentially the largest source of investment funds and carried with it the needed technical skills, managerial experience, and organizational talents. To encourage such a movement the President recommended specifically that the Export–Import Bank Act be amended so as to authorize the Bank " . . . to guarantee United States private capital invested in productive enterprises abroad which contribute to economic development in foreign countries against risks peculiar to such investments."[1]

In the Hearings on the bill before the Senate and House Banking and Currency Committees, Administration spokesmen pointed out that although net private direct long-term investment by the United States, after having been negative during the years 1937–44 inclusive, had increased from $100 million in 1945 to all time highs of about $660 million in 1947 and $800 million in 1948,[2] these investments were concentrated in the Near East, Venezuela, and Canada and were to a large extent in one industry—petroleum, while the foreign policy of the United States required large investments in other areas and in many industries.[3]

The Executive branch recognized that, in addition to attractive investment possibilities in the United States, there were many obstacles to a large, continuous, and more diversified international flow of capital whose removal was the responsibility primarily of the foreign countries. Important here, it was said, were the following: restrictions on management and employment practices

[1] S. 2197, 81st Cong., 1st Sess.
[2] These figures are exclusive of reinvested earnings. More recent data show the figures for 1947 as $666 million and for 1948, $793 million. Net investments in 1946 were $141 million.
[3] For details on United States private direct investment abroad see pages 100 ff.

and on conversion of earnings into foreign exchange, the past record and present threat of nationalization and expropriation without effective compensation, discriminatory taxation, extreme political instability, and fear or threat of war. The United States, it was stated, was helping meet these problems by its efforts to promote peace and by making special efforts to negotiate tax conventions and "Treaties of Friendship, Commerce and Navigation." The Administration maintained, however, that more tangible assurance was needed by United States investors, for even the best intentions of a foreign government could not assure that dollars would be available to those investors whose projects were profitable, and so it was proposed that the United States should issue guaranties against risks "peculiar" to foreign investment, these guaranties to be given only if the investments were acceptable to the government of the recipient country.

In the Hearings, Administration spokesmen stated that the major "peculiar" risks were non-convertibility of earnings, confiscation or seizure, and destruction by war. It was made clear, however, that, despite the wide authority requested for the issuance of guaranties, in the beginning at least such guaranties would be restricted to convertibility and probably limited to convertibility of current earnings. The Administration was not prepared to discuss details and urged great flexibility in the law on the ground the proposal was an experiment.

Although there was no specific restriction in the proposed law, it was stated in the Hearings that only new direct investments would be covered, that no protection would be offered against devaluation, that the Export-Import Bank would charge a fee designed to cover possible losses, and that it would carefully investigate every proposed guarantee on a case-by-case basis to determine if it were a "sound business" proposition. Under the proposed legislation, Export-Import Bank guaranties would be limited to the amount of its uncommitted funds—approximately $970 million at the time of the discussion. This limit included both the regular lending functions of the Bank and the possible issuance of guaranties, but it was stated that sometime in the future the authorized maximum of outstanding commitments by the Bank might need to be raised.

Under-Secretary of State Webb testified that, before the Export-Import Bank would go ahead with a specific guarantee to a particular United States investor, the State Department would attempt to obtain from the foreign government an appropriate "Treaty of Friendship, Commerce and Navigation" designed to insure an appropriate "climate;" the United States Government might also insist on working out a program by which, if the Export-Import Bank had to pay off on a guarantee, the Bank might expect to collect dollars for that local currency over a period of time.[4] It was not suggested that the Bank would hold a preferred position over other Americans holding local currency derived from similar sources, but some private persons have expressed the fear that such would be the case.

It was planned that in the beginning at least this type of assistance would be restricted largely to the Middle East, Far East, Africa, and Latin America, and assurances were given that every effort would be made, through investment treaties, to see that old investments were not discriminated against. The importance of agricultural as well as industrial investment was recognized, but almost no attention was given the former.

The Senate and House Committees reported favorably on the Bill in September and October and replaced the Administration's proposal to give authority to the Export-Import Bank to guarantee "against risks peculiar to such investments" with authority to " . . . guarantee United States private capital invested in productive enterprises abroad which contribute to economic development in foreign countries by assuring either or both (i) the conversion into United States dollars of foreign currency derived from an investment and (ii) compensation in United States dollars for loss resulting from expropriation, confiscation or seizure [by action of public authority]," (House bill only).[5] There was no Congressional debate on the measure in 1949.

Except for representatives from the Detroit Board of Commerce and a brief appearance by Mr. Aldrich, who supported the

---

[4] For arguments favoring a much more bold guarantee program see testimony of N. A. Littell in *Hearings before the Senate and House Banking and Currency Committees*, 81st Cong., 1st Sess., on S. 2197 and H.R. 5594. *The Economist*, July 2, 1949, p. 23, reported that the State Department had urged a broader program but had been overruled by the Treasury.

[5] S. 2197 and H.R. 5594, 81st Cong., 1st Sess.

proposal, potential investors did not participate in the Hearings. However, Congressman Herter, following discussions with business groups, did testify; also many reports were issued by various business organizations on different aspects of Point Four. Although there are sharp differences, the majority's views, which are not new and were not met by the ITO Charter or the draft Economic Agreement of Bogota, in summary are the following: (1) the United States Government must make it unmistakably clear that its efforts will be directed mainly to encouraging foreign nations to create a favorable climate abroad for private investment; (2) any future long-term financial assistance from the United States Government will be available only to those countries which first subscribe to a "code of fair treatment" for foreign investors; (3) aid will be limited further to "economically sound" projects, which contribute to the economic development of an area, which do not displace or "unfairly" compete with similar facilities operated by private enterprise, and for which private capital is not available on reasonable terms. Transportation, communication, harbors, irrigation, and perhaps electric power were fields generally mentioned as appropriate for government investment.

As regards what constitutes fair treatment, most of the business proposals include as a minimum: (a) no discrimination on grounds of nationality, (b) full access to domestic courts, (c) agreement not to introduce legislation placing restrictions on nationality of shareholders, composition of directors or selection of administrative, technical, and executive officers, (d) except where restrictions were authorized by the International Monetary Fund, freedom to transfer into currencies acceptable to investors the current earnings, depreciation, amortization, and payments necessary for upkeep or removal of assets (some of the business groups propose "unqualified commitments" to convert, while others urge a priority second only to a very limited list of essential imports), and (e) immediate and fair compensation by the foreign government if it expropriates foreign property, deprives the owners of normal control over their properties, imposes restrictions on their property or business so as to deprive the foreign owner of any substantial beneficial interest therein, or destroys or substantially impairs the business or property by engaging in competition with it—the funds to be freely transferable at the rate of exchange prevailing at time of expropriation. They also stressed the necessity of bilateral tax agreements to prevent double taxation, and some of them strongly urged agreements that taxation be confined to the country in which the money was earned.

Business groups frequently argued that only after foreign nations had committed themselves to the above should the United States Government even consider providing investment guaranties. It was their belief that if investment guaranties were provided first, or possibly at all, many foreign nations would feel it unnecessary to agree to the above measures. They also had fears that guaranties would result in "undue regulation" or "involvement" of the government in private undertakings.[6]

Congressman Herter and Senator Saltonstall introduced bills in their respective chambers in the late summer which incorporated many of the published views of the business groups and comprised many aspects of both the technical assistance and capital assistance features of Point Four.[7] Their measures proposed the establishment, within the Department of State and under the general supervision and control of the Secretary of State, of a Foreign Economic Development Administration, aided by a business advisory group, with broad responsibility over all aspects of the Government's policies on international investment. This organization would help foreign nations (not just "underdeveloped" areas) formulate programs of economic development, make available technical assistance on a bilateral basis in the fields of agriculture, health, sanitation, and education, and would recommend United States Government loans for the limited purposes noted

[6] For some statements of the business community's views see "The Bold New Plan," National Association of Manufacturers, Economic Policy Division Series No. 11, May 1949; "Intelligent International Investment," United States Council of International Chamber of Commerce, April 1949; "Draft International Code of Fair Treatment for Foreign Investments," International Chamber of Commerce, April 1949; "Private Enterprise and the Point IV Program," National Foreign Trade Council, Inc., New York, May 1949; and "Point IV," *Fortune*, February 1950, pp. 181 ff.

[7] H.R. 6026 and S. 2561. The Herter bill was actively discussed during the House Hearings on the Administration's technical assistance proposals but was not formally introduced into the hearings on investment guaranties.

above. However, this assistance would be extended only to nations which had entered into bilateral investment treaties and tax conventions including the provisions mentioned above. There was no provision for investment guaranties in the Herter proposals.

In the light of these wide differences of view between the Government and many of the potential investors it appeared at the end of the Congressional session in October that the Program might be indefinitely delayed. After Congressional adjournment, therefore, meetings were held between State Department officials on the one hand and Mr. Herter and representatives of the business community on the other with the aim of developing a measure which would command wide approval.

[In May 1950, as this goes to press, no further action has been taken by Congress on the investment guarantee proposals other than to broaden ECA's guarantee authority to cover expropriation or confiscation by the government of a participating country. Congress has, however, following bitter debate in the Senate, just approved an "Act for International Development" as a separate title of the legislation extending the European Recovery Program. Congress has not yet, however, debated the question of appropriating funds to implement this enabling legislation. The approved measure represents a substantial compromise between the original Administration and Herter proposals. So far as specific authorizations are concerned, it accepted much of the former's provisions regarding technical assistance, but with respect to broad policy findings and declarations it included much of the latter's emphasis on foreign countries' responsibilities for creating a favorable "climate" for private investment if the objectives of technical assistance are to be achieved. Thus, technical assistance is authorized in a wide variety of fields, both bilaterally and via international organizations, but it is also specified that in considering requests for technical assistance "due regard" will be given to steps taken by the requesting country aimed at encouraging the inflow of foreign capital. It is specifically stated that international investment can make a substantial contribution only if investors are given reasonable opportunities to remit earnings and withdraw capital, receive non-discriminatory treatment, are not deprived of property without prompt, adequate, and effective compensation, have freedom to control and operate their enterprises, etc. An advisory board is to be created, but its authority apparently will be restricted to the technical assistance program and not be extended to all aspects of the Government's policies on international investment. The developments leading up to this will be treated fully in a succeeding survey.]

Investment Treaties

Although not formally included in their legislative proposals, an integral part of the Administration's Point Four Program was efforts to improve the "climate" for private foreign investment. Important here are the bilateral "Treaties of Friendship, Commerce and Navigation"—now often referred to as "investment treaties." For over one hundred years the United States Government has been developing such treaties, which attempt to define how United States businessmen may conduct their affairs in foreign countries, but, as noted above, it has not succeeded in obtaining the kind of economic conditions throughout the world which satisfy private investors. Many of the existing treaties were signed in the nineteenth century and so were drawn up at a time when nationalization and government controls and operations of the type used today were virtually unknown.

Multilateral attempts to create a favorable climate for private foreign investments were made in the ITO Charter and at the Bogota Conference in 1948. The Administration submitted the Havana Charter to Congress in May 1949,[8] and repeatedly urged its approval, but hearings were not held and there was a growing sentiment in the business community that the Charter was weighted heavily in favor of the debtor and was also inadequate because it was so vague and contained so many escape clauses.[9]

During 1949, as prospects for early Congressional approval of the Havana Charter grew dimmer, the State Department seriously attempted to negotiate, or renegotiate, several bilateral treaties, or informally sounded out the possibility of more formal negotiations; but it appears that accomplishments were not impressive. Under-Secretary Webb stated that these efforts were designed to assure potential investors that their property " . . . will not be expropriated without prompt, adequate and effective compensation; that investors will be given a reasonable opportunity to remit their earnings and withdraw their capital; that they will have reasonable freedom to manage, operate, and control their enterprises; that they will enjoy security in the protection of their

[8] The Economic Agreement of Bogota was under discussion at the executive level during the year and was not presented to Congress for approval.
[9] See especially the "Draft International Code of Fair Treatment for Foreign Investments," op. cit.

persons and property and non-discriminatory treatment in the conduct of their business affairs."[1] He also testified that in some areas it was very difficult to elicit interest in such treaties because the United States as a regular practice gives foreign investors and businessmen quite good treatment and, as a result, foreign countries see little point in negotiating new treaties.

Between the war and the end of 1948, treaties had been signed with Italy and China.[2] Ratifications of the Chinese treaty were exchanged in November 1948; the ten-year treaty with Italy, regarded as something of a post-war model, was signed in 1948, and ratifications were exchanged in Rome in July 1949. The more important innovations in the Italian Treaty were that it (a) generally strengthened the provisions for guaranteeing impartial treatment in business operations, including assurances that property would not be seized without prompt and effective compensation and that entry of managers and technicians needed to operate foreign enterprises would be facilitated, (b) accorded "national treatment" in the matter of certain social security benefits, (c) endeavored to maintain a competitive basis for publicly owned or controlled enterprises, and (d) provided for submission of disputes to the International Court of Justice.

On November 23, 1949 a "Treaty of Friendship, Commerce and Economic Development" was signed with Uruguay, following formal negotiations which had begun in March; it was awaiting ratification at year's end. This was the first comprehensive commercial treaty signed with any Latin American country since 1927. In most respects this treaty is similar to those signed with

[1] Statement in *Hearings before House Banking and Currency Committee on H.R. 5594, op. cit.*, p. 31.
[2] While no treaty has been signed with the Philippines, the Philippine Trade Act of 1946 specifies that for the period July 4, 1946–July 3, 1974 United States citizens and business enterprises shall have the same rights as Philippines or any other persons to the disposition, exploitation, development, and utilization of natural resources in the Philippines. This provision, which necessitated certain amendments to the Philippine constitution, came in for heavy criticism in the Philippines but entered into force in April 1947 following a plebiscite and action by the Philippine Congress to amend the constitution. This Trade Act also provided that the peso-dollar exchange rate could not be changed and that no restrictions could be placed on the convertibility of pesos into dollars or on the transfer of funds from the Philippines to the United States except by agreement with the President of the United States.

Italy and China, but it is somewhat broader in scope in matters relating to the encouragement of economic and industrial development, and even its title reveals the new effort to lay the ground-work for expanded private investment. An important innovation was a clause which aims at an equitable distribution of "hard money" in the event it has to be rationed. On January 21, 1950 a "Treaty of Friendship, Commerce and Navigation" was signed with Ireland, which was similar in most respects to the treaties with Italy and Uruguay, but it included a provision by which American investors would be bound by the Irish statute which stipulates domestic ownership of over 50 percent of the original capital of manufacturing, processing, and insurance enterprises operating in Ireland;[3] it also included a clause recognizing the right of Ireland to continue the advantages accorded to imports from members of the British Commonwealth.

It was reported in the press in November and December that a joint Argentina-United States committee on commercial studies had made considerable progress in its discussions looking toward, among other things, the possibility of negotiating a new treaty to replace the existing one which had been ratified in 1853. In early 1950 Argentine officials announced a willingness to enter into more formal discussions. Discussions with India for an investment treaty reached an impasse during the year, apparently in large part because of the popular distrust of foreign enterprises in India, and talks were at least temporarily in abeyance at the year's end.

Tax Reforms and Conventions

The United States Government has given no indication that it was contemplating exempting income from foreign investment from the United States corporate income tax, as some of the business community urged. In fact, the Government has reported that " . . . investigations of the subject indicate that United States taxes have little weight in the corporate investors' appraisal of foreign investment opportunities."[4] Nevertheless, study was

[3] The Irish Government can grant exceptions to this law, and it has agreed to apply the law in a liberal spirit.
[4] *Point Four, op. cit.,* p. 69. For a careful discussion of "Tax Stimulants to Foreign Investment" see the address delivered by L. L. Ecker-Racz, Treasury Department, before the National Tax Association at Boston, *Proceedings* of the 42nd Annual Conference on Taxation, September 19–22, 1949, pp. 142–151.

given to revising and liberalizing United States taxes in order to stimulate the flow of foreign investment, and in his January 23, 1950 tax message to Congress President Truman said, "Among the steps which should be taken at this time are those to postpone the tax on corporate income earned abroad until it is brought home, to extend and generalize the present credit for taxes paid abroad, and to liberalize the foreign residence requirements for exemption of income earned abroad."[5]

Serious efforts were made during 1949 to enter into tax agreements with several foreign countries to remove double taxation and also to prevent fiscal evasion.[6] In many cases two conventions are involved, one relating to taxes on income and the other to taxes on estates and inheritances. At the beginning of 1949, estate tax conventions were in force between the United States, Canada, and the United Kingdom, while the United States had income tax conventions in force with Canada, Denmark, France, the Netherlands, Sweden, and the United Kingdom. Similar conventions between the United States and Belgium, South Africa, and New Zealand had been signed and were awaiting approval by the United States Senate, which did not act on them during the year.

On June 13, 1949 two tax conventions were signed between Norway and the United States, and in mid-September two similar conventions between the United States and Ireland were signed in Dublin. All four of these were submitted to the Senate and were awaiting approval at the end of the year. Ratification instruments for an estate and inheritance tax convention with France, which had been signed in 1946 and approved by the Senate in 1948, were exchanged on October 17, 1949.

During the year discussions on these problems were held with Brazil, Colombia, Cuba, and Argentina and there were also discussions looking toward a revision of the conventions with Canada.[7]

[5] *New York Times,* January 24, 1950. Earlier the President had sent to Congress a National Advisory Council report setting forth specific changes it deemed desirable (see *New York Times,* January 21, 1950).

[6] In general, double taxation is eliminated by means of allowing a credit against the United States tax for the tax paid to the foreign country. If the foreign rate is lower than the United States rates the difference must be paid to the United States Treasury.

[7] In February 1950 two conventions were signed with Greece following discussions which had taken place in large part in 1948.

B. UNITED STATES GOVERNMENT LOANS AND CREDITS

As explained in the previous section, the international investment policy of the United States Government in 1949 was primarily directed to encouraging private long-term foreign investment, and concern was expressed lest any large increase in government loans seriously prejudice foreigners' ability to attract private American capital in the future. For the first year since the war, there occurred an abrupt decline in net official long-term foreign investments to a level below net private long-term capital outflow. With respect to short-term capital, however, there was a net outflow on government account and a net inflow on private account, with the result that total net capital movements from the Government slightly exceeded those from private sources, as was shown in Table XII on page 66.

Long-Term

Net long-term loans and credits by the United States Government, which had accounted for approximately half the total Government aid to foreign nations from the end of the war through 1948, began to decline sharply after the inauguration of the European Recovery Program and accounted for about 8 percent of net Government aid extended in 1949, the rest being in the form of grants. During the year, long-term official foreign credits utilized totalled only $668 million, while principal and interest collections on outstanding credits totalled $197 million and $97 million respectively.[8] Of the total new credits, nearly two thirds represented ECA loans, handled by the Export-Import Bank, and nearly one quarter represented loans by the Export-Import Bank in its regular program. The remainder included the loan to build the U.N. headquarters in New York, commodity credits by the Army to the occupied areas, and miscellaneous credits utilized in

[8] Table XII and Table XXVI show this net capital outflow as $482 million instead of the above $471 million. This slight discrepancy may be due to the fact that preliminary data were included in the official balance of payments estimates (the source of the first figure) and/or to attempts to enter items in the balance of payments at the time they are assumed to have taken place rather than when they appear in the records of the Government agencies.

the winding up activities in connection with the post-war surplus property, lend-lease, and merchant ship programs. Had it not been for that part of ECA assistance which was extended on a credit rather than a gift basis, principal and interest collections by the United States Government on outstanding obligations would have exceeded new loans extended during 1949 by $51 million.

i. ECA LOANS

The 1948 Economic Cooperation Act specified that $1 billion of the aid authorized for the first year of the Marshall Plan was to be in the form of loans or investment guaranties; of this ECA later set aside only $27.7 million for investment guaranties. For reasons discussed earlier, the Administration asked that none of the 1949–50 funds be earmarked for loans, but Congress did finally specify that $150 million of the authorized aid should be extended on a credit basis.

The Export-Import Bank acts as the agent of ECA in extending these loans, but the countries to receive them and the terms and conditions are specified by ECA after consultation with the National Advisory Council (NAC). As a matter of policy the terms have been lenient. For most of the loans granted through 1949 the principal is repayable in 35 years starting in June 1956; the interest rate is 2½ percent per annum with payments waived until 1952. These loans can probably be described as "fuzzy." The loan agreements contain provisions for a discussion of the postponement of the payments and for an alteration of terms in the event of adverse economic conditions or for any other reasons, and the loan agreements with Denmark, Norway, and Turkey make provision for possible repayments in local currency.

It appears that ECA makes no distinction in approving procurement authorizations as between aid extended on a grant and on a credit basis. In fact, ECA aid in many cases has been provided on an indeterminate basis, with allocation between grant and credit subsequently determined. The European nations showed an expected reluctance to having a part of their aid classified as credits, but in 1948 and 1949 loan agreements were reached for $971.2 million of the funds provided in the original act and $900.9 million had been utilized; agreements had not been reached by the end of the year on any of the $150 million earmarked for loans in the 1949 legislation.[9] ECA loans, allotted and utilized, are shown in Table XIII.

TABLE XIII

Loans under Economic Cooperation Act, 1948 and 1949

(in millions of dollars)

	Allotted		Utilized	
	1948	1949	1948	1949
Belgium-Luxembourg	50.0	9.5	0	50.9
Denmark	25.0	6.0	17.3	13.7
France	170.0	2.0	127.5	44.5
Iceland	2.3	0	1.9	0.4
Ireland	60.0	26.3	0	63.9
Italy	50.0	17.0	37.5	29.5
Netherlands[a]	95.0	51.7	47.8	97.9
Norway	35.0	0	11.8	23.2
Sweden	10.0	10.4	0	0
Turkey	30.0	8.0	0	20.1
United Kingdom	310.0	3.0	232.5	80.5
Total	837.3	133.9	476.3	424.6

a. Including Indonesia.

Sources: *Eighth* and *Ninth Semi-Annual Report to Congress,* Export-Import Bank of Washington, Washington, D.C., p. 13 and Appendix J, respectively, for data on allotments. For data on loans utilized, *Foreign Transactions of the U.S. Government,* Department of Commerce, Washington, D.C., March 1950, Appendix Table 8.

Note: The data on loans "utilized" are defined as "aid extended on a credit basis" and differ substantially in the distribution between the two years from the "disbursements" reported by the Bank. This difference arises from the fact that frequently ECA extended assistance on an indeterminate basis and then later classified it as a "credit," with the Bank making the disbursement at the time of the classification rather than when the aid was actually rendered. Department of Commerce data are used in order to make this table consistent with other official tabulations included in this study.

In addition to the above, ECA also extended directly during 1949 a total of $0.6 million in loans to France (French Morocco) in connection with a deficiency-materials project. Half of this was in dollars and the other half in counterpart funds.

[9] No statements are available as to the criteria used by NAC and ECA in determining what portion of its aid each country was allocated on a loan basis other than very general statements that consideration was given to such factors as prospective dollar deficits and the relative ability to service loans.

ii. EXPORT-IMPORT BANK TRANSACTIONS

Disbursements made by the Bank under its regular program (excluding disbursements by agent commercial banks which are here treated as private transactions) amounted to only $163 million in 1949, while loan repayments totalled $101 million and interest collections by the Bank another $61 million, as is shown in Table XIV.   Thus, this sixteen-year old institution, which had

TABLE XIV
Export-Import Bank Operations, 1949
(in millions of dollars)

Area	Loans Author- ized	Loans Can- celled	Loans Disbursed			Principal Collected by Com- mercial Banks	Inter- est Col- lected[1]	Loans Out- standing Dec. 31, 1949
			by EIB	by Bks. at EIB Risk	by EIB			
ERP Europe[2]	0	*	60	0	39	0	45	1638
Other Europe[3]	20	0	9	4	5	17	4	142
Latin America	63	19	77	1	25	9	11	334
Middle East[4]	104	0	12	0	1	0	*	22
Far East[5]	26	0	5	17	31	17	1	42
Other and Un- allocated[6]	28	*	1	*	0	*	*	2
Total	241	19	163	22	101	43	61	2180

* Less than one half million dollars.
1. Interest retained by agent banks of the EIB is not included.
2. Austria, Belgium, Denmark, France, Greece, Italy, Netherlands, Norway, Sweden, Turkey.
3. Czechoslovakia, Finland, Poland, Yugoslavia.
4. Egypt, Israel, Saudi Arabia.
5. China, Japan, Philippines.
6. Afghanistan, Canada, Ethiopia, Liberia, Portuguese West Africa.
Sources: Compiled from the *Seventh* and *Ninth Semiannual Report to Congress*, Export-Import Bank of Washington, 1949 and 1950 (mimeographed) Appendices C, and *Foreign Transactions of the U.S. Government*, Department of Commerce, March 1950, Appendix Tables 8, 9, and 10. These documents are the source for most of the information included in this section.
Note: Amounts disbursed and collected by agent banks of the Export-Import Bank—shown separately in the above table—are treated as private transactions in all other parts of this survey.

been a very important source of emergency aid to foreign nations in the two and a half years immediately following the war,[1] con-

[1] In anticipation of the Bank's being a primary source of extraordinary financial assistance by the United States to foreign countries during the

tributed but one million dollars to financing the export surplus of the United States. Its record pointed up the obvious but sometimes forgotten difficulties of relying on capital flows to solve the American balance of payments problem.

Except for the Administration's proposal to authorize the Export-Import Bank to finance the investment guaranties under the Point Four Program (see pages 80 ff), there were no important new trends in policy during the year, the Bank having in 1948 withdrawn from the field of "emergency" financing and more or less returned to its pre-war policies.

New loans totalling $241 million were authorized[2] by the Bank during the year and were mostly in "underdeveloped" areas. All of them were of the "project type" rather than the "general purpose" or "balance of payments" loans which had been so important in the period between the end of the war and the beginning of the Marshall Plan. With few exceptions the loans were "tied" to United States exports; indeed, many of the loans originated from direct applications of American exporters. Each loan was carefully scrutinized by the Bank to insure that it was a "sound business" proposition and that the financed exports of equipment, materials, and services would contribute directly to expansion of productive capacity of the importing country and to an improvement in its current balance on international account. During most of its life, the Bank has encouraged private American companies to supply a part of the foreign capital needed, and at least five of the loan authorizations in 1949 were parts of larger foreign investments in which United States corporations or their subsidiaries participated.[3]

The largest, $100 million, and fourth largest, $20 million, of the 1949 loan authorizations were to Israel and Yugoslavia re-

---

period of post-war reconstruction, the Export-Import Bank Act of 1945 raised the limit on outstanding loans and guarantees from $700 million to $3500 million, removed the prohibition on loans to countries in default on their obligations to the United States Government, and removed the statutory limits on its life.

[2] The Export-Import Bank lists a loan as "authorized" when it has been approved by the Bank's officials even though it has not been yet formalized by a signed loan agreement. A loan is "utilized" when actual disbursements are made.

[3] Republic Steel Corporation, Bethlehem Chile Iron Mining Company, International General Electric Company, Dahican American Lumber Corporation, and Saudi Arabian Industries Corporation.

spectively, giving evidence of the nice coordination between Export-Import Bank loans and the foreign political policy of the Government. Only 26 percent of the total value of the new authorizations were to Latin American countries, but disbursements by the Bank on both the new and previous authorizations accounted for some 95 per cent of total United States Government aid to that area during the year.

At the end of 1949 the Bank had loans outstanding of $2180 million and undisbursed authorizations totalling $431 million. Of the Bank's lending authority of $3500 million there remained available for future disbursement $1320 million, of which $889 million were uncommitted. On several occasions during the year the Administration reported it might be necessary some time in the future to increase the Bank's lending authority, but no specific recommendations to this effect were made.

iii. UNITED NATIONS LOAN

Congress authorized in 1948 the granting of an interest-free loan by the State Department for helping to finance the permanent headquarters of the United Nations in New York City. It authorized an appropriation of no more than $65 million and specified that repayments were to start on July 1, 1951 and be completed not later than 1982. The RFC was authorized to advance up to $25 million, pending appropriations. On June 23, 1949, Congress finally appropriated the $65 million which were to remain available until June 30, 1955. $2.7 million had been disbursed in 1948 and another $19.9 million were disbursed in 1949.

iv. DEFENSE DEPARTMENT LOANS

In June 1948 Congress authorized a new credit program for financing the purchase of cotton and other natural fibers and their processing in the areas occupied by the Army.[4] A $150 million revolving fund, as a public debt transaction, was authorized from which the Army Department was to extend credits with a maximum maturity of 15 months. None of these credits was

[4] This program was intended to replace the commodity credit program of the Agriculture Department which from the end of the war through 1948 had supplied $214 million of commodities—mostly raw cotton—to Germany and Japan. Full repayment for these credits had been received by the end of 1948.

utilized in 1948, but, during 1949, $26.7 million were used to supply raw cotton to Japan. There were no principal repayments during the year, and interest collections were only $0.2 million.

V. LEND-LEASE AND RELATED CREDIT TRANSACTIONS

On March 14 the Government reached final agreement with Canada and France regarding several wartime claims. With respect to Canada a payment of $3.7 million was made by the United States as reimbursement for excess deposits made by the latter with the United States Treasury during the war to finance the purchase of defense goods. With this payment all claims and accounts between the two countries connected with the conduct of the war and arising out of the procurement of supplies and services by one government for the other were settled or waived. The settlement with France involved two agreements. One established the "knock for knock" method of handling maritime claims and litigation arising out of operations during or immediately after the war and was, essentially, a mutual waiver of intergovernmental claims. The other reduced the obligations of France to the United States for settling lend-lease and surplus property accounts from a tentative $720 million set in May 1946 to a firm $653.3 million, and provided for the final settlement of a large number of other outstanding claims. In addition, $2.1 million were paid to the French Government as a refund on excess deposits by the French beyond amounts required for cash procurement of lend-lease articles.

An agreement was signed with Ethiopia on May 20 for final settlement of lend-lease, reciprocal aid, and other financial claims arising out of World War II. The Ethiopian debt was set at $200,000; it was provided that this could be paid by delivery, at United States request, of real property and/or Ethiopian dollars to the United States Government to be used for certain specified purposes in Ethiopia. Any balance at the end of five years was to be paid to the United States in United States dollars.[5]

On September 27 an understanding was reached with Russia for the return of certain United States Navy vessels, but no agree-

---

[5] Nothing in this agreement affects the obligation of Ethiopia to return to the United States an amount of silver bullion equivalent to the 5.4 million ounces transferred under Lend-Lease.

ment was reached during the year on several of the major lend-lease issues with Russia and China. In addition to those mentioned above, lend-lease activities during 1949 were primarily concerned with winding up operations.[6] Although $4.6 million of lend-lease property credits were actually utilized by foreign nations in 1949,[7] this was less than the $6.5 million in principal repayments and $9.6 million (including $1.5 million from Russia) in interest and commissions collected by the Government on outstanding lend-lease credits.

vi. SURPLUS PROPERTY AND MISCELLANEOUS CREDIT TRANSACTIONS

By mid-1949 the Government had also, for all practical purposes, completed its disposal of foreign war surplus property and of merchant ships. On June 30 the Office of Foreign Liquidation Commissioner was abolished with certain residual functions being taken over by other agencies of the Government.[8] During 1949, $24 million of surplus property credits were utilized, while principal collections by the United States Government on outstanding credits totalled $23.9 million and interest collections totalled $13.9 million. Less than half a million dollars of Maritime Commission credits were utilized during the year, while principal and interest collections on outstanding foreign credits amounted to $19.4 million and $7.8 million respectively.[9]

The War Assets Administration, which had in the period since the war extended small amounts of credits to foreign governments for the purchase of surplus property located in the United States,

[6] For details, see the President's 1949 quarterly *Report to Congress on Lend-Lease Operations.* In the Third Deficiency Appropriation Act of 1949 Congress included $100,000 for Treasury liquidation activities in fiscal year 1949–50 and extended through June 30, 1950 the availability of $1 million from the unexpended balances of previous lend-lease appropriations for payment of certain patent claims.

[7] This represents delayed billings and expenditures by the United States Navy for the construction of a port in Liberia.

[8] From its inception the OFLC had disposed of surplus property located in foreign areas whose procurement cost was estimated at $10.4 billion. The Government had received approximately 19 percent from these sales, a large part of which were on a long-term credit basis. Surplus property credits "utilized" represents the value of sales contracts signed.

[9] The Maritime Commission credits for the purchase of merchant ships had been utilized to an amount of $229 million up to the end of 1949. "Utilized" here represents the principal amount of mortgages received from foreign sales of merchant ships.

was also liquidated in 1949; its residual functions were assumed by the General Services Administration.[1]   During the year $4.4 million of its credits were used, and collections of principal and interest totalled $0.4 million and $0.1 million respectively.   The Reconstruction Finance Corporation extended no new foreign loans during 1949 but collected $45.6 million of principal and $4.8 million of interest on outstanding obligations, almost entirely the war time loan to the United Kingdom secured by marketable dollar securities.

vii. TOTAL UNITED STATES GOVERNMENT LONG-TERM CREDITS

From the creation of the Export-Import Bank in 1934 through December 31, 1949, the United States Government extended $11.5 billion of foreign loans and credits, excluding $3.4 billion of subscriptions to the International Bank and Fund.   Approximately $1.6 billion of these had been repaid by the end of 1949, leaving an outstanding balance of $9.9 billion.   Since World War I items may be considered no longer active, this represents the total foreign obligations to the United States Government on that date. Over 95 percent of these outstanding obligations had been incurred since June 1945, and, on the basis of the $9.8 billion of outstanding credits on June 30, 1949, the projected annual payments of principal and interest will reach $329 million and $189 million respectively by 1952.

The long-term foreign loan and credit transactions during 1949 by the United States Government, by program and area, are shown in Table XV.

Short-Term

During the first three post-war years (1946–1948) there was a net reduction of $306 million in the short-term foreign claims of the United States Government, but there was a net outflow of an estimated $174 million in 1949, as is shown in Table XII on page 66.   A large part of the reduction in the early years represented liquidations of foreign currencies acquired during the war, and there were also some net repayments of short-term advances made

[1] The WAA had entered into credit agreements of $127.3 million with foreign governments but only $18 million had been utilized through 1949, and the balance had been cancelled. Data on loans "utilized" refer to deliveries.

TABLE XV
Long-Term Foreign Loans and Credits of the
U.S. Government, by Program and by Area, 1949
(in millions of dollars)

	Uti-lized[1]	Prin-cipal Col-lected[2]	Interest and Com-missions Collected[3]	Outstand-ing Indebted-ness[4] Dec. 31, 1949
By Program—Total	*668*	*197*	*97*	*9901*
A. Current and Active Programs				
Export-Import Bank[5]	163	101	61	2187
Economic Cooperation Adminis-tration	425	0	0	902
Defense Department:				
Natural Fibers Revolving Fund[6]	27	0	*	47
State Department:				
United Nations Building Loan	20	0	0	22
B. Completed or Nearly Completed Programs				
Treasury Department:				
Special British Loan	0	0	0	3750
Lend-Lease Credits	5	7	9	1586
Surplus Property Credits	24	24	14	1035
Maritime Commission	*	19	· 8	192
Reconstruction Finance Corpora-tion	0	46	5	163
General Services Administration	4	*	*	17
By Area—Total	*668*	*197*	*97*	*9901*
ERP Participants	496	108	74	8365
United Kingdom	81	47	4	4831
France	53	24	48	2053
Netherlands	99	6	7	447
Italy	67	5	6	351
Other	196	26	9	683
Other Europe[7]	10	7	8	446
Far East[8]	33	42	4	552
Middle East[9]	28	4	*	67
Latin America	77	34	11	399
Other and unallocated[10]	24	2	*	72

* Less than one half million dollars.

1. "Utilized" means cash disbursements for loans and value of goods delivered under the various property credits, or principal amount of mortgages received, or sales contracts, or billings. For ECA loans these data are "amount

by Government agencies. Most, if not all, of the net increase in 1949 consisted of an accumulation of deposits of counterpart funds may by the ERP nations in special accounts for use by the United States Government (see p. 28 ff.).

C. PRIVATE FOREIGN INVESTMENT

The importance of private foreign investment has recently been reemphasized by the reliance of the President's Point Four Program on the emergence of a large and continuous outflow of private capital. But experience since the war with respect to private capital movements shows that there are difficult problems to resolve before an adequate volume and an optimum distribu-

---

of aid extended on a credit basis" and differ from "disbursements" as reported by the Export-Import Bank; this discrepancy apparently arises because ECA frequently pays for and ships goods prior to determining whether they will be classified as "grants" or "credits."

2. Principal collected represents the payments received and applied to the reduction of outstanding indebtedness, excluding repayments of agent-bank loans of the Export-Import Bank.

3. Interest and commissions collected represents the payments actually received. Those received and retained by agent-banks of the Export-Import Bank are not included.

4. Outstanding indebtedness represents utilizations from beginning of program through 1949 less principal repayments.

5. Excludes $22 million of disbursements by commercial banks on loans guaranteed by the Export-Import Bank and $43 million of principal repaid to agent-banks. These are included as private transactions in the official balance of payments statements. In the outstanding loans is included a participation of $7 million by another agency as well as outstanding agent-bank loans guaranteed by the Export-Import Bank.

6. $20 million of the outstanding indebtedness represents the estimated amount of surplus property delivered to China prior to 1949 by the Army subject to future settlement.

7. Czechoslovakia, Finland, Hungary, Poland, USSR, Yugoslavia. In "utilized" is $0.8 million by Russia representing billings for lend-lease aid furnished prior to March 31, 1947.

8. Burma, China, India, Indonesia, Japan, Korea, Philippines, Thailand.

9. Egypt, Israel, Saudi Arabia, Lebanon, Iran.

10. Australia, Canada, Ethiopia, Liberia, New Zealand, Union of South Africa, United Nations.

Source: Compiled from data in *Foreign Transactions of the U.S. Government*, Department of Commerce, Washington, D.C., March 1950, pp. A-28 ff. For explanation of slight discrepancies between this table and Tables XII and XXVI see footnote 8 on page 90.

Note: Excluded from this table are short-term indebtedness to the United States and aid extended on a basis which may or may not call for ultimate repayment. Aid rendered on the latter basis is included in "grants" in the official statistics.

tion, from the point of view of increasing standards of living abroad, may be obtained.[2]

Long-Term

Despite the increasing attention being placed on the desirability of, and methods for encouraging, a large outflow of private capital from the United States, *net* foreign long-term private investment (excluding reinvested earnings, for which data are not available) fell from an all-time high of $909 million in 1948 to an estimated $656 million in 1949, as shown in Table XVI. This

TABLE XVI

Net Movements of Private Long-Term United States Capital, 1946–1949
(in millions of dollars) (outflow (+); inflow (−))

Year	Total	Direct	Portfolio
1946	+26	+141	−115
1947	+744	+666	+78
1948	+909	+793	+116
1949[P]	+656	+669	−13

p. Preliminary.
Sources: 1946–1948 data, *The Balance of International Payments of the United States 1946–48*, Department of Commerce, 1950, pp. 130–131. 1949 data, *Survey of Current Business*, March 1950, p. 7.
Note: Portfolio investments consist of the holdings of miscellaneous foreign securities which do not involve any controlling interest by the American investor. Direct investments represent the extension of American business into foreign countries and consist largely of foreign branches and subsidiaries of United States companies. Included in the portfolio data are purchases of debentures sold or guaranteed by the International Bank of $243, $8 and $20 million in 1947, 1948, and 1949 respectively.

decline was apparently attributable in large part to the completion or curtailment of foreign expansion programs, especially by the oil companies which, as noted on pages 132–133, were facing the prospect of a contraction in their markets. Curtailment of foreign investment seems once again to have paralleled a reduction in domestic private investment in the United States. A similarity

[2] It should also be emphasized, although it rarely was in the public discussions, that there is no simple, uniform, or one-directional effect of capital movements on the balance of payments of the borrower (or lender) and that the effects cannot be accurately assessed in advance. Such capital movements may immediately alleviate or increase the pressure on the balance of payments of the recipient nation, and in the longer run the production and trade to which the investment gives rise may affect the supply and/or demand for dollars, relieving or intensifying exchange difficulties.

in the broad outline of changes in the volume of domestic and foreign investment since the first war suggests common factors affecting each. In addition, as commented upon above, political instability and uncertainties about economic controls abroad continued to constitute serious deterrents to a larger volume of private foreign investment. The United States Government's offer of investment guaranties and its attempts to improve the "climate" for investments abroad through "Treaties of Friendship, Commerce and Navigation" and the relatively large average returns on direct foreign investments were not sufficient to offset these negative forces.

Details concerning the 1949 investment are not yet available. From the experience of the previous four years (1945–1948) it would seem probable that almost all of the direct investment in 1949 was by a relatively small number of corporations out of the cash balances of the investing company and in the form of the expansion of the existing enterprises. The investments were probably concentrated in the petroleum industry (which investment since the war has hitherto been encouraged by the United States Government) and mainly in the Middle East, South America, and Canada. The post-World War II record contrasts sharply with the experience of the 1920's when purchases of foreign dollar bonds in relatively small amounts by large numbers of persons accounted for some 60 percent of American long-term foreign investments; direct investments were distributed over many countries and industries, with public utilities accounting for one-third of the total; and nearly half the direct investment funds were obtained by selling securities to the public.

In view of the unhappy experiences of both lenders and borrowers of the over $8 billion of foreign securities sold in the United States for new capital during the period 1919–1930, there have been few attempts to float foreign securities in the United States since the last war. During the five years ending December 31, 1949 only the International Bank and the Governments of Canada, Norway, Belgium, and the Netherlands sold dollar bonds in the United States market for the purpose of raising new capital. Even so, practically no net investment in such bonds resulted since these sales (plus certain refunding operations) were almost matched by foreign redemptions and amortizations, especially by Canada and the Latin American Republics.   American banks were reasonably active during the post-war period in the field of long-term credits, sometimes guaranteed by the Export-Import Bank, but net outflow was negligible as was net movement in other portfolio securities.

It has been estimated that in 1949 there was a gross inflow of portfolio investments of $193 million, which was in large part offset by an outflow of $160 million plus $20 million of purchases of obligations guaranteed by the International Bank.   The trend in private long-term investments since the first world war is shown in Table XVII.   The large decline from 1929 to 1940 was due in part to reductions in the market value of securities and in part to repurchases, at default-induced prices, by foreign countries of large amounts of their obligations.

TABLE XVII

Value of Private Long-Term United States Investments Abroad at Year-End, Selected Years

(in billions of dollars)

	1919	1929	1940	1945	1948
Direct Investments	3.9	7.7	7.3	8.4	11.4
Portfolio Securities[a]	2.6	9.1	2.8	3.8	3.9
	6.5	16.8	10.1	12.2	15.3

a. Not included are portfolio investments of certain real property, estates, and trusts which have been estimated to total approximately $0 billion in 1919, $1.2 billion in 1929 and $1.5 billion in 1948.

Source: *Survey of Current Business*, Department of Commerce, Washington, D.C., November 1949, pp. 18 and 20.

Note: Value of direct investments is estimated book value of American interests in foreign enterprises. Reinvestment of earnings of foreign subsidiaries is included except for the period 1931–37 for which data are not available. Value of portfolio securities is market value.

Of the $3 billion increase in net *direct* long-term investments during the three years 1946–48 (Table XVIII), only some $1.6 billion represented capital movements, with the remainder principally reinvested earnings.   Nearly three-fourths of these new capital movements were in the petroleum industry.   In general it can be said that, since the last war, most direct investment has been to develop natural resources for export rather than to develop markets for United States exports or to increase foreign production for local consumption.

TABLE XVIII
*Factors Affecting Value of United States
Private Direct Investments Abroad, 1945–1948*
(in millions of dollars; capital inflow (−))

	Value, end of 1945	1946–48			Value, end of 1948
		Capital movements	Reinvested earnings	Other factors[a]	
All industries	8,370	1,650	1,259	100	11,379
Manufacturing	2,671	162	714	56	3,603
Distribution	672	118	131	10	931
Agriculture[b]	518	54	55	—	627
Mining and smelting	1,063	44	23	16	1,147
Petroleum	1,538	1,205	301	3	3,047
Public utilities	1,357	−88	13	5	1,287
Miscellaneous	551	155	21	10	737

a. Other factors affecting the change in value include some allowance for re-valuation of assets because of fluctuations in foreign exchange rates during 1946.
b. Includes fishing.
Source: *Survey of Current Business*, Department of Commerce, Washington, D.C., November 1949, p. 21.
Notes: Capital movements represent the net of known new investments less liquidations. Reinvested earnings are the undistributed portion of the net earnings of foreign subsidiaries. Value is the American equity in direct investments abroad and includes expropriated property for which compensation has not yet been received and properties in Germany and Japan. No allowance has been made for war damage.
   More recent data (e.g. in Table XVI) show the total for capital movements for 1946–48 as $1600 million, but details needed to revise this table are not available.
   In this table, detailed figures have been rounded so they will not necessarily add up to the totals.

Of the total United States private direct long-term investments abroad at the end of 1948, $4.2 billion were in Latin America, $3.2 billion in Canada, $2.4 billion in Europe, and $1.6 billion in the rest of the world. These should be compared with figures of $3.1 billion, $2.5 billion, $2.0 billion, and $0.8 billion respectively at the end of 1945.

The average rate of earnings on private direct investments abroad since the war has been surprisingly high. After foreign taxes the ratio of earnings to total American equity in direct investments rose from 6.2 percent in 1940 to 8 percent in 1945 and had reached 15.6 percent by 1948, when they totalled over $1.5

billion on direct investments valued at approximately $10 billion at the end of 1947.[3] These high rates were in part, of course, a reflection of the world-wide inflation. They appear to compare favorably with those shown by domestic United States corporations, but such comparisons are dangerous.

The rate of earnings on direct investments varied greatly from industry to industry in 1948, with petroleum easily holding the top position, reflecting the great demand for petroleum products and the development abroad of large reserves which could be exploited relatively cheaply. The rate of return by major industry groups ranged from 25.6 percent for petroleum down to 2.4 percent on public utility investments, with manufacturing yielding 17.6 percent, distribution 14.7 percent, agriculture 11.9 percent, and mining and smelting 10.6 percent. The average yield on portfolio securities has been much lower. In 1948 the average rate of return on foreign bonds payable in dollars held by United States residents was about 3 percent of the par value, and 3.8 percent of the market value, of such bonds.

Income[4] from total private American investments abroad was slightly in excess of $1.2 billion in 1949, an all-time peak, which was more than double the 1945 figure. Direct investment income reached a record of $997 million in 1948, as compared with a pre-war high of $474 million in 1928 and $426 million in 1945. Estimates for 1949 are not yet available but preliminary estimates of total income from foreign investments indicate the return on private direct investments was probably slightly in excess of 1948.

After the war, income receipts on foreign dollar bonds held by American investors continued the decline which began in 1931. They totalled $70 million in 1945, $65 million in 1946 and $59 million in 1947 but rose slightly to $61 million in 1948 as nearly $7

[3] If the value of investments in those countries to which there was no free access—e.g., Eastern Europe, Germany and Japan—were excluded the overall rate of return during the year 1948 would have been over 17 percent.

[4] "Income" on foreign investments for balance of payments purposes is defined by the Department of Commerce to include branch profits, interest, and common and preferred dividends. "Earnings," as used in the two previous paragraphs, are defined to include "income" plus the American equity in the undistributed profits of foreign subsidiaries. These undistributed profits of foreign subsidiaries constitute the reinvested earnings shown in Table XVIII.

million of interest were paid by the International Bank. Data for 1949 are not yet available, but presumably receipts were approximately $60 million. The gradual decline was the result, noted above, of the absence of any large new loans plus continued amortization and refunding of the outstanding indebtedness. Interest and dividend receipts from other foreign investments, mostly long-term loans by banks and commercial firms, local currency bonds, and some corporate stocks, were $90 million in 1948 and had been at approximately this figure for much of the postwar period.

Data are not available on how much of the United States income on foreign investments was actually transferred into dollars. It is popularly believed that exchange controls abroad prevented the conversion of much of this income, but the Department of Commerce has reported " . . . for the most part there was sufficient dollar exchange available after the war to accommodate the transfer of income to the United States."[5] It recognizes, however, that in some countries and for some individual companies exchange controls and inability to transfer constituted serious problems. It was also recognized that even if in the recent past there was relative freedom to transfer earnings, the absence of advance assurance of transferability constituted a serious deterrent to new investment.

Short-Term

During 1949 there was a net inflow of private United States short-term capital estimated at $182 million. This may be compared with a total net outflow of $651 million for the previous three years, as was shown in Table XII, page 66. In the first year and a half after the war there was a large outflow of short-term capital as the United States resumed the normal process of financing exports. This outflow, largely commercial bank credits, began to decline in 1947 as difficulties were encountered in ob-

[5] Abelson, M:, "Private United States Direct Investments Abroad," *Survey of Current Business*, November 1949, p. 22. Much of the information in this section was taken from this report and from Chapter 3 of *The Balance of International Payments of the United States 1946–48*, Department of Commerce, Washington, D.C., 1950. The reader wishing more details is referred to these sources.

taining dollars for goods shipped to many areas, and in 1948 there was a small inflow of such capital which was, however, over-balanced by short-term loans on gold to foreign central banks by the Federal Reserve Bank of New York. During 1949 there was apparently a further large liquidation of foreign claims arising directly from exports. Income on foreign short-term investments rose steadily from $3 million in 1945 to $13 million in 1948 but presumably declined in 1949.

D. THE INTERNATIONAL BANK FOR RECONSTRUCTION AND DEVELOPMENT

The International Bank, in whose affairs the United States holds a dominant position,[6] was not an important factor quantita-tively in the international financial affairs of the United States during 1949.[7] There was much criticism from private sources in the United States (although not on the whole from the finan-cial press) and from both private and official sources abroad of the cautious lending policies of the Bank, but official United States policy was that the Bank was not to be an outlet for gifts or quasi-gifts from the United States.

The Bank authorized $219.1 million of loans during the year, but actual disbursements were only $61.8 million in United States dollars plus $6.1 million in other currencies (Table XIX). The Bank received $23.7 million in commissions, interest charges, and commitment and other service charges. A large but unspecified part of these receipts was in dollars. Principal repayments dur-ing the year, the first since the founding of the Bank, totalled $1.3 million. The Bank does not "tie" its loans. And on the basis of the record from its inception through 1949, although almost all the Bank's disbursements were in United States dollars, only about three-quarters of the dollar disbursements were in the United States.

[6] By virtue of its voting strength and the fact that most of the operations are in dollars contributed by the United States to the Bank's capital or ob-tained by selling securities in the American market, which sales require prior approval of the National Advisory Council.

[7] For an excellent discussion of the International Bank see Basch, A., "International Bank for Reconstruction and Development 1944–1949," *International Conciliation*, November 1949. Mr. Basch, an official of the Bank, speaks with the usual disclaimer.

TABLE XIX
Disbursements by International Bank, 1947–1949
(in millions of dollars or equivalents)

Currency Disbursed	1947	1948	1949	Total
U.S. Dollars	299.9	193.2	61.8	554.9
Belgian Francs	0.3	1.7·	0	2.0
Swiss Francs	0	4.0	0	4.0
Canadian Dollars	0	0	5.1	5.1
Pounds Sterling	0	0	1.0	1.0
	300.2	198.9	67.9	567.0

Source: *International Financial Statistics,* International Monetary Fund, Washington, D.C., January 1950, p. 17.

During its first year of operation, 1947, the emphasis of the Bank was entirely on European reconstruction. It authorized four loans totalling $497 million,[8] and all of these were to Western European countries. All except $12 million were "general purpose" or "balance of payments" loans in the sense that they were not for specific projects, although the Bank did give its approval to the goods to be purchased. During 1948 the Bank was, in its words, "changing gears," and loans authorized totalled only $28 million, of which $12 million were to four Dutch shipping companies and $16 million were for two development projects in Chile.

With ERP under way the Bank concentrated most of its attention in 1949 on development loans in underdeveloped areas and stated that its objectives were essentially the same as those of President Truman's Point Four Program. During the year, twelve loans for specific projects were authorized, of which eight, accounting for nearly 80 percent of the total funds, were to governments or institutions in areas generally called underdeveloped. Although the Bank anticipated that as Marshall aid was reduced and finally ceased in 1952 it would be called upon to consider financing long-range projects in Europe, it planned to place most of its emphasis during the next few years on loans to underdeveloped areas, including European overseas territories.[9] The program for loans to such overseas territories received something of a set-back as the year ended when negotiations between the

[8] In 1949, $0.2 million of the loan to Luxembourg were cancelled.
[9] *Fourth Annual Report, 1948–1949,* International Bank for Reconstruction and Development, Washington, D.C., September 13, 1949.

TABLE XX

Loan Authorizations by the International Bank, 1947–1949
(in millions of U.S. dollars)

Date	Member Country Concerned	Principal Amount	
1947			
May 9	France	250.0	
Aug. 7	Netherlands	195.0	
Aug. 22	Denmark	40.0	
Aug. 28	Luxembourg[1]	11.8	496.8
1948			
March 25	Chile[2]	16.0	
July 15	Netherlands[3]	12.0	28.0
1949			
Jan. 6	Mexico[2]	34.1	
Jan. 27	Brazil	75.0	
Mar. 1	Belgium	16.0	
July 26	Netherlands[4]	15.0	
Aug. 1	Finland	12.5	
Aug. 18	India	34.0	
Aug. 19	Colombia	5.0	
Sept. 29	India	10.0	
Oct. 17	Yugoslavia	2.7	
	Finland	2.3	
Dec. 14	El Salvador	12.5	219.1
Total			743.9

1. This loan authorization was originally for $12.0 million but $0.2 million were cancelled in 1949.
2. Two separate loans.
3. Six separate loans.
4. $6.2 million of this loan were cancelled, at the request of the Netherlands, in April 1950.
Source: *International Financial Statistics,* January 1950, International Monetary Fund, Washington, D.C., p. 17.

Bank and the British Government's Colonial Development Corporation for a $5 million loan were abandoned because the Colonial Development Corporation was unwilling to accept some of the Bank's non-financial convenants. The exact nature of the difficulties has not been made public. The press reported that the Bank wanted more of a voice in the Corporation's affairs than the latter would accept, while the Bank stated it was asking only acceptance of its "standard" requirements.

During 1949 the Bank, presumably with United States approval, made it a policy to stress that there was "no quick and easy way to raise productive levels and living standards" in underdeveloped areas. It emphasized the severe limitations on the capacity of such areas to absorb foreign capital for genuinely productive purposes as a result of low levels of education and health, political instability and irresponsibility, incompetent government administration, and limited resources and local captal. In its *Fourth Annual Report* the Bank reached an oft-quoted conclusion: " . . . the principal limitation upon Bank financing in the development field has not been lack of money but lack of well-prepared and well-planned projects ready for immediate execution."[1] Despite these obstacles, the Bank considered development loans to be a fertile field for future Bank activity, and laid special stress on the contributions of the many technical missions it sent to various countries during the year. It also warned against too much emphasis on industrial, at the expense of agricultural, development.

The Bank also made it clear in 1949 that it did not intend to be used primarily for anti-cyclical activities. In response to U.N. inquiries and plans concerning action to achieve or maintain economic stability and full employment, the Bank pointed out that there might well be conflicts between economic development and stability and that " . . . the Bank's primary function is to provide for a smooth and continuous flow of international investment . . . therefore, it cannot conserve its resources simply in order to release more funds in times of incipient depression."[2] This policy was subject to continuing attack, and in late December a group of experts (including two Americans) appointed by the U.N. Secretary General to consider measures for full employment, recommended that a new and separate department of the Bank be created to lend, from funds borrowed from governments, such amounts to governments as were necessary to provide, along with private lending, a stable total of international long-term investment. The United States representative to the U.N. Economic

---

[1] In reply to criticism in February 1950 by delegates to the U.N. from some of the underdeveloped countries that the Bank was following a much too conservative loan policy, President Black pointed out that the Bank had to get most of its funds from the United States market and that this would be very difficult if its standards were lowered.

[2] U.N. ECOSOC Doc. E/1111, 31 January 1949, p. 175.

and Employment Commission indicated in January 1950 that the United States would oppose this proposal.

During the year the Bank, as a matter of policy and with full United States support, pressed member countries for consent to use in its lending operations that portion of the Bank's paid-up capital represented by the 18 percent local currency contribution. The United States had consented to the use of its paid-up subscription. The United States considered that other nations should make a part of their foreign investments via the mechanism of the International Bank and that efforts should be made to make the Bank truly international in character. In 1947 Belgium had consented to the use of the equivalent of $2 million in Belgian francs, and in 1949 the respective governments agreed to the use of up to 8 million Canadian dollars, 500 thousand British pounds, and some 600 thousand Danish kroner. The British and part of the Canadian permissions were in connection with the Bank's loan to the Brazilian subsidiaries of certain Canadian companies.

It was, however, recognized that in the foreseeable future most of the funds requested from the Bank would be United States dollars and that only the United States was likely to engage in large capital exports.[3] During 1949 the Bank borrowed only $19.9 million in the United States market and this by selling the balance ($3.9 million) of the mortgage notes received from a 1948 loan to some Dutch shipping companies and $16 million of sinking fund bonds of the Kingdom of Belgium received under the 1949 loan to Belgium. Both of these issues carried the Bank's full guarantee and were easily sold to mutual savings banks. The Bank reported that although this operation permitted a testing of the market and gave the Bank some valuable experience, it did

[3] At Bretton Woods it was anticipated that the Bank would obtain most of the dollars it needed, beyond the United States paid-up capital and the gold and dollar contributions of other members, by issuing in the United States market securities of various countries carrying the Bank's guarantee. In 1947, however, the Bank, uncertain over the United States market, had resorted only to direct borrowing and floated two issues of its own bonds in the United States market, one of $100 million ten-year bonds and one of $150 million twenty-five-year bonds. In 1948 the Bank also sold its own Swiss franc bonds to the Bank for International Settlements to an amount equivalent to about $4 million. In 1948 the Bank did sell to United States, mutual savings banks and commercial banks from its portfolio $8.1 million of the $12.0 million of mortgage notes received under its loan to four Dutch shipping companies.

not intend to rely on portfolio sales frequently but would depend more on selling its own bonds.

In recognition of the reliance of the Bank on the United States as a primary source of investment funds and to encourage the Bank to assume greater responsibility in financing reconstruction and development abroad, the Administration requested Congress in early 1949 to amend certain of the Securities Acts, the National Bank Act, and the Bretton Woods Agreements Act so as to broaden the market for Bank securities by permitting national banks and state banks which are members of the Federal Reserve System to *deal* in and underwrite obligations issued by the Bank and to exempt the obligations issued by or fully guaranteed by the Bank from the Securities Acts of the United States.[4]   It was argued that the commercial banks would not invest heavily in these securities unless they could not only hold them but also deal in them—that is, could sell quickly and so provide for the liquidity or shiftability in assets required by commercial banks. Exemption from the Securities Acts was asked on the grounds that the public was amply protected anyway and the marketing system of the commercial banks was geared to deal in securities which were exempt and was not adapted to meet the requirements pertaining to securities subject to these Acts.[5]   The measure was approved on June 29, 1949.

In late December the Bank announced that early in 1950 it planned to call for redemption, at a price of 101, its $100 million ten-year 2¼ percent bonds, which had been sold in July 1947, and would offer a refunding issue of serial bonds in the same amount at competitive bidding.   This action was designed further to test the credit of the Bank, to reduce interest charges, and

---

[4] A similar request had been made in 1948 but ran into some opposition over the provisions for exemption from the Securities Acts.   The new proposal took account of the previous objections.   From 1946 to the end of 1949 the Bank and United States authorities were successful in obtaining state and national legislation and administrative action permitting the Bank's securities to be bought by commercial and mutual savings banks whose deposits were more than 93 percent of the total of such deposits and insurance companies whose assets amounted also to some 93 percent of all such assets in the United States.

[5] For a detailed discussion of these issues see *Hearings before Committee on Banking and Currency, House of Representatives, 81st Cong., 1st Sess., on H.R. 4332.*

to adjust the maturity on Bank securities to fit in with loan repayments.[6] It reported no net additional borrowing in the near future was contemplated.[7]

The Bank also gave consideration during the year to selling a small amount of dollar bonds in Europe, but no such action was taken. It was thought that the sale of dollar bonds in Europe might be a method of mobilizing for productive purposes some of the dollars being hoarded by European residents.[8]

[6] The Bank announced on January 25, 1950 that it had sold to a United States banking syndicate $100 million of its bonds maturing serially from 1953 to 1962 in equal annual installments. The winning bid was 100.559 for the specified 2% interest coupon, indicating a net interest cost to the Bank of 1.92%. The proceeds were used to retire on February 17 at 101 the $100 million 2¼% bonds sold in 1947 and due in 1957.

[7] In early March 1950 the Bank sold to a group of Swiss banks an issue of Swiss franc bonds totalling 28.5 million Swiss francs (U.S. $6.6 million).

[8] Mr. McCloy testified that a "goodly" number of the $250 million of bonds sold in 1947 were purchased by European buyers. Department of Commerce data on private United States investments indicates that some $7 million of these bonds were purchased by non-Americans.

III POLICIES TOWARD EXCHANGE RATES AND GOLD

A. EXCHANGE RATES

Devaluation

THE United States steadfastly maintained during the year that the question of exchange rate alterations was one which each country must decide in consultation with the International Monetary Fund. While there is no acceptable evidence that the United States put direct pressure on other nations to revalue their currencies, there was no doubt as to its interest in the question or its view that devaluation was desirable in many countries.[1] During the February Hearings on extending the Economic Cooperation Act, both ECA spokesmen and Secretary Snyder stated that devaluation of many European currencies might be necessary in the near future and that this question would be "reviewed" during the year with many foreign countries. Secretary Snyder, speaking for the National Advisory Council (NAC), told the Congressmen that, with the United States supplying billions of dollars in aid, foreign exchange rates were a matter of grave and direct concern to the United States in so far as exchange rate policies tend to retard exports or misdirect trade, thus increasing Europe's deficit with the Western Hemisphere. At the same time United States officials often warned against the assumption that devaluation alone would solve the balance of payments problems of Europe.

[1] For various official statements see *A Report on Recovery Progress and United States Aid, op. cit.*, p. 17; *Semi-Annual Report to the President and to the Congress for the period October 1, 1948–March 31, 1949*, National Advisory Council, Washington, D.C., 1949, p. 15; and the *Hearings before the Committee on Foreign Affairs, House of Representatives, 81st Cong., 1st Sess., on H.R. 2362.*

As the year progressed, both Mr. Snyder and Mr. Hoffman publicly dropped the broadest hints that the time had come to devalue most European currencies; correlatively, the main theme of the 1949 Annual Report of the Executive Directors of the International Monetary Fund was "currency revaluation." This report was agreed to by the United States Executive Director, whose activities, by statute, are guided by NAC.[2] In his presidential address at the annual meeting of the Governors of the International Bank in September, Mr. Black stated in unmistakable terms that a devaluation of many European currencies was necessary.[3]

It was generally recognized that the crucial rate was that between the dollar and the pound sterling, and that a change here would be the signal for many others. It was officially stated on several occasions that the United States put no pressure on the British to devalue, but it was reported in the press that just prior to the British-Canadian-United States financial talks in September, which preceded the sterling devaluation, " . . . everyone in Washington had been bracing himself for a long and hard tussle over devaluation."[4] Such a tussle, however, was not necessary, since the British informed senior American officials at the beginning of these talks that they were going to devalue; this action was welcomed by the latter as a constructive step.

Because of the confidential nature of the Fund's operations, an outsider cannot know whether the September devaluations were taken with no more than perfunctory reference to the International Monetary Fund. The Fund officially stated at the

[2] When there is no evidence to the contrary it is assumed that the Fund's action, if not its inaction, has the approval of the United States Government. This does not mean that the United States necessarily initiates the policies of the Fund. R. F. Mikesell, an authority on the Fund, has written that the United States " . . . has insisted that the lending policies of the Fund bear some relation to the general foreign financial aid program of the United States" and implied that the same considerations for coordination of the Fund and United States international financial policies apply to the other operations of the Fund. See his "The International Monetary Fund, 1944–1949," *International Conciliation*, November 1949, for a careful study of the Fund's operations.

[3] Mr. Black also urged in general terms much of what Mr. Hoffman was to ask in his October 31 "integration" speech to the OEEC Council (see pages 192 f).

[4] *The Economist*, London, September 24, 1949, p. 668.

time that the devaluations were taken through its machinery, but the statements of officials of several governments—especially the French and British—strongly suggest that consultations with the Fund were no more than token and that the crucial devaluation, that of sterling, was sprung on it without observing more than a semblance of consultation.[5] And to many outsiders it appears that the other devaluations " . . . sprang in considerable measure out of efforts, after Britain had acted, to adjust to a *fait accompli*."[6] At the same time it must be recorded that its *Fourth Annual Report* showed the Fund was alert to the possibility and was not taken by surprise. It should also be recognized that, of necessity, devaluations must be handled quickly; it is, therefore, the Fund's responsibility to be fully prepared to consider proposals on short notice. Further, it is possible that the Fund's staff may have held confidential discussions with individual member governments and exerted some influence on their final action, but there is no public evidence that such was the case. The Fund did state that the devaluations were in conformity with its views, but this could be true even though the decisions were taken unilaterally. Since the Fund did not publicly raise any objections to the new rates, the important question of how effective it could be in altering major decisions with which it disagreed was not publicly demonstrated, nor perhaps tested.

The published record concerning the September devaluations does suggest that the Fund was a less potent organization for coordinating international monetary policies than had been hoped when it was established. But even granting the Fund's imperfections, the United States clearly wishes to preserve it as the preeminent international organization concerned with such problems. This attitude was indicated in NAC's objections in January 1950 to certain parts of the ECA-sponsored "European

[5] ECA stated, in its *Sixth Report to Congress*, p. 8, that the United Kingdom submitted its proposals to the Fund on Friday and, with the Fund's concurrence, the new rate went into effect on Sunday. Indeed, in his radio speech on September 18 announcing the devaluation, Sir Stafford Cripps said that the decision taken " . . . had to do with matters that were entirely our own concern and upon which there was no question of our consulting others, even our best friends." (*New York Times*, September 19, 1949.)

[6] "Monthly Letter on Economic Conditions," National City Bank of New York, October 1949, p. 110.

Payments Union," which they believed were in conflict with the objectives and responsibilities of the Fund (see page 150).

Whatever the United States influence—either direct or via the Fund—on the other devaluations, her responsibility in the German, Austrian, and Japanese devaluations was even greater and more direct. The devaluation of the D-mark was mishandled. Apparently no preparations had been made; after the sterling devaluation the Germans were told that while the Allied High Commission alone had the right to set the exchange rates they would permit the Germans to make up their minds first. (The record does not show whether this was the result of the three occupying powers being unable to agree.) The Germans proposed a 25-percent devaluation to 22.5 cents per mark. The French raised strong objections to such a devaluation—on the grounds that it would directly increase their difficulties in selling Saar steel in Germany and, further, would increase the cost differentials for Ruhr coal.[7] Finally, the Allies rejected the German figure and set the rate at 23.8 cents—a devaluation of 20.6 percent.

In Austria, devaluation was delayed for a month. The press reported this was because of a difference of opinion between ECA officials and the Austrian Government, but the fact that the Austrian elections were being held may also have been important. The Americans were reported favoring a greater devaluation than the Austrians, and the former's view finally prevailed. The Fund sent a mission to Austria in the summer which held prolonged discussions on the problem; it approved the final arrangements, but the public has no way of knowing whether there were any disagreements between the Fund and ECA officials. As finally approved, the Austrian system provided for a single export rate, three rates for imports, and a special rate for invisibles.

A single rate of 360 yen per dollar was finally established in April for the Japanese yen, on the recommendation of NAC and as part of a broad stabilization program which had been agreed

---

[7] Ruhr coal for export was priced, and had to be paid for, in dollars, and the French argued that if, after devaluation, both the dollar price and the internal German price remained unchanged the differential in favor of German manufacturers would be increased. It was finally agreed to reduce the dollar price by the full amount of the devaluation and leave the internal price unchanged.

upon in late 1948. Prior to that time there had been no explicit rate for commercial transactions and the implicit rates varied greatly from commodity to commodity. No alteration was made during the rest of the year.

Multiple Rates

In the establishment of the Fund a basic aim, for which the United States pressed strongly, was the elimination of multiple exchange rates. However, the Fund continued in 1949 to be lenient in its attitude toward this practice.[8] Although the Fund did refuse in December to approve new exchange measures put into effect in Nicaragua involving a multiplicity of rates, it gave its reluctant blessings to multiple rates in at least four other cases during the year, justifying this action on the ground that these were first steps in simplifying even more complex exchange systems. In addition to approving the Austrian rates, the Fund in November did not formally object to the institution of a system in Paraguay involving four separate buying rates and four separate and different selling rates. The Fund earlier had raised no serious objections, when the issue was presented to it, to Uruguay and Ecuador maintaining, for the time being, multiple rates. On the other hand, the Fund has consistently opposed exchange practices which lead to disorderly cross rates,[9] and it welcomed reforms in this respect by France and Greece following the September devaluations.

Fluctuating Rates

There were evidences late in the year that the United States was reconsidering its stern policy of advocating fixed over fluctuating exchange rates. ECA seemed to be doubtful whether a policy of fixed rates over long periods of time was desirable, at least for Europe; it gave unofficial approval to the "Fritalux" plan (see page 144) which envisaged fluctuating rates among the members. Collaterally, in his famous "integration" speech

[8] In 1949 multiple exchange rates were in effect in more than one-third of the Fund's membership.

[9] See *Annual Report of the Executive Directors for the Fiscal Year Ended April 30, 1948,* International Monetary Fund, Washington, D.C., 1948 and *Annual Report of the Executive Directors for the Fiscal Year Ended April 30, 1949,* International Monetary Fund, Washington, D.C., 1949 for statements of the Fund's position on disorderly cross rates as well as careful official statements on its other policies.

of October 31 (see page 142), Mr. Hoffman said that, to achieve the conditions he was urging, ERP countries would have to "provide means for necessary exchange rate adjustments" where these were the only feasible alternatives to exchange controls.

There was an indication that the Fund also was altering slightly its previous policy of rigorously insisting on fixed exchange rates for all members at all times. In late November, Peru reported to the Fund that it considered a change in the parity of its currency to be necessary but could not at that time set a new parity; it, therefore, proposed the establishment of a single free foreign exchange market for all trade transactions with the rate to be determined solely by market forces. The Fund stated it would not object to the plan as a "temporary measure," on the understanding that as soon as "circumstances warrant" a new fixed par value for the sol would be established.[1] This action cannot be interpreted to mean the Fund was prepared to embrace fluctuating rates as a general policy, but it was a clear indication that the Fund recognized there were situations in which a fixed rate was inappropriate.

Lending Policy of the Fund

During 1949 the Fund sold, with the approval of NAC, $101.5 million of U.S. dollars to Brazil, India, Australia, Yugoslavia, Egypt, and Ethiopia.[2] Thus, from its inception in March 1947 through 1949 nineteen members had drawn on the Fund's resources to an amount equivalent to $783.4 million, of which all was in dollars except for the equivalent of $11.4 million in Belgian francs and $6 million in pounds sterling. Sales of dollars would

[1] *International Financial News Survey*, International Monetary Fund, Washington, D.C., November 18, 1949, p. 157.

[2] A par value for the Yugoslav dinar had been agreed to on March 24, 1949. On June 17 the Fund agreed to a new par value for the Mexican peso and at the same time the United States signed an agreement with Mexico supplementing the United States-Mexican Stabilization Agreement of May 1947, under which Mexico had already utilized $37 million of the $50 million available under that agreement. The new agreement increased to $25 million the balance available from the United States Stabilization Fund for the purchase of pesos to stabilize the dollar-peso exchange rate. Secretary Snyder stated that any operations under this bilateral agreement would be closely coordinated with the activities of the Fund.

Thailand became a member of the Fund and Bank on May 3, 1949, raising total membership to 48. At the September meeting of the Board of Governors the application of Haiti for membership was approved but she did not formally join in 1949.

doubtless have been larger in 1949 had it not been for the April 1948 decision by the Fund, which almost prohibits dollar sales to countries receiving ERP aid.[3] In the fall of 1949 there were rumors that the Fund was considering dropping this restriction, but these were disposed of in October by Secretary Snyder who stated, in effect, that the United States Treasury was opposed to any such change.

1949 witnessed the first repurchases by members of their own currencies to a total equivalent to $3.6 million. In May and November, Costa Rica bought back the equivalent of $2.2 million worth of colones with dollars and gold. In August, Belgium repurchased the equivalent of $946,500 of francs by paying into the Fund an equivalent amount of gold and dollars.[4] Shortly thereafter, Nicaragua repurchased the equivalent of $500,000 of cordobas with dollars. Despite these repayments, the record through 1949 of the lending operations of the Fund suggests that a large amount of its loans have been to finance fundamental and long-term rather than short-term disequilibria in members' balances of payments.[5]

A summary of transactions by the Fund for 1949 and for the period from its inception through 1949 is shown in Table XXI.

[3] It appears that, as a consequence of this, the European members of the Fund took a less active interest in its operations. Conversely the writer has seen no evidence that the Fund seriously concerned itself with the Intra-European Payments and Compensations Scheme (see pages 136 ff.) under which the Bank for International Settlements was selected as agent. However, a possible serious conflict of responsibilities and operations was foreseen between the Fund and the more ambitious ECA-sponsored European Payments Union proposed in December 1949, with the result that NAC raised serious objections to the latter in January 1950 (see page 150). At its own request the Fund did take part in the 1950 negotiations in Paris regarding the proposed European Payments Union.

[4] On January 30, 1950 it was announced that Belgium had repurchased an additional $20.6 million of its francs with dollars and gold.

[5] In late December a group of experts, including two American economists, appointed by the Secretary General of the United Nations to consider measures for full employment, recommended, among other things, that if a nation suffered a recession it should make available to the Fund for sale to other nations an amount of its currency equal to the fall in imports less any fall in exports, in the given year as compared with a reference year. (See National and International Measures for Full Employment, United Nations, December 1949). In January 1950 the United States representative to the United Nations Economic and Employment Commission indicated the United States opposed this proposal.

TABLE XXI
International Monetary Fund Exchange Transactions, 1947–1949
(in millions of U.S. dollar equivalents)

	1947–1948	1949	Total
Currency Sold	*681.9*	*101.5*	*783.4*
U.S. dollars	664.5	101.5	766.0
British pounds	6.0	0	6.0
Belgian francs	11.4	0	11.4
Currency Bought	*681.9*	*101.5*	*783.4*
Australian pounds	0	20.0	20.0
Belgian francs	33.0	0	33.0
Brazilian cruzeiros	0	37.5	37.5
Pounds sterling	300.0	0	300.0
Chilean pesos	8.8	0	8.8
Costa Rican colones	1.3	0	1.3
Czechoslovakian korunas	6.0	0	6.0
Danish kroner	10.2	0	10.2
Egyptian pounds	0	3.0	3.0
Ethiopian dollars	0.3	0.3	0.6
French francs	125.0	0	125.0
Indian rupees	68.3	31.7	100.0
Mexican pesos	22.5	0	22.5
Netherlands guilders	75.3	0	75.3
Nicaraguan cordobas	0.5	0	0.5
Norwegian kroner	9.6	0	9.6
Turkish liras	5.0	0	5.0
Union of South Africa pounds	10.0	0	10.0
Yugoslav dinars	0	9.0	9.0
Gold[a]	6.1	0	6.1
Currency Repurchased	*0*	*3.6*	*3.6*
U.S. dollars	0	2.6	2.6
Gold	0	1.0	1.0
Currency Resold	*0*	*3.6*	*3.6*
Belgian francs	0	0.9	0.9
Costa Rican colones	0	2.2	2.2
Nicaraguan cordobas	0	0.5	0.5

a. Sold by Norway in 1948 in exchange for U.S. dollars. Article V, Section 6(a) of the Agreement of the International Monetary Fund provides: "Any member desiring to obtain, directly or indirectly, the currency of another member for gold shall, provided that it can do so with equal advantage, acquire it by sale of gold to the Fund."

Source: *International Financial Statistics*, International Monetary Fund, January 1950, p. 12.

B. GOLD

During 1949 the United States held to its policy that " . . . the most important use of gold is for the domestic and international monetary functions of the Government . . . " and that a large gold stock " . . . gives impregnable international strength to the dollar."[6] This policy involved the maintenance of a fixed price in the face of much pressure from certain producing countries for a higher price, and the limiting of international transactions to those between central monetary authorities. It also involved disapproval of subsidized gold production abroad on the ground that while the United States was willing to buy gold freely at $35 per ounce in order to maintain gold as an international standard it was not in this country's interest for other nations to subsidize gold as a means of reaching equilibrium in their balance of payments with the United States.[7]

During the year the question of gold policy became a public issue on two occasions. The first resulted from the Union of South Africa's drive to take advantage of the premium prices for gold which existed in both legal and illegal markets all over the world, and the other followed the extensive devaluations in September which led to rumors that the United States was also planning to devalue.

South African Proposals

In early February the South African Minister of Finance announced that his country was, as an experiment, going to sell abroad 100,000 ounces of semi-processed gold for industrial and similar purposes at premium prices. The Fund took immediate exception to this action, received a strongly worded reply from the South Africans, and then issued the strongest statement of its career.[8] Publicly supported by Secretary of the Treasury

[6] Letter from W. McC. Martin, Jr., Acting Secretary of the Treasury, to Senator Maybank, dated May 4, 1949 and included in *Hearings before the Committee on Banking and Currency, U.S. Senate, 81st Cong., 1st Sess.,* on S. 13 and S. 286, pp. 4–6.

[7] For an official view of this policy see Secretary Snyder's December 1947 statement reprinted in *Department of State Bulletin,* December 28, 1947, p. 1268. The Fund has discouraged but not prohibited such subsidy payments in 1949.

[8] See its Press Release, February 24, 1949, reprinted in *International Financial News Survey,* March 3, 1949.

Snyder, the Fund stated that it had had a firm policy since June 18, 1947 of disapproving *external* gold sales at premium prices unless there were adequate safeguards to insure that the gold was actually used for *bona fide* industrial, professional, and artistic purposes and not for speculation or hoarding. The Fund did not believe such safeguards existed in the present case; it stated that since the United States was prepared to satisfy all verifiably genuine demands for non-monetary gold at approximately $35 an ounce, there was strong evidence that the South African sales at a premium price would get into private hoards. This result was objectionable, the Fund reported, because it reduced the proportion of newly-mined gold available for international monetary reserves and resulted directly or indirectly in a leakage or diversion of foreign exchange reserves to the disadvantage of countries importing the gold. Although not stressed in the 1949 controversy, the policy statement of June 18, 1947 argued that external gold sales at premium prices directly or indirectly involved exchange dealings at depreciated rates and so disturbed the exchange relationships of its members.[9]

Later, Mr. Gutt, Managing Director of the Fund, went to Capetown to discuss the sale of semi-processed gold. He an-

[9] During the year there were in the United States newsworthy, but presumably small, internal sales of gold in its natural state to private persons, at prices ranging up to $46 per fine ounce just prior to the September devaluations and falling to around $39 per ounce at year's end, by such large firms as Bache & Company of New York. Such sales are authorized by Section 19 of the Treasury Department regulations issued under the Gold Reserve Act of 1934, which defines gold in its natural state as "gold recovered from natural sources which has not been melted, smelted, or refined or otherwise treated by heating or by a chemical or electrical process." Internal sales at premium prices were extensive during the year in several countries, especially in Asia. The United States also provided Greece with gold sovereigns for internal sales at premium prices as an anti-inflationary device.

The Fund stated during the controversy that it had not objected to internal gold sales at premium prices. It is hard to discern the basis for this policy distinction between internal and external sales. Internal sales probably go into private hoards just as surely as external sales and represent the same reduction in international monetary reserves and diversion of foreign exchange earnings. Internal sales might not, however, be subject to the same criticism of effectively depreciating the nation's currency as would external sales at premium prices. In its June 18, 1947 statement the Fund recognized these problems but apparently has not considered them serious.

nounced on May 11 that an agreement had been reached whereby adequate safeguards would be applied to assure that South Africa's gold exports would not get into hoarding or speculative channels.[1]

The South Africans, regarding gold in their discussions with the Fund as a commodity and not as an international currency, also asked for an increase in the official gold price on the grounds that since all other prices had risen, maintaining the $35 per ounce price for gold was creating a state of disequilibrium and disturbing the pattern of world trade. To this the reply was that " . . . the Fund strongly objects to the statements of Mr. Havenga with reference to the present price of gold."[2] In its 1949 Annual Report the Fund stated that the United States in fact determined the gold price and that under existing conditions a rise would merely increase United States exports in exchange for additions to its gold stocks which were already two-thirds of the world's reserves. It said further that, in so far as the United States was prepared to maintain an export surplus, " . . . it can do this more effectively through its foreign aid program. . . . " Finally, it was argued that a rise in the price of gold at that time would not correct the maldistribution of gold and could not be regarded as " . . . a substitute for the measures in the sphere of exchange and payment policies which have to be taken if international balance is to be restored."[3] The devaluation of the South

---

[1] A full implementation by the Union of South Africa and the Fund of this policy seems quite impossible under today's conditions. From February 1949 through February 1950 the South Africans supplied 1.3 million ounces to the premium market.

[2] Press Release, February 24, 1949, *op. cit.*

[3] *Annual Report of the Executive Directors for the Fiscal Year Ended April 30, 1949*, International Monetary Fund, Washington, D.C., 1949, p. 39.

At the September meeting of the Board of Governors of the Fund the South Africans again pleaded for a higher gold price. Secretary Snyder once again rejected this plea, saying " . . . I do not perceive any considerations of monetary policy which would justify me in proposing to my Government a change in the dollar price of gold." (*Semi-Annual Report to the President and to the Congress for the Period April 1–September 30, 1949*, National Advisory Council, Washington, D.C., 1950, p. 33.) The reasons were presumably those put forward earlier by the Fund. On September 16 the Board of Governors disposed of the South African request to permit member countries to sell up to 50 percent of their newly-mined domestic gold at premium prices by ordering the Executive Directors to study the problem and report back to the Board of Governors. In early May 1950

African pound in late 1949 served to meet their demand for a higher price, at least in terms of South Africa's own currency, but it is to be expected that South Africa at least may again apply pressure on the Fund and the United States to change their gold policy since there is little prospect that many countries in the near future will be able to provide for convertibility of their currencies into gold and so make gold a genuine international standard of value.

Dollar Devaluation Rumors

Following the devaluation in September, there was a temporary resurgence in the United States of certain small groups advocating the establishment of a "free market" for gold and others urging that the United States should return to a policy of free convertibility of dollars into gold. These provoked a full-dress rebuttal by the President of the New York Federal Reserve Bank in early November; public discussions virtually ceased thereafter.[4]

During the same period rumors, both in the United States and abroad, that the United States was contemplating devaluing the dollar via decreasing its gold content reached such proportions that on October 5 Secretary of the Treasury Snyder issued a formal denial of any intention to revalue gold.[5] But even this did not convince many persons, and on November 10 President Truman gave "positive" assurance that there would be no alteration in the price of gold while he was in the White House. This statement put to rest, for the time being at least, most of the speculation on the gold price.[6]

---

the Executive Directors released a report (not unanimously agreed to) recommending the rejection of the proposal. This drew strong criticism from Mr. Havenga and the issue promised to be again the subject of debate at the September 1950 meeting of the Board of Governors.

[4] See *Monthly Review*, Supplement, Federal Reserve Bank of New York, December 1949 for Mr. Sproul's excellent statement.

[5] The power of the President to change the gold content of the dollar expired on June 30, 1943 and so Congressional action would be required for such a step. The Secretary of the Treasury still has legal authority to alter the buying and selling price for gold but this authority is limited by United States obligations as a member of the Fund to one-fourth percent above and below the par value for purchases and sales of gold; also under the Bretton Woods Agreement Act the par value of the dollar can be changed only with the approval of Congress.

[6] During this period the central banks of Italy and Belgium converted part (amounts not disclosed) of their reserves of liquid dollar assets into gold; the Bank of France, needing to replenish its dollar account in October,

Foreign Gold Transactions

Net purchases of gold by the United States from foreign countries during 1949 totalled $230 million, as compared with $1.5 billion in 1948 and $2.8 billion in 1947. The sharp fall in foreign sales of gold to the United States in 1949 resulted primarily from (a) the tightening of import and exchange controls, as many nations felt their gold and dollar reserves were at or below safe minima, (b) the large flow of Marshall aid, (c) the completion of some of the post-war reconstruction and the recovery of production and trade abroad, and (d) the extensive devaluations during the year.[7]

Foreign gold transactions by the United States varied greatly during the year both with respect to time and to countries. From January until September 18 the United States made net purchases of $462 million, but the devaluations were followed by net sales of $232 million. Nearly 90 percent of gross United States foreign purchases were from the United Kingdom and the Union of South Africa. Although Italy was easily the largest single purchaser, sizeable amounts were also sold to Argentina, Venezuela, Thailand, Belgium and Switzerland. The net foreign gold transactions by the United States during the year are shown in Table XXII.

In addition to these net purchases from foreign countries, the United States made net sales to the Bank for International Settlements of $34 million and domestic consumption was probably some $32 million in excess of domestic output. Thus, total official United States gold holdings increased by $164 million during the year. Despite this increase in gold holdings, the *percentage* of the total official world gold reserves held by the United States declined for the first time in many years as foreign production per-

did so by borrowing $100 million against gold collateral instead of merely selling gold. In some of the press this was interpreted as a move to protect themselves against a possible rise in the dollar price of gold; but the French had so borrowed before, and the Italian move may have been directed to strengthening public confidence in the lira following the devaluation.

[7] It should be remembered that foreign purchases and sales of gold are closely related to their combined gold and dollar position. It is common practice to purchase gold when dollar balances exceed customary levels and to sell gold when dollar balances fall below such levels.

mitted foreign holdings to increase by $250 million in spite of net sales of $230 million to the United States.[8] The distribution of world official gold holdings is given in Table XXIII.

TABLE XXII
Foreign Gold Transactions by the United States, 1949
(net purchases (+); net sales (−))
(in millions of dollars)

ERP Countries (other than United Kingdom)	−215
Other Europe	−8
United Kingdom	+446
Union of South Africa	+195
Canada	+3
Latin America	−137
Asia	−55
Total	+230

Source: "Foreign Gold and Dollar Holdings in 1949," *Federal Reserve Bulletin,* March 1950, p. 272. The reader is referred to this article for a careful analysis of the changes in the gold and dollar assets of foreign countries during the year under review. It is the source of much of the information included in this section.

Note: The total excludes net sales of $34 million to the Bank for International Settlements.

TABLE XXIII
Estimated Official World Gold Holdings, 1929–1949
(exclusive of Soviet Union)
(in billions of dollars)[a]

	United States		Other	International Monetary	
End of	Amount	Percent of Total	Other Countries	Monetary Fund	Total
1929	6.6	*37.9*	10.8	0	17.4
1937	12.8	*51.0*	12.3	0	25.1
1945	20.1	*59.6*	13.7	0	33.8
1947	22.9	*66.4*	10.4	1.3	34.6
1948	24.4	*70.0*	9.1	1.4	34.9
1949	24.6	*69.7*	9.4	1.4	35.4

a. Calculated in present dollars.
Sources: *Annual Report for the Fiscal Year Ended April 30, 1949,* International Monetary Fund, Washington, D.C., 1949, pp. 40–41, and *International Financial Statistics,* International Monetary Fund, Washington, D.C., April 1950, p. 16, and "Foreign Gold and Dollar Holdings in 1949," *Federal Reserve Bulletin,* March 1950, p. 273.
Note: NAC estimated USSR holdings at $2.7 billion as of June 1948.

[8] Excluding Russia, foreign gold production in 1949 has been estimated at about $750 million; it is assumed that most of the unaccounted-for $270 million went into private hands via the various free and black markets.

IV · DOLLAR AREA - STERLING AREA
FINANCIAL DISCUSSIONS

DESPITE constant pressure on the European nations to meet their problems by joint European action through OEEC, the United States in 1949 held separate discussions with the British and Canadians on the particular problems of the sterling area. France and other European nations resented this action, but the United States explained that the financial relationships between the sterling area and the dollar area involved problems which " . . . concern in the first instance the governments which are the centers of these two currency systems."[1]

Loss of Reserves

In the late spring it became evident that the sterling area's gold and dollar reserves were declining at an unexpected and alarming rate and were reaching a level below that considered as minimum necessary working reserves (Table XXIV).[2] The problem was worsened by the knowledge that ECA aid was going to be reduced. In early June the British authorities ordered all pur-

[1] "Joint Communique," September 12, 1949. Reprinted in the *Department of State Bulletin*, September 26, 1949, p. 473 ff.

[2] The important immediate causes of the decline after March were increased imports by sterling area countries, a sharp falling off of sterling area exports to the United States as business activity here receded somewhat and as post-war shortages of automobiles and certain other durable goods disappeared, and a widespread belief that with the return of a buyers' market in the United States the United Kingdom could not maintain the sterling exchange, with the result that purchases from the sterling area and payments for past purchases were delayed and there was an acceleration in requests for payments for goods sold in the sterling area. Although details are not available, capital flight was also important.

chasing departments to postpone dollar purchases to the maximum extent practicable.[3]

TABLE XXIV
Sterling Area Gold and Dollar Reserves, Selected Dates
(in millions of dollars)

December 30, 1946	2696
December 30, 1947	2079
December 30, 1948	1856
March 31, 1949	1912
June 30, 1949	1651
September 18, 1949	1330

Source: "British Economic Record," British Information Service, New York, January 15, 1950. The September 18, 1949 figure was taken from the *Semi-Annual Report to the President and to the Congress for the period April 1- September 30, 1949*, National Advisory Council, Washington D.C., 1950, p. 20.

The United States officially stated it regarded this loss of reserves as serious both for the British Empire and the rest of the world. From July 8 to 10 Secretary Snyder, who was visiting the various Treasury Representative offices in Europe, held discussions in London with British and Canadian officials, which were described by the British Treasury as " . . . a general exchange of views . . . on the balance of payments difficulties between the dollar and sterling areas and the measures which could be taken . . . " to correct the disequilibrium.[3] These discussions apparently produced no new ideas and were very general in nature. Arrangements were made, however, for technical and fact-finding discussions by the three governments (these began in Washington on August 27) to be followed in September by further "ministerial discussions." Four days after the London talks ended the United Kingdom ordered a 25-percent quantitative reduction in imports from the dollar area as compared with

[2] Further difficulties were created in OEEC when, despite the reduced total of ECA aid to be distributed, Britain successively raised her request from $940 million for the second year of ERP to $1114 million, and finally to $1518. She was tentatively allocated $962 million in late August by OEEC, and this was reduced in October to $920 million following ECA's earmarking of $150 million as a special pool to underwrite trade and payments liberalization.

[3] British Treasury Communique, July 10, 1949. Reprinted in *Department of State Bulletin*, August 8, 1949, p. 197.

1948. At the same time the Commonwealth governments, whose Finance Ministers had been meeting in London prior to and during Secretary Snyder's visit, began general undertakings to carry out similar reductions.

September Agreements

Prior to the September discussions, the United States made it clear that suggestions for action must come from the British and that the problem would have to be considered within the framework of the United States foreign economic policy, aimed at enabling international trade and payments to develop on a multilateral basis. At the beginning of the discussions (September 7–12), the British revealed that they had already decided to devalue the pound. The conclusions reached in the discussions were mostly "polished and well-balanced commonplaces." Unlike previous conferences on the sterling crises, no decision was made on new gifts or loans. It was made clear that the British were expected to take their place in a system of multilateral trade. But, perhaps most important of all, the United States gave such assurances as the Executive branch can that it would accept the responsibilities of a creditor nation with respect to increasing imports and encouraging a larger capital outflow.

So far as immediate positive action was concerned, the United States agreed: (a) to permit the United Kingdom greater flexibility in using Marshall dollars for purchases outside the United States; (b) to open to natural rubber a substantial additional area of competition; (c) to review the stockpile program, especially for tin and rubber; (d) to simplify United States customs procedures and continue the policy of reducing tariff barriers; and (e) to permit the United Kingdom greater freedom in reducing trade restrictions with countries with which it has no balance of payments difficulties, even though that might involve discrimination against the United States.[4] These were apparently all the positive steps which the United States negotiators thought they could take without Congressional approval, and they were unwilling at that time to go to Congress on this problem. It was decided that further study was required on (a) the production

---

[4] In the 1946 loan agreement the British undertook not to discriminate against imports from the United States.

and distribution of petroleum products,[5] (b) the question of blocked sterling balances, in conjunction with all the interested parties,[6] and (c) shipping. Finally, provisions were made for continuing consultations on the whole range of problems between the two currency areas. (The United States, following conferences with French officials who resented the bilateral nature of the discussions with the British, later said that the agreements regarding stockpiling, customs procedures, and eligibility requirements for the spending of ECA funds would also apply to the other ERP nations.)

Implementation

Some of the agreements were not long delayed in implementation. Three days after the conference ended ECA announced that Great Britain would be permitted to use $175 million of Marshall Plan funds to buy Canadian wheat.[7] But it was also provided that Britain was to purchase $30 million of wheat and $8–10 million of other surplus agricultural commodities from the United States, purchases which had not been previously planned. A few days later the Department of Commerce issued a directive lowering the minimum percentage of synthetic rubber to be used by manufacturers from 33⅓ percent to 25 percent. It was estimated at the time that this would result in a shift from synthetic to natural rubber consumption of some 50,000 tons per year. Although United States stockpile purchases were reported to have

[5] These represented a heavy dollar charge on the sterling area. In early February 1950 the British Government estimated that, prior to the import restrictions introduced later that month, the net dollar drain from oil transactions during 1950 would be about $625 million, of which $350 million would arise from net payments to American oil companies and $275 million would represent the net dollar expenditures from the world-wide operations of the British oil companies. (Memorandum by British Government reprinted in *Journal of Commerce*, February 14, 1950.)

[6] Article X of the 1946 Financial Agreement had included some specific provisions regarding these balances, but they had not been effectively translated into action.

[7] Several members of Congress expressed the opinion that this action was illegal or at least contrary to the spirit of the law, indicating their great concern over off-shore purchases of goods in ample supply in the United States. ECA maintained that since the British had a contractual obligation to buy wheat in Canada they could not have transferred the purchases to the United States so that the ECA action did not adversely affect the interests of the American wheat producers.

increased somewhat during the rest of the year, precise data on foreign purchases are not available (see pages 162 ff.). The United States also began to tackle more energetically the problem of simplifying the customs administration (see page 159).

The State Department announced on September 15 that meetings were beginning between representatives of the governments of the United States, the United Kingdom, and Canada regarding the production, refining, and distribution of petroleum and petroleum products, with a view to developing means of reducing the dollar drain on the sterling area. It was stated that discussions would continue for some time and would involve analyzing oil transactions affecting the sterling area in the light of the "legitimate interests" of the countries and companies concerned. During the year the British Exchange Control Board placed an increasing number of restrictions on the transfer and use of sterling obtained by American companies selling oil to third countries. In late December the United Kingdom, and several other members of the sterling area, announced that beginning January 1, 1950 they would exclude imports from dollar companies whenever oil from sterling companies could be substituted. Shortly after this decision was announced, the State Department reported that the study group established in September had been carefully analyzing the problem, that no easy solution had been found, that discussions were continuing, and that "We have indicated to the British our concern at their present action in this field and our desire to discuss this question of displacement in order to minimize any dislocations which might be occasioned to the United States companies."[8] Subsequently, the British postponed the effective date of these restrictions to February 15. Further discussions were held amid much agitation by American oil interests, and in early February the British authorities modified the earlier proposals so as to limit the reduction in sterling area imports from American companies to four million tons of refined petroleum a year (thus permitting continued imports of over nine million tons of refined products from American companies per year), and to leave undisturbed the previous arrangements for crude oil imports on the understanding the United States companies would attempt

[8] *Department of State Bulletin,* Washington, D.C., January 2, 1950, p. 30.

to reduce its dollar content. The British offered not to introduce any additional restrictions during the life of the Marshall Plan and suggested that the American companies might in the meantime increase their sales in the sterling area beyond the amounts permitted under these new restrictions if the companies increased their dollar purchases of goods and services from sterling area countries.[9] This proposal was not acceptable to the American companies and discussions continued, but the reduction of four million tons of refined products imported per year from the American companies went into effect on February 16.

The oil problem is one of extreme complexity involving many parts of the world besides the United States and the sterling area, and no mutually satisfactory solution was in sight at the year's end. One immediate effect of the British action promised to be extensive examination by Congress in 1950 of the petroleum question, in all its aspects, when it would be asked to extend ECA for a third year. It must be noted that, despite the wide interest in this problem, the British February restrictions were estimated at then current prices to result in a direct yearly reduction of only about $70 million in purchases from the American companies and a net dollar saving to the sterling area of about $55 million.

The problem of blocked sterling balances was subject to more or less continuous study following the September discussions. These balances constituted a very serious problem for the United States in several respects. In the first place, when they led to unrequited exports they increased the British need for dollar assistance. Their release also created an easy market for British exporters and so tended to discourage attempts to sell in the dollar area. Further, the existence of these balances was an important factor in the inability or unwillingness of the United Kingdom to participate fully in the United States-sponsored "integration" of European economies. So long as Britain was honoring these debts she was to an important extent unable to export to the Continent or, alternatively, to pass on to the Continent in pay-

[9] For details of the British February proposals see *Journal of Commerce*, February 14, 1950. As a possible longer range solution the British suggested the possibility of integrating the American companies into the sterling area fiscal and legal system so as to reduce the dollar costs of their sales in the area. For a "sterlingization" proposal by Standard Oil (N.J.) see *Journal of Commerce*, February 2, 1950.

ment for imports sterling area currencies which the Continent needed to pay for imports of food and raw materials. But, if the balances were frozen or written off, then the economic problems of those nations holding the balances (especially India, Pakistan, and Egypt) would be increased. The United States could not ignore the possible consequences of such action. There were several unofficial suggestions in the United States during the year that it assume an active role in "reorganizing" these debts.[1] The press reported that official studies, however, had not "spawned any policy proposals" other than the old suggestion that the rate of release be cut down.[2]

The sterling-dollar area disequilibrium in all its aspects was the subject of continuing discussion and study as the year ended; there was every prospect of its continuing to be a serious problem for some time to come.[3] In addition to the political issues involved, a mutually satisfactory solution was rendered difficult, if not impossible, not because of technical problems but because it would call for important reallocations of resources in each area which neither Britain nor the United States was anxious to make, and because of the basic differences in view as to the role to be played in the adjustment process by free market forces and direct controls.

[1] See, for example, *The Statist*, London, December 24, 1949 pp. 758 ff. and *New York Times*, December 15, 1949.

[2] *New York Times*, January 14, 1950.

[3] The press reported that in addition to the problems mentioned above, the United States had also been urging the British to reduce governmental expenditures inside the United Kingdom, (*New York Times*, February 26, 1950.)

V · EUROPEAN ECONOMIC INTEGRATION

INTRODUCTION

THE statement that "It is further declared to be the policy of the people of the United States to encourage the unification of Europe . . . "[1] was added in 1949 to the law extending the Economic Cooperation Administration, thus emphasizing and making explicit a goal which was implied in the original Act. Accordingly, during the year ECA policy for Europe changed from one of urging self-help and some cooperation to one of insisting on economic "integration." This was defined by Mr. Hoffman to mean freer, more competitive, and larger trade among the ERP recipient nations with the goal of a single producing and trading area. These conditions, it was argued, would set in motion forces contributing greatly to a solution of the area's balance of payments problem with the Western Hemisphere. There was evidence during the year that economic integration was seen by some officials as one of the first steps in a broader long-term foreign policy program of United States encouragement of economic, political, and military federation in Western Europe.

In 1948 much praise had been given by ECA to the Marshall Plan countries for the economic cooperation represented by the work of OEEC in recommending a division of United States aid, analyzing the problems of the area as a whole, formulating joint economic programs, and preparing "plans of action" designed to make Europe viable by 1952. In 1949 ECA made it clear that it expected much more during the second year of the Marshall Plan. Very early in the year the ECA ceased pressing the member countries to prepare an overall four-year "Master Plan" for Europe, which had seemed so important and promising in 1948 and had

[1] Public Law 472, 80th Cong., as amended by Public Law 47, 81st Cong., Sec. 102 (a).

served the purpose of focussing attention on many of the area's problems, because the plans of the individual nations appeared to be developing along lines of national autarchy and promised to result in a Europe less, rather than more, economically unified.

A. ACTION TAKEN

Intra-European Payments Scheme

During the first several months of 1949 the main subject of concern for the policy makers of ECA and OEEC was revising the scheme for intra-European payments with the view of using this device not only to increase intra-European trade but to make it more competitive. With strong United States support an Agreement for Intra-European Payments and Compensations had been signed in Paris on October 16, 1948. This technical and complicated scheme was designed to increase intra-European trade (which had bogged down in part because of the absence of credit facilities and the consequent tendency toward the bilateral *balancing* of trade) by having intra-European creditors extend grants to their European debtors in return for dollar aid. Those nations which, according to their recovery plans, it was estimated would have a surplus in their balance of payments with their European trade partners were required to extend a grant (drawing rights) to the debtor countries as a condition for receiving an equivalent amount of dollars (conditional aid) from ECA. Thus, the general principle was that Western Hemisphere and intra-European deficits were dealt with in a combined operation.[2]

For the year ending June 30, 1949 specific drawing rights totalling the equivalent of $810.4 million were provided (later reduced to $805.5 million). Most European countries gave drawing rights to some nations and received drawing rights from others, but six of the group were net creditors for Europe as a whole and six were net debtors.[3] By June 30, 1949, when the

[2] For an excellent discussion of the operations of this scheme see *Bank for International Settlements 19th Annual Report*, Basle, June 13, 1949, pp. 200 ff. It should be noted that to obtain the net assistance each country received from ECA, one should add to the total dollars received the drawing rights received and subtract the drawing rights granted.

[3] Both the 1948 and the 1949 agreements also provided that the agent for the scheme—the Bank for International Settlements—should each month

original agreement expired, only $677 million of the authorized drawing rights had been used (equal to about 14 percent of the ECA aid for the period), and approximately $1 billion of surpluses and deficits had been settled by payments in gold, dollars, or other third currencies, or were financed temporarily by use of credit margins.[4]

ECA was convinced that this elaborate scheme had made substantial contributions to increasing intra-European trade, but some of its shortcomings became clearly evident in early 1949. The more important were seen to be that (a) the drawing rights mechanism did not provide incentive for creditors to import and debtors to export;[5] (b) inflexibility and rigidities resulted from the necessarily unreliable advance estimates of bilateral trade balances; and (c) the division of Europe into two broad groups, one whose members were predominantly creditors and the other predominantly debtors in their trade relations with other participants, presented a basic obstacle. It should also be noted that this scheme ameliorated only slightly the basically bilateral character of the prevailing intra-European trade relations and rested squarely on United States aid, which foundation was to be removed in 1952.

In April ECA told the European nations that the new payments agreement should provide for transferability of drawing

---

perform the maximum possible amount of multilateral compensation before applying the drawing rights. These compensations or clearings were of two types: "first category," performed automatically, involved a round-robin cancellation or offsetting of debit and credit balances in intra-European trade accounts; "second category," performed only with the consent of the countries concerned, involved acceptance by the creditor nations of a new debtor in place of an old debtor. For a description and a discussion of these operations see R. W. Bean, "European Multilateral Clearing," *Journal of Political Economy*, October 1948 and R. F. Mikesell, "Regional Multilateral Payments Arrangements," *Quarterly Journal of Economics*, August 1948.

[4] Another $104 million of balances had been compensated for by the first category and second category compensations mentioned in the previous footnote. A small amount of the $128.5 million unused drawing rights were cancelled but the bulk of them were carried over to the second year.

[5] Indeed, many argued that it gave wrong incentives by encouraging debtors to have deficits and creditors to have intra-European surpluses when their major problem was to increase exports to the dollar area. See e.g., JHW, "The Revision of the Intra-European Payments Plan," *Foreign Affairs*, October 1949.

rights among participating countries and that some provision should be made for permitting the holders of drawing rights to convert them into ECA dollars for expenditure anywhere. These recommendations were based on the belief that the intensification of competition resulting from giving debtor nations a choice of where to buy would result in reduction and realignment of costs and prices, and would contribute to an increase in European productivity, and therefore would result in an improvement in Europe's dollar earning ability. It was also hoped that such a change would be a step in breaking away from Europe's network of bilateral agreements. European opposition to this proposal was widespread. England offered very strong objections on the grounds that it would make any advance planning of dollar expenditures difficult and might also involve a drain on the United Kingdom hard currency reserves, especially if drawing rights England had extended were spent by the debtor in Belgium or Switzerland. Some debtor countries objected because they feared the effect might be for the European creditors to reduce imports in order to establish an export surplus which would guarantee them the conditional ECA aid.[6]

After long and heated discussions, agreement in principle was finally reached in July. It was provided that 25 percent of the drawing rights received by any debtor could be freely transferred anywhere in the ERP area, if bilateral drawing rights or other agreed resources were not available, and that the ECA conditional aid would follow the drawing rights during the life of the agreement. To meet the objection that the original plan was too

[6] A further problem arose from the fact that ECA had earlier adopted a principle that dollar aid to any country should not exceed its dollar deficit, while Belgium's intra-European surplus was in the first half of 1949 running at about twice her dollar deficit. ECA finally compromised this principle and agreed, on the assumption that Belgium's European export surplus would be $400 million, to give Belgium $112.5 million more than her estimated dollar deficit provided Belgium would extend $87.5 million equivalent in long-term credits to Britain, France, and the Netherlands. That is, Belgium was estimated to have for the year 1949–50 a European export surplus of $400 million and a dollar deficit of $200 million. She would receive $312.5 million ECA aid and herself extend long-term credits of $87.5 million. It was further provided that the loss of dollars to Belgium by other countries would not exceed $40 million. (See *The Economist*, July 9, 1949 and JHW in *Foreign Affairs, op. cit.*, for a more detailed discussion of this problem.)

rigid, provisions were included for a periodic review of operations and possible modification of drawing rights. ECA stated that it accepted this limited scheme reluctantly and hoped that action would be taken in other areas to reduce drastically quantitative restrictions on intra-European trade.

On September 7 an Agreement for European Payments and Compensations for 1949–50 was finally signed in Paris, and debts accumulated since June 30 were brought into it. This agreement provided for the equivalent of $517.1 million in bilateral drawing rights and $284.9 million in multilateral drawing rights.[7] It was recognized that the devaluations of European currencies which took place two weeks later would significantly affect the European trade and payments patterns. Discussions for revising certain of the drawing rights were held, but decisions were postponed until a clearer picture of the effects of the devaluations and the reductions of quantitative barriers on trade was available.

Customs Unions

ECA also encouraged the formation of customs unions in Europe, but was disappointed at the slow rate of progress during 1949. In March the Benelux economic union was postponed from January to July 1950, largely because of the wide disparity in internal monetary conditions between Holland and Belgium. (At year's end it appeared a further postponement might be necessary). The pre-union, originally scheduled for July, was postponed until the fall of 1949. On March 26, 1949 the French and Italian officials, with American blessings, signed a Customs Union Treaty which anticipated the gradual mutual reduction of trade barriers, with a goal of free trade in 1955. This agreement, however, was not ratified by either parliament during 1949,

---

[7] This $284.9 million of multilateral drawing rights was to be a dollar pool created by crediting to it dollars equal to 25 percent of the total drawing rights extended by all nations except Belgium, plus 25 percent of the $200 million allocated to Belgium to cover its Western Hemisphere deficit, plus the entire $112.5 million set aside for Belgium as mentioned above. Whenever the Bank for International Settlements made use of multilateral drawing rights it was to inform ECA of this, and the latter would then make a firm allotment to the creditor of conditional aid from the dollar pool. The Text of the agreement may be found in *Sixth Report to Congress*, Economic Cooperation Administration, Washington, D.C., January 1950, Appendix A.

and prospects for early action are poor. A Scandinavian customs union was discussed but later abandoned.

Liberalization of Trade and Payments

By the summer of 1949 ECA had become convinced that with European production in most sectors at or above pre-war and with internal price stability in most countries having been restored, its first objective—that of preventing an economic collapse—had been achieved. It believed that more energetic action should be taken by the European countries in relaxing trade and payments restrictions and in increasing trade and competition within the area than had been achieved with the payments scheme or was in prospect with the then planned customs unions. Soon the words "economic unification" were being used by Mr. Hoffman to describe the action which Europe must take.[8]

Several steps were taken in this direction before Mr. Hoffman's formal call for integration of the European economies. In response to ECA's growing concern over the many quantitative restrictions on trade within Europe the OEEC Council, after long discussions, approved on July 4 a British proposal calling for each country by October 1 to notify the OEEC of (1) a list of goods on which it had or was prepared unilaterally to grant, vis a vis other member countries, open general import licenses (or "global quotas" equal at least to the sum of previous bilateral quotas), and (2) a list of additional goods upon which import quota restrictions would be relaxed in return for specific relaxations by others. This plan, however, contained a great many escape clauses, and the British Parliament had been told that relaxations would not be applied if they would (a) cause balance of payments difficulties, or (b) involve any loss of gold, or (c) harm any "legitimate" interests of British industries.[9] In September and October most of the countries removed from import quota restrictions some goods imported from certain countries, but the action was far short of what Mr. Hoffman had been talking about when he asked in August for a "vastly freer movement of goods and currencies" within Europe.[1]

[8] See, for example, his speech at Battle Creek, Michigan on September 15 and his press conference on August 29.
[9] See *The Economist*, August 20, 1949, p. 420.
[1] ECA Press Release, August 29, 1949.

In the summer, ECA earmarked $150 million of its 1949–50 appropriations as a special fund to be used primarily to underwrite genuine efforts to liberalize intra-European trade and payments.[2] A short time later Mr. Hoffman notified OEEC that, while he would accept its recommendations for distribution of ECA aid for the last half of 1949, beginning in 1950 the aid would be distributed not according to need as in the past but according " . . . to the performance of the participating countries . . . in effectively using the aid and realizing the objectives . . . of the Economic Cooperation Act."[3] This decision to apportion the aid according to merit was given more specific meaning when the OEEC Council decided in November—presumably with ECA approval—that the distribution of whatever aid Congress provided for fiscal year 1950–51 would be automatic and would be based on the proportions actually granted each country during 1949–50. The member countries were told by the OEEC Council that they must start with the assumption that the total aid for each (except Greece) would be reduced in 1950–51 to 75 percent (and in 1951–52 to 50 percent) of that received in 1949–50, and to prepare their plans and policies accordingly.[4] This meant that ECA was abandoning the approach of the previous two years when it had asked each country to draw up an estimated balance of payments based on its economic programs and had then used the resulting deficits, after careful screening and pruning, as the basis of requests for appropriations. It was hoped this new approach would give each country additional incentives to tackle its balance of payments problems more vigorously since the previous practice had a tendency to give a nation more as its deficits grew. Although not publicly stressed by ECA, this procedure would permit a recipient nation, directly or indirectly, to use ECA aid to increase its dollar reserves; this also represented a change in the general policy of ECA—one which might be difficult to justify

---

[2] A small part of this fund was to be used to encourage economic development in overseas dependent areas and for investment projects in continental Europe which were international in character.

[3] *New York Times*, September 4, 1949, quoting from Mr. Hoffman's September 3 note to OEEC.

[4] This 25 percent reduction in total aid for fiscal year 1951 was based on ECA estimates that the recipient countries could and should have a 10-percent increase in dollar earnings and an 11-percent decrease in dollar requirements as compared with the previous year.

to Congress but which was probably the necessary prelude to any substantial moves by the European countries to relax direct controls on imports and payments. Later ECA qualified this OEEC decision, and introduced a greater element of distributing the aid "according to merit," by stating that it planned to withhold from this automatic distribution at least $600 million in fiscal year 1950–51 for use in supporting the proposed "payments union" discussed below and otherwise to aid those who liberalized their trade and payments.

The efforts of ECA to get the recipient nations to approach their problems on an area rather than a national basis suffered a temporary set-back on September 18 when the British devalued without effective consultation with any European country and when the sterling area problem was discussed trilaterally with the United States and Canada.[5]

The growing dissatisfaction of the Americans with European progress in liberalizing trade and payments within the area was brought into sharp focus on October 31 when Mr. Hoffman told the OEEC Council in Paris that it must face the prospect of receiving no further Marshall Plan aid unless there was some quick action on the "integration of the Western European economy," the substance of which "would be the formation of a single large market within which quantitative restrictions on the movement of goods, monetary barriers to the flow of payments and, eventually, all tariffs are permanently swept away."[6] He argued that such an integration would accelerate the development of large scale, low-cost industries, make effective use of all resources easier, and increase productivity, thus improving Europe's competitive position vis a vis the rest of the world and increasing her standard

[5] The devaluations, however, did improve the prospects for more liberal trade policies. Since Switzerland did not devalue at all and Belgium only 12.3 percent, as compared with the British and most other countries' devaluations of approximately 30.5 percent, it could be expected that there might be some relief from the persistent creditor position of the two former countries which had made most European nations afraid to risk freeing trade from direct controls for fear of losing gold or dollar reserves. Both Italy and Germany in 1949 were also creditors on European account and their devaluations were only 9.6 percent and 20.6 percent respectively.

[6] For text of this speech see New York Times, Nov. 1, 1949. Press reports stated that most Europeans professed not to know what Mr. Hoffman meant by integration but feared that whatever it was the implied timetable was much too fast.

of living.[7]   To achieve such a "mass market" he said it would be necessary to (1) " . . . bring about a substantial measure of coordination of national fiscal and monetary policies"; (2) " . . . provide means for necessary exchange rate adjustments, subject . . . to the general supervision of the International Monetary Fund, where these are the only feasible alternatives to imposing direct exchange controls"; (3) prevent the full impact of temporary payments discrepancies from falling "upon the reserves of the individual country"; and (4) " . . . insure that strains are not imposed . . . through conflicting policies and practices."[8]

Mr. Hoffman urged that steps be taken at once by the region as a whole, but he stated that much could be done in addition by smaller groups within Europe.   He acknowledged that complete integration would take some time and would not be easy; yet he hoped to see specific action by early 1950 in three areas: (1) widescale removal of quantitative restrictions on trade (late in the year ECA urged their complete removal by the end of 1950), (2) the elimination of the system of maintaining export prices for fuel and basic materials at higher levels than domestic prices,[9] and (3) the development of a "realistic plan" to create a genuine integration of European economies.

To this speech the OEEC Council responded two days later with a decision that member countries should "adopt the objective" of removing import quotas so that by December 15 at least 50 percent of each nation's private imports (government purchases were excluded) from the other member nations *as a group* should be free from such quantitative restrictions.   This propor-

[7] In later speeches Mr. Hoffman repeatedly stressed his conviction that the "mass market" he was urging would restore competition within Europe and thus would result in lower costs and prices and improve her dollar earning capacity.

[8] In its *Sixth Report to Congress,* the ECA mentions but does not stress the all important fact that it would be necessary to permit a reallocation of productive resources within each country.

[9] These practices were not eliminated during 1949.   It is to be noted that during this period one of the more serious offenders with respect to dual pricing for coal and coke was Germany, and for this the United States itself must assume large responsibility.   Following the devaluations in September the Allied High Commission ordered a reduction in differentials but no significant action was taken during the year.   Contrarily, about the same time United States firms expanded their dual pricing practices but in the form of lower prices for exports than for domestic sales.

tion was to apply to each of three categories (foodstuffs, raw materials, and manufactures) and was, it appears, substantially accomplished.[1] The Council also promised to try to widen the area of currency transferability among its members, to "reexamine" the problem of absorbing in Europe or elsewhere the persistent surplus of manpower in certain member countries, to "report . . . on progress . . . and . . . proposals" for "closer economic arrangements" with one another, to "enquire into ways" to eliminate dual prices and to submit by December 15 reports on what each could do to relax controls over invisible transactions.[2]

The British Government quickly made it clear that, while it supported the general ideas of the Americans and would cooperate, it could not fully integrate Britain's economy with that of Europe because of her responsibilities to the sterling area and the Commonwealth. At first the Americans seemed to accept this reluctantly. It appeared that regional groupings within the area might be the first stage in European integration.

B. ACTION PROPOSED

Regional Blocs

The French had for some time been planning a regional economic bloc. This effort received new impetus from the Hoffman speech. From available data it appears that the original plan was to form with the Benelux countries and Italy a bloc ("Fritalux," "Benefit," or "Finebel") involving (1) the elimination of quantitative import restrictions beyond the 50 percent called for by OEEC, (2) the creation of a clearing bank to make possible the interconvertibility of their currencies, and (3) the provision for a free movement of their exchange rates so as to maintain approximately balanced payments among the member countries. The bank's resources would be obtained by a pooling of the five

[1] Apparently this action was not very important since, for the most of the items covered, either licenses had not previously been required or were easily obtainable or tariffs provided heavy protection. It was reported in the press that objections to any large removal of quantitative restrictions on imports had by this time become more a matter of protecting domestic industries than a reflection of balance of payments difficulties.

[2] *Text of OEEC Council Decision,* November 2, Economic Cooperation Administration, Washington, D.C., 1949. See also *New York Times,* Nov. 3, 1949 and *The Economist,* Nov. 5, 1949, pp. 985–987.

countries' drawing rights and by using some of the $150 million which ECA had set aside as a special reserve to encourage trade liberalization. It was reported that this plan had "gone over big" with ECA. Difficulties were encountered immediately, however, when the Benelux countries proposed that tariffs as well as import restrictions be lowered. The French and Italians were unwilling to agree to this. A much more acute problem arose, however, with respect to the inclusion of Germany. A very important new development in United States policy became evident at this time when the United States made it clear that it favored the "integration of Germany in an economically united Western Europe."[3] The Netherlands also favored bringing Germany into the proposed regional bloc, but the French and Italians were, to say the least, reluctant. The American view was that, by interlocking the capital structure of French and German industry, French military and political fears could be allayed without blocking Germany's capacity to recover. But the French did not like to contemplate the fate of their heavy industries if they were exposed to free competition from Germany. A French proposal that members of the bloc foster, under government supervision, investment agreements among basic industries in member countries was received coolly by the Americans who, despite French assurances to the contrary, saw this as a move toward cartels.[4]

On December 9 the experts of the Benelux countries, France, and Italy finally reached tentative agreement on the first modest steps which involved (a) increasing to 60 percent the proportion of total mutual private trade to be freed from import quota restrictions, (b) a very limited provision for currency conversion, (c) agreement in principle regarding coordination of internal

[3] Mr. Hoffman, quoted in *New York Times*, December 7, 1949.
[4] The press reported in November that moves in Europe to remove quantitative restrictions on imports were being effectively blocked by the cartel-like action of private European industrialists who were beginning to limit competition between different countries by dividing up markets, agreeing on prices, restricting plant expansion, and agreeing on products in which each should specialize. Such action would, of course, defeat much of the new ECA policy; on this issue ECA might, it was reported, find itself facing a tougher adversary than government controls. Both ECA and the State Department indicated concern over this development. (See *Department of State Bulletin*, December 12, 1949, p. 910, and *New York Times*, November 21 and December 5, 1949.)

financial policies, and (d) a limited provision for modifying exchange rates if necessary to prevent balance of payments discrepancies that might otherwise lead to gold movements. This agreement did not go very far but it would, it was hoped, be something which Mr. Hoffman could invoke when he asked Congress for additional funds in 1950. The plan was, however, not accepted by the respective governments during 1949. Enthusiasm for it died down following the United States proposal for a "payments union" mentioned below but was revived in February 1950 following the failure of the OEEC Council to reach agreement on this more ambitious scheme.

The continental group did not invite Germany to join them, but they did hold discussions with the British.[5] Nothing resulted, but, during December at British initiative (reportedly as a direct result of United States demands for greater cooperation with the Continent), short and inconclusive exploratory talks were held by the United Kingdom with three Scandinavian countries looking toward the removal of certain currency restrictions that were hampering the flow of goods and services between the two areas. Additional talks took place in early 1950, and on January 30 it was announced that agreement had been reached on a very limited financial union, "Uniscan," providing for continuing consultations and for some minor relaxation of restrictions on payments among the four countries.

ECA Proposals

i. OEEC AUTHORITY

ECA was not at all satisfied with the above responses to the October 31 declaration, and just before the year ended it advanced two new proposals designed to hasten the integration of the entire area. One was to strengthen the authority of OEEC—previously almost entirely "experts" with only the occasional

[5] As the year ended there was a growing conviction in Europe that full British participation was necessary to establish any effective free trade area in Europe because of the importance of the sterling area as a source of supplies and a market but that, until something was done to reduce the claims on current United Kingdom production from holders of blocked sterling balances, Britain could not permit either uncontrolled imports from or exports to the Continent nor could she provide for convertibility of her currency. Further, it was felt British participation was necessary to prevent Germany from becoming the dominant power.

presence of ministers—by providing for frequent and possibly continuous participation by men of Cabinet rank and by appointing an outstanding political leader as its permanent head.[6]   In late December the European countries agreed that the ministers would meet at least once a month, but there were sharp differences of opinion, especially between the Americans and British, on the desirability of a permanent political chief and, if so, the man.   The United States strongly urged the appointment of Mr. Spaak of Belgium.   He was unacceptable to the British, and in late January 1950 agreement was reached that there should be such an office but that it should be filled by Dr. Stikker of Holland.[7]

ii. PAYMENTS UNION

The second proposal by ECA was to establish a monetary payments union including the sterling area and all ERP nations. Details of this proposal, alternatively referred to as a "clearing union," "payments union," and "currency union," were not officially released; from press reports and summary official statements[8] it appears the essentials of the scheme, which would replace the intra-European payments and compensation system discussed above, were that a new payments union would be established, through which members would make settlements with one another partly in gold or dollars and partly in credit.   Each country's account at the clearing house would be kept in terms

[6] Earlier a nine-member consultative group of ministers of cabinet rank had been formed to assist the chairman in supervising the affairs of OEEC between Council meetings. This had apparently not worked satisfactorily but had underlined the need for more political authority in OEEC.

[7] The basic issues here, it seems, were (1) should real authority be vested in a regional organization or left to each country? and (2) if authority were given to the regional group should the senior official be one broadly sympathetic with British economic policies and objectives or one generally favoring greater reliance on free market forces? It would appear that the United States view was accepted with respect to (1) but rejected with respect to (2).

[8] See *New York Times, The Statist,* and *The Economist,* late December 1949 and following months, for a running account of the discussions on this issue; see also *European Recovery Programme, Second Report,* Organization for European Economic Cooperation, Paris, February 1950, pp. 228–232 for a discussion of "Future Payments Arrangements," obviously occasioned by ECA proposals; and *Senate Document No. 144,* 81st Cong., 2nd Sess., March 8, 1950.

of some new common unit, and participants would settle their net multilateral surpluses or deficits with the union rather than bilaterally with each other. That is, the European currencies, including sterling, involved in current account transactions among the members would be fully transferable. This, combined with a rapid reduction and substantial elimination by the end of 1950 of quantitative restrictions on intra-European trade would, it was hoped, permit and encourage multilateral trade within the area and remove the bilateral shackles of the existing payments and compensation arrangements.

Technically, it seems that a European debtor, instead of receiving "drawing rights" of fixed amounts of the currencies of its anticipated creditors (as in the 1948 and 1949 schemes), would have the right to draw from the union up to a fixed total *any* European currencies. Conversely, a creditor would provide its own currency, up to a stated limit, to the clearinghouse as it was called for. Under this arrangement ECA, instead of providing "conditional aid" directly to anticipated creditors, would turn a specified amount of dollars over to the union;[9] these dollars could then be "earned" from the clearinghouse by the creditors as and when they supplied their own currencies to the union.

Another new and a basic feature of the plan was that after intra-European debtors (creditors) had exhausted their drawing rights (conditional aid) and a small revolving credit or "swing margin" to cover seasonal discrepancies, debtors (creditors) would automatically pay (receive) dollars or gold into the union in increasing (decreasing) percentages of any deficits (surpluses). For any deficit (surplus) beyond a certain quota, determined as a fraction of each country's total trade with all other members, debtors would pay into the pool 100 percent in gold or dollars while creditors would have to finance such surpluses entirely with credit; i.e., creditor nations would receive only a claim in European currencies in the union. It was anticipated that these provisions would be a stimulus to both debtors and creditors to keep their European accounts more nearly in balance.[1] It was

---

[9] Such payments would be progressively reduced and would cease when ECA aid ended.

[1] In addition to the dollars paid over to the union in the form of conditional aid, it was planned that ECA would set aside part of its appropriations to help make up any initial differences between gold or dollars

argued further that these payments would link this area to the dollar area and be a step toward general convertibility of all currencies.

A supervisory board would be created, including a representative of ECA so long as it was supplying dollars to Europe, which would have some authority over the settlements mechanism and would presumably apply some pressure on individual countries to make necessary, but painful, internal financial and economic adjustments. It was reported that all ERP nations accepted this proposal "in principle," but during the technical discussions in January 1950 important differences developed, again mostly between ECA and the British experts. It has been unofficially reported that the main British worries were (a) that the ECA scheme would, in actual operation, permit participating countries holding sterling balances to convert them into gold or dollars at the expense of British reserves; and (b) that the establishment of a successful new monetary area would not only reduce or eliminate the use of sterling in settling intra-European balances but might even result in some countries leaving the sterling area and, thus, not only might deprive the United Kingdom of a source of invisible income and lead to pressure for larger unrequited exports but might also weaken further the existing political ties. In addition, it may be that the British feared the loss of important controls over their trade which were provided by their many bilateral agreements and which served to supplement their internal controls. Specifically, the British were reported to have insisted on (1) retaining the existing bilateral payments agreements with their overdraft facilities, (2) lengthening the time period before gold payments were required, (3) establishing the principle that a country should, over a period of time, import as much as it exports rather than accumulate gold, (4) permitting a gold-losing country to reimpose quantitative restrictions on imports from gold-receiving countries, and (5) restricting the union to purely technical functions and severely limiting the authority of the union's management to apply sanctions on its members.[2]

---

paid into the union by the debtors and paid out to the creditors. Further, ECA anticipated that in order to relieve the strain on some debtors it might be desirable to extend some dollar loans conditioned on the debtors' taking steps necessary to correct deficits.

[2] It is interesting to remember that in the discussions preparatory to establishing the International Monetary Fund the British favored greater

These qualifications were of basic importance since they involved the question of whether a soft currency bloc was being created or whether the scheme was an important step toward general convertibility.

Further complications arose in January when, apparently as a result of a deplorable lack of internal United States coordination, the National Advisory Council entered important reservations to the ECA scheme. Again the exact nature of these has not been made public but the press reported that NAC stated that it could approve the plan only (a) if the agency created to administer the clearing union did not conflict with the responsibilities and operations of the Fund, (b) if the United States was not represented on this agency since this would be inconsistent with our representation on the Fund, and (c) if safeguards were introduced to prevent the maintenance or erection of barriers by the region against imports from the rest of the world and the United States in particular. These reservations are closely related to the whole question of European economic integration. They were reported to reflect NAC's concern over the basic problem of whether we should abandon the world-wide approach to the problem of currency convertibility and multilateral trade, as represented by the Fund and the General Agreement in Tariffs and Trade (GATT), in favor of a regional approach and whether the latter, if adopted, would delay or prejudice general convertibility and multilateral trade.

These objections, while presumably very embarrassing to ECA, since it had ardently pressed its scheme with the Europeans, were apparently taken into account in a revised ECA draft. But, at the late January meeting of the OEEC Council, agreement could not be reached by ECA and the European nations. The final decision of the Council was to give a general endorsement to the idea but to let the experts go on discussing its specific terms with the hope that agreement could be reached by the end of June. This meeting of the OEEC Council also failed to take any effective decisions to eliminate dual pricing. With respect to further reduction of import quotas it decided, after long dis-

---

automatic operations than did the United States. (See Mikesell, R. F., "The International Monetary Fund, 1944–1949," *International Conciliation*, (November 1949, pp. 843–847.)

cussion, to urge the member countries, as soon as a new payments scheme comes into force, to increase by another 10 percent the value of total private imports from member countries which would not be subject to quantitative import restrictions, and to aim at a liberalization of 75 percent of their imports on private account from other participating countries by the end of 1950.[3]

Earlier in the month Mr. Hoffman had prophesied before a Congressional committee that the clearing union plan would be in operation within ninety days, and he made no attempt to hide his disappointment at the January decisions of OEEC. But he made it clear that ECA intended to apply new pressures for acceptance of its proposals. And, in February 1950, when requesting Congress to extend ECA for a third year, Mr. Hoffman asked for specific legislative authority to withhold, at the start, from allocations to individual countries not less than $600 million of the 1950–51 appropriations. These funds would be used " . . . to encourage the aggressive pursuit of a program of liberalized trade and payments."

Note on Bilateral Agreements

For the record, action by the United States on certain specific bilateral trade agreements should be noted in connection with this integration policy.[4] The State Department during the early summer had expressed concern over the Anglo-Argentine five-year trade and payments agreement, and made representations to the British which resulted in some relaxing in the rigidity of the terms of this contract.

During most of the year, however, a rigorous bilateral policy was pursued by the United States authorities in Germany and Japan. In Germany the Joint-Export-Import Agency,[5] under predominantly

[3] For text of this resolution and a discussion of the integration problem as seen by Europeans see *European Recovery Programme, op. cit.,* Chapter 23.

[4] For a detailed description and discussion of the bilateral agreements in force throughout the world in early 1949 see the statement prepared by the State Department and reprinted in *Congressional Record*, September 8, 1949, p. 12916 ff.

[5] For early 1947 to mid-1949 the JEIA handled directly all of Germany's foreign trade. In keeping with America's general policy of restoring greater authority to the Germans the JEIA in mid-1949 began to reduce its functions to a licensing and control organization and the negotiation of trade agreements. With the establishment of the Allied High Commission in September its Foreign Trade and Exchange Committee became a part of the JEIA and was to assist in the latter's liquidation, taking over any control functions that warranted retention.

United States influence, entered into many trade agreements which approached barter deals. Most of these rigorously restricted "non-essential" imports, and the insistence on an exact balancing of accounts was complicated by using dollars for settling any trade deficits. Bilateral trade agreements were signed or extended in 1949 with at least 24 nations, including five with countries behind the "iron curtain." Several of these were signed after Mr. Hoffman's October 31 speech asking for greater freedom of trade. Many of these, however, relaxed or removed import quota restrictions and provided for geater flexibility as regards commodities traded and for the early balancing of accounts. It appeared in early 1950 that as a result of these more liberal import policies Germany was developing serious deficits on current account. At the very end of 1949 the press reported the Allies were objecting to certain "barter" deals proposed by the Bonn Government with South American countries.

The Supreme Commander for the Allied Powers (SCAP), acting on behalf of Japan, also followed the practice of concluding bilateral trade and payments agreements which usually provided for balancing of trade between the two signatories, excluding the import into Japan of "non-essentials," and settling balances with dollars. During 1949 such bilateral agreements were extended or initiated with at least 13 countries plus the sterling area and, excluding United States Government-financed imports, over half of Japan's imports were under these arrangements. And at year's end it was announced that while trade would be turned over to private traders in January 1950 even a larger percentage of the trade would be restricted to trade agreement countries. It is interesting to note that, with the exception of this network of trade and payments agreements concluded by SCAP, there were few bilateral trade agreements in the Far East.

VI · IMPORT POLICY

INTRODUCTION

BOTH the Administration and important sectors of the business community recognized during 1949 more clearly than ever before that the United States also had a deep-seated balance of payments problem but in the form of a large current account surplus.[1] The favorable balance of goods and services totalled $6.3 billion in 1948, $11.3 billion in 1947, and $7.8 billion in 1946 but had existed in every single year since 1914; for the thirty-six years it totalled $101 billion. (Excluding the war years 1914–1918 and 1941–1945 the export surplus was $52 billion.) Approximately 15 percent of this total had been paid for with gold imports, 10 percent by private gifts, 10 percent by long and short-term capital flows on private account, and the balance by government loans or grants. It became apparent during 1949 that most quarters did not like to anticipate either an indefinite continuation of gifts or the domestic and international consequences of a sharp reduction in exports. As the United States already possessed some 70 percent of the world's monetary gold stocks, the only major alternatives were seen as expanded investments and enlarged imports. As was shown in Chapter II, considerable attention was directed to the problem of larger investments abroad. While much work was done on what might be regarded as efforts to educate the

[1] For a statement of "Industry's View" see "The Foreign Trade Gap," a report by George Halm and Harry Hawkins sponsored and published by the National Association of Manufacturers, July 1949. Perhaps the clearest short statement by a government official was Secretary Acheson's speech at the National Foreign Trade Council Convention on November 2 at New York City. A fuller official discussion of the problem can be found in *Report of the ECA-Commerce Mission,* Economic Cooperation Administration, Washington, D.C., October 1949.

public as to the desirability of larger imports and the necessity of viewing international trade policies from the standpoint of the whole economy and not just particular industries competing with imports, specific measures to expand imports were not very impressive. However, certain old freer trade policies were restored or continued, and first steps were taken in some new directions.

A. IMPLEMENTATION BY AGREEMENT

Increasing European Dollar Exports

One of the basic objectives of the ERP program is to increase Europe's dollar earnings, and much attention was given this problem by ECA officials during the year. Efforts were directed to several aspects of the problem in addition to that of increasing Europe's production of exportable goods. Rightly or wrongly, larger exports to the dollar area was one of the important reasons American officials urged exchange rate devaluations and was a fundamental part of the objectives in the program for European "integration." Repeated exhortations were made to the Europeans to study the American market more closely and to do more effective advertising, packaging, and product adaptation to American tastes. International trade fairs were encouraged. In May, a special ECA-Commerce Department Mission, popularly called the "Taylor Mission" after its chief, was sent to Europe for a ten week period to study and discuss ways of increasing Europe's exports to the Western Hemisphere. ECA encouraged European governments to offer special incentives to dollar exporters. It looked with approval on the export credit guarantee schemes of the United Kingdom, France, Italy, and the Scandinavian countries; on the Dutch practice of permitting exporters to the dollar area reasonably free use of a portion of their dollar earnings; on the preferential treatment given in Britain, Sweden, and Denmark to dollar exporters in obtaining imports; and on the practice in France, Denmark, and Britain of extending more liberal credit facilities to those exporting to the dollar area.

Reciprocal Trade Agreements Act

Congress in 1948 had extended the Reciprocal Trade Agreements Act for only one year instead of the customary three. It also had introduced the so-called "peril points" which required the President to notify Congress whenever he proposed reducing the tariff rate below the minimum, as determined by the Tariff Commission, necessary to avoid threat of serious injury to a domestic industry. In his State of the Union Message of January 5, 1949, the President urged Congress to restore the Act to full effectiveness and to extend it to June 12, 1951.[2]

It was generally recognized in the Hearings and Congressional debate that the "peril points" provisions provided much more protection than did the standard escape clause under which the United States reserved the right to withdraw or modify any concession which caused or threatened to cause serious injury to domestic producers. This was primarily because the former would operate on the basis of *estimates* as to *possible* effects and so would encourage extreme caution in making reductions. It also served to concentrate attention only on specific domestic industries without any regard for national or international considerations. During the Hearings and Congressional debate, Administration spokesmen and supporters argued that the one year limitation of authority did not give sufficient time for important negotiations and was interpreted abroad as a weakening of United States determination to continue the policy. It was also maintained that the 1948 Act would hamper the effectiveness of United States participation in the negotiations which were scheduled to begin in April 1949, at Annecy, France to bring eleven more countries into the General Agreement on Tariffs and Trade (GATT).

The major issue in both houses was the attempt, chiefly by Republicans, to continue in force the "peril points" procedure. This restriction was finally defeated by a vote of 43 to 38 in the

[2] Several times during the year ECA, as well as the State Department, took occasion to point out that although our tariffs had been reduced a great deal since 1933 and were at approximately the 1914 level on the average, they were still very high given the United States exporting and creditor position and, further, that the average of the tariff was frequently misleading since rates were often very high on the particular goods which otherwise might be imported in large quantities. (See Appendices Q and R of *Report of ECA-Commerce Mission* cited above for some details on the restrictiveness of the American tariff. For a recent brief unofficial statistical appraisal of the tariff, see Prest, A. R., and Roy, A. D., "The United States Tariffs," London and Cambridge Economic Service *Bulletin*, February 1950, pp. 2–8.)

Senate and 241 to 151 in the House. The difference in support for the measure should be carefully noted: the House voted in February while the Senate vote was taken in September, and during the interval there was a growing concern over the recession in the United States. An attempt in the Senate to include a provision limiting imports of petroleum products to 5 percent of the total domestic demand of the same quarter of the preceding year was defeated by only one vote, and a proposal to authorize import quotas on furs was defeated by only three votes.

Although the old law expired on June 30, the new measure was not finally passed until September 15 in the Senate (the House had passed it on February 9) and was approved by the President on September 26. The law repealed the 1948 Act and extended until June 12, 1951 the previous law authorizing the President to make tariff reductions up to 50 percent of the rates in effect on January 1, 1945. Some observers have expressed the opinion that had the British devaluation been announced one Sunday earlier the Senate would not have approved the bill. The close vote on the "peril points" provision gives evidence that Congress was as yet not as convinced as the Administration that the United States should encourage larger imports as a matter of policy.

The Annecy Conference

The Administration continued to place great emphasis on the multilateral approach to the reduction of trade barriers. With strong United States support more than 500 delegates and assistants, representing 34 countries, assembled in Annecy, France from April 11 to August 27 for the largest meeting ever convened to discuss tariff barriers and other problems of international trade. The conference included two separate but related activities. It was the third session of the 23 original contracting parties to GATT; the agenda included various matters relating to the operation of the agreement and to the terms on which new countries would be admitted to GATT.[3] More important, it was a meet-

[3] GATT is operating under interim machinery until the International Trade Organization, which provides permanent machinery for consultation, is approved. For a detailed discussion of the items considered and action taken in this part of the conference see Willoughby, W., "The Annecy Conference on Tariffs and Trade," *Department of State Bulletin*, November 21, 1949.

ing for tariff negotiations among eleven countries[4] wishing to accede to GATT and between each of these and each of the 23 countries which had agreed to mutual tariff reductions at Geneva in 1947. The original members did not negotiate any new concessions among themselves.

In preparation for these tariff negotiations, the United States followed the customary reciprocal trade agreement procedures and in late 1948 published a list of the commodities on which tariff concessions might be considered; public hearings were held in December 1948 and January 1949.

The discussions at Annecy were long drawn out. Enthusiasm was dampened considerably by the failure of Congress even to consider the International Trade Organization (ITO) and the fact that it did not extend the Reciprocal Trade Agreements Act (the legal authority for United States concessions) until after the conference ended. For many weeks the new governments put forward what were regarded as only "bargaining tariffs," and the conference was not concluded until late August.

The United States finally obtained concessions on products which the ten acceding countries imported from it in 1947 to a value of $537 million, or nearly 39 percent of their total imports of all products from this country in that year. The concessions granted by the United States, other than "bindings," were very modest. On the basis of 1948 figures, United States duties were reduced in direct negotiations with the acceding countries on imports from them valued at $60.9 million, or approximately 15 percent of total imports from these countries. Existing duties were bound on imports totalling $4.2 million in 1948, and existing duty-free treatment was bound on $78 million of 1948 imports. In addition, each acceding country obtained the benefit of American concessions granted at Annecy to other acceding countries; contractual assurance was given of continuance of the benefit of concessions previously made to countries party to

[4] Denmark, Dominican Republic, Finland, Greece, Haiti, Italy, Liberia, Nicaragua, Sweden, Uruguay, and Colombia. During the discussions Colombia withdrew from the negotiations and later the United States and Colombia, by mutual consent, ended their fourteen year old trade agreement as of December 1, 1949, which, it was agreed, had been entered into when economic and fiscal conditions in Colombia were substantially different than they were in 1949.

GATT and to earlier trade agreements. Altogether, it has been estimated that United States imports from all sources totalling slightly more than $250 million in 1948 were affected by the concessions (including bindings) negotiated at Annecy and not previously negotiated at Geneva.[5]

On December 7 the State Department announced that the tariff concessions negotiated with Haiti would become effective on January 1, 1950. The governments of none of the other nine new countries signed the Annecy Protocol during 1949, but by April 30, 1950 Greece, Sweden, the Dominican Republic, Italy, Finland, Liberia, Nicaragua, and Denmark had taken such action. In March 1949 the agreement with Chile negotiated at Geneva in 1947 was put into effect.

It was announced in November, 1949 that a "third round" of negotiations for reducing tariff and other trade barriers would take place in 1950 and that it was intended to invite Germany to this conference.

The Havana Charter

Since 1941, the United States has been actively sponsoring the project of an international trade organization designed to establish a code of international conduct for dealing with problems of world trade and to create an international agency to help implement this code. The Charter of the International Trade Organization was approved at Havana in 1948, and on April 28, 1949 the President transmitted the Charter to Congress, urging approval of United States membership and provision of funds to implement it. The proposal was sent to the foreign relations committees, but hearings were not even begun during 1949 despite several pleas for action by the Administration. The Executive branch promised to press for Congressional approval early in 1950, but there was growing evidence during the year that for a wide variety of reasons important sectors of American banking and commerce were unwilling to support the Charter and probably would urge Congress not to approve it.[6] [The House

[5] For additional details on the Annecy Conference see *The Department of State Bulletin*, Washington, D.C., issues of March 20, April 24, September 19, October 17, November 21 and 28, and December 19, 1949.

[6] For a discussion of many of the criticisms of the Charter see Wilcox, C., *A Charter for World Trade*, Macmillan, 1949, especially Chapters 18

Committee on Foreign Affairs finally opened Hearings on April 19, 1950.]

B. UNILATERAL IMPLEMENTATION

Tariff Administration

Considerable attention was given in 1949 to the restrictions on imports resulting from United States customs procedures, which were described in one official report as frequently antiquated, inequitable, slow and complex.[7] This problem was discussed during the September United States-United Kingdom-Canada financial discussions, and the United States stated that it was already contemplating steps to simplify customs administration.[8] During the autumn a good deal of study was given to the problem, and discussions with Canadian officials began in mid-December. Some minor reforms in the way of preshipment chemical analysis were instituted, and plans were under way to provide for a simplified import bond. Involved in this whole problem were the protectionist attitudes of many customs personnel; reforms here probably would be slow. It was reported in December that Secretary Snyder had instructed customs inspectors to extend a more friendly hand to importers.

[After long delays in the Bureau of the Budget, reportedly occasioned by objections from the chemical industry, a bill for customs simplification was submitted to Congress in early May, 1950. Especially important were provisions relating to valuation procedures which, if approved, could result in an effective lowering of rates.]

---

and 19. See also, Brown, W. A., Jr., *The United States and the Restoration of World Trade*, The Brookings Institution, 1950.

[7] *Report of the ECA-Commerce Mission, op. cit.* See Appendices N, Q and S in this report for some very interesting details on United States customs procedures. See also the text and Appendix T for a discussion of the obstacles to imports created by the "Buy American" laws and restrictions on federal, state and local government purchases. For a study of tariff administration by a business organization, see *Invisible Barriers to Trade and Travel*, International Chamber of Commerce, Brochure 130, Paris, August, 1949. The reader is also referred to Smith, R. E., *Customs Valuation in the United States*, University of Chicago Press, 1948 for a recent unofficial study of tariff administration.

[8] In 1947, Congress had provided the Treasury Department with funds for studying the problem of simplifying and reducing the costs of customs administration.

VI. IMPORT POLICY
Direct Import Controls

During 1949, such emergency or war-introduced direct import controls as were still enforced in the United States were diverted from their immediate post-war purpose of facilitating the United States fulfillment of its responsibilities for ensuring an equitable world-wide distribution of scarce essential food items. They were used almost exclusively to protect the United States market from imports of agricultural commodities which were in surplus at the government-supported prices.

During the war, import controls were broad and extensive but, along with most economic controls, they were largely eliminated shortly thereafter. In the Second Decontrol Act of 1947, primarily concerned with export controls (see Note below) authority was extended to the Executive branch to control imports of fats and oils (excluding petroleum products), rice, and rice products.[9] These import controls have been administered by the Department of Agriculture.

From the end of the war through 1948, these import restrictions were used entirely to implement allocations made by the International Emergency Food Committee to the United States and 34 other member nations. In general, United States imports were restricted to the allocated amounts, it being thought that otherwise the favorable financial position of the United States would result in a disproportionate share of fats and oils, sorely needed by deficit areas, being attracted to the United States and in rice being imported on a speculative basis, despite the existence of a large export surplus.

On February 10, 1949, in response to greatly increased world production, the International Emergency Food Committee discontinued the international allocation of fats and oils.[1] But by this time United States production—especially of butter but

[9] Authority was also given to control imports of nitrogenous fertilizer materials and pig tin. Apparently the United States did not find it necessary to invoke controls on the former to discharge its international commitments and the control authority was allowed to expire on June 30, 1949. The RFC was the sole importer of tin from the end of the war to December 1, 1949, when the Department of Commerce eliminated all controls, except for reporting requirements, on the importation, distribution, and inventories of pig tin.

[1] Butter had never been allocated by the IEFC, but the available supplies were taken into account in allocating other fats and oils.

also of many other edible and inedible fats and oils—had reached such levels that the Government held large stocks under its price support program with the result that import restrictions were maintained to facilitate the orderly liquidation of Government stocks.[2]   On July 1, 1949, authority was extended for another year to restrict the imports of fats and oils, rice, and rice products, but the purpose now was frankly one of protecting the domestic market.

The virtual embargo during 1949 on the import of fats and oils[3] was in sharp conflict with the Government's general policy of freer trade and increasing United States imports; the case of butter was the source of no little embarrassment to both ECA and the State Department.   Mr. Hoffman had been urging ERP countries to increase their exports to the United States; following the September devaluations, Denmark found United States importers were prepared to buy large quantities of Danish butter but were unable to obtain import licenses.   Government negotiators had granted tariff reduction to Danish butter in the Annecy negotiations, but these concessions were effectively withdrawn by the refusal of the Department of Agriculture to grant import licenses, as were previous concessions to New Zealand.[4]

Equally in conflict with the policy of encouraging imports was the cartel-like control exercised over sugar imports.   By terms of the Sugar Act of 1948, effective from January 1948 through December 1952, the Secretary of Agriculture in December of each year estimates the total amount of sugar "needed to meet the requirements of consumers in the continental United States" during the following year.   This determination shall be made so as to provide "such supply of sugar as will be consumed at prices

[2] See the various quarterly reports by the Secretary of Commerce to the President and Congress on *Export Control and Allocation Powers,* Washington, D.C., for details on these direct United States import controls.

[3] Butter, oleomargarine, cottonseed, cottonseed oil, lard, flaxseed, linseed oil, sunflower seed, sunflower oil, soy beans, soy bean oil, peanuts, peanut oil, peanut butter, tallow, and cheap soaps.

[4] It should also be noted that imports of certain agricultural products—cattle, butter, milk and cream, potatoes, and shelled walnuts—as well as fillets of cod, were subject in 1949 to tariff quotas, with the tariff in most cases doubled for any imports in excess of the quotas.   In the Geneva Agreement of 1947, the United States reserved the right to impose tariff quotas on woven wool fabrics.

which will not be excessive to consumers and which will fairly and equitably maintain and protect the welfare of the domestic sugar industry." Against this total, a quota of 2.3 million tons is reserved in the statute for domestic producers, approximately 2 million tons for Hawaii, Puerto Rico and the Virgin Islands, and nearly 1 million tons for the Philippines. Any difference between total estimated consumption and these quotas (or amounts marketed, if less than the quotas) is then allocated to other foreign countries, with Cuba receiving the lion's share. In 1948 and 1949, the quotas assigned to domestic producers exceeded their production.

In addition to high tariffs and special excise and processing taxes, restrictions on imports of many other farm products are provided by the sanitary regulations, which have been notoriously effective in protecting the United States cattle industry. Further, the Agricultural Adjustment Act authorizes the application of quotas or import fees by the President whenever imports of agricultural commodities threaten to render ineffective or materially interfere with any program of the Department of Agriculture. The Agricultural Act of 1948 expanded the scope of this authority, and during 1949 import quotas were used to restrict imports of wheat, wheat flours, cotton and cotton waste.[5]

Stockpiling

In their search for ways of maintaining United States exports other than by continued gifts, many spokesmen for both the Government and private sectors of the economy placed increasing emphasis during 1949 on the stockpiling of strategic and critical materials by the United States.[6] While expenditures for these purposes did increase during 1949, at year's end it appeared that these cash purchases might taper off rapidly in the future, in part because the planned stockpile would be completed within a few years,[7] in part because of pressure from the Congress to

[5] For an interesting discussion of several of these problems see Hickman, C. A., *Our Farm Program and Foreign Trade*, Council on Foreign Relations, 1949.

[6] A "review" of our stockpiling program was included in the action promised by the United States during the United States-United Kingdom-Canadian financial discussions in September as noted above.

[7] Certain items, e.g., rubber, must, be rotated if deterioration is to be avoided.

purchase for the stockpile from domestic rather than foreign sources wherever possible, and in part because of a new program for bartering surplus agricultural commodities held by the Commodity Credit Corporation (CCC) for strategic materials.

Although some sixteen separate government agencies were involved in the stockpiling program, expenditures in 1949 came largely from two sources: purchases by the Federal Supply Service (formerly the Bureau of Federal Supply) on instructions from the Munitions Board and purchases by ECA out of counterpart funds.[8] The latter, of course, do not involve payment in dollars.[9]

Prior to the last war, only minor and almost casual efforts had been made to build up in the United States a reserve of strategic and critical materials. Following the expensive and unpleasant experiences during the war in obtaining adequate quantities of certain items, the maintenance of stocks of strategic and critical materials as an essential element of national security became an accepted national policy.[1] To date very little official attention has been given to the desirability of building up stockpiles from foreign sources as a requirement for an expanding civilian economy or to retard the depletion of domestic resources.

i. LEGISLATION AND PURCHASES

The basic post-World War II stockpiling legislation was the Strategic and Critical Materials Stockpiling Act of July 23, 1946 under which the Federal Supply Service has received annual appropriations for the procurement, storage, rotation, and disposal of the strategic stockpile, the composition and size of which is determined primarily by the Munitions Board. During the first two years, Congress appropriated $200 million in cash and $75

[8] For details on the stockpiling program, see the semi-annual *Stockpile Report to the Congress*, Munitions Board, Washington, D.C.

[9] For a detailed description of the legislative history and administrative aspects of the stockpiling program, see *Senate Report No. 140*, "ECA and Strategic Materials," March 22, 1949, 81st Cong., 1st Sess. The Atomic Energy Commission stockpiles fissionable materials, but no data are available on the extent or nature of these operations.

[1] Strategic and critical materials for these purposes have been defined by the Munitions Board as those raw or semi-processed materials that are required for essential uses in a war emergency and whose procurement in adequate quantities, quality, or time is sufficiently uncertain for any reason to require prior provision for their supply.

million in contract authorizations for these purposes, but during this two year period only $87 million had actually been spent, primarily because of a Government policy that requirements for industrial conversion should be met before materials were immobilized in the Government's stockpile. In July 1948 the President approved an acceleration in stockpiling, and in June Congress provided for the fiscal year ending June 30, 1949 a cash appropriation of $300 million ($75 million of which was to liquidate the previous contract authorizations) plus $300 million in new contract authority. In September 1948, the Munitions Board listed 67 commodities[2] which it deemed it essential to stockpile and estimated that the total cost would be approximately $3.7 billion; it hoped to have these accumulated by 1952.[3] In mid-1949, because of price declines, the estimated cost was reduced to $3.2 billion, but during the second half of the year the stockpile goals were raised so that the planned cost was estimated at $3.8 billion; it was then recognized that the program would not be completed in 1952.

By the end of 1948, the total stockpile on hand was valued at $821 million, of which only $175 million represented new purchases under the post-war legislation, $580 million had been transferred from the surplus property held by the War Assets Administration, and $66 million was a carry-over from the pre-war stockpile.[4] However, the authorities had been so active during the last half of 1948 in placing orders that 90 percent of the funds and contract authority granted by Congress had been obligated by the beginning of 1949—some of it in long-term contracts designed to encourage an expansion in production.

In early 1949, the Administration asked Congress for a supplemental appropriation of $40 million cash plus $270 million in contract authorizations for the rest of the fiscal year 1949; for fiscal

[2] Subsequently two were removed and three new ones added.

[3] In early 1949, plans of the Joint Chiefs of Staff assumed war requirements of these strategic items would total $12.4 billion, of which it was estimated $4.5 billion could be obtained as needed from domestic sources, $4.2 billion could be imported in time of war and $3.7 billion should be stockpiled.

[4] The January 23, 1950 Stockpile Report to Congress, Munitions Board, Washington, D.C., lists the surplus and pre-war stockpile at less than these figures, apparently as a result of deterioration, price changes, and the fact that some of them did not meet stockpile specifications and were being reprocessed.

year 1949–50 it requested a cash appropriation of $564 million (of which $250 million would be to liquidate prior contract authorizations) and an additional $211 million in new contract authorizations. These two requests met almost no opposition in Congress, but they were not approved until late June (with the cash appropriation reduced by $39 million and the contract authority increased by $39 million) with the result that during the first half of 1949 new commitments fell off sharply but deliveries and payments on previous orders reached new highs.

With the new funds, the Munitions Board and the Federal Supply Service began again in early summer to place new contracts with emphasis on creating a balance in the stockpile. But Congress was becoming increasingly worried over the large expenditures of the Government and was upset over the placing of a long-term contract for copper from foreign sources while certain United States copper mines were closing down for the lack of a market. As a result, in the legislation providing appropriations for the military establishment signed on October 29 a section was included rescinding $100 million of the $520 million of contract authorizations which had been approved in June.[5] Further, the Senate Appropriations Committee in its report on the legislation "directed" the Munitions Board to " . . . exhaust every possibility of securing the needed minerals and materials in the United States before looking to foreign sources . . . "[6] and directed that " . . . any foreign contracts entered into in the future shall be for a short term and should contain language to allow such contracts to be cancelled, if that becomes necessary."[7] While such directives are not law they most surely will be taken very seriously by the Munitions Board; this policy, unless reversed, may result in a sharp curtailment of purchases abroad.[8]

During the year 1949, the Federal Supply Service made new

[5] The Senate Appropriations Committee had recommended a $275 million reduction.

[6] Procurement for stockpiling was already subject to the "Buy American Act." See *Report of the ECA-Commerce Mission, op. cit.*, pp. 214–216 for a statement of liberality in interpretation of the Act as regards stockpile purchases.

[7] *Senate Report No. 745*, 81st Cong., 1st Sess.

[8] A bill to stimulate exploration for and conservation of strategic materials in the United States and authorizing the establishment of a Mineral Conservation Board passed the Senate in October but failed to win approval in the House.

commitments of $333.2 million and actually disbursed $553.3 million, much of the latter against previous contracts. No official estimates of the amount of the stockpile purchases made abroad appear to have been published, but it has been stated in the press that from 1947 to mid-1949 approximately 80 percent had been from foreign sources.

ii. ECA PARTICIPATION

ECA legislation contains several provisions designed to increase foreign production of and to procure for the United States supplies of strategic materials; the more important provisions are as follows: (1) ERP aid can be extended on the condition that it be repaid by the transfer of strategic and critical materials to the United States; (2) both dollars and counterpart funds can be used to increase production of such materials abroad; (3) at least five percent of the counterpart funds (see pages 30 and 31) can be used to purchase such materials for account of the United States (and for other local currency requirements of the United States).

During 1948, ECA entered into only four agreements, out of counterpart funds, in an amount equal to $21.6 million, most of these being with the United Kingdom. Congress was very critical of this record. During the hearings in 1949 on extending the ECA Act, ECA officials stated their poor record was due to their lack of authority to enter into long-term contracts, the limited supply of such materials in ERP countries, the long time required to work out development projects, and the reluctance of producers (both domestic and foreign) to contribute to a large Government stockpile which would overhang the market and so be an ever-present threat to lower prices. Although ECA apparently wanted to be relieved of responsibility for stockpiling, Congress decided otherwise and amended the law reemphasizing ECA's obligation to make use of its bargaining power to increase foreign production of such materials and authorized ECA, with the approval of and within the appropriations available to the Federal Supply Service, to enter into long-term contracts of up to twenty years for the purchase of such goods. (The subsequent directive of the Senate Appropriations Committee, noted above, would appear to restrict this latter authority.)

During 1949 ECA made strenuous efforts to buy strategic

materials with counterpart funds but during the year committed only the equivalent of $29.2 million for such commodities, raising the total since the beginning of ECA to $50.8 million.[9] Actual expenditures through 1949 totalled the equivalent of only $36.3 million. In addition to these purchases, ECA encouraged increased production of such goods abroad and through 1949 had allocated $6.1 million of its dollar funds (to be repaid by future deliveries of strategic materials) for general territorial surveys and developmental projects plus approving the use by ERP countries of the equivalent of $38.2 million of counterpart funds for promoting the production of deficiency materials.

iii. COMMODITY CREDIT CORPORATION ACTIVITY

Finally, it must be noted that when Congress comprehensively amended the Commodity Credit Corporation (CCC) charter in June it authorized CCC to exchange, via commercial channels wherever practicable, surplus agricultural products in its possession for strategic materials produced abroad.[1] Congress thought such barter deals would not only increase our stockpile reserves but would also improve the internal market for domestic farm products. For any goods which the Munitions Board accepts for transfer to the stockpile, CCC is to be reimbursed, in an amount equal to the fair market value of the strategic and critical materials, out of funds appropriated to the Federal Supply Service for stockpiling purposes. Data are not yet available as to whether any such trade was carried out in 1949, but it has been unofficially reported that negotiations have taken place looking toward a barter with India involving some $80 million of mangenese and mica in exchange for wheat. A law approved on June 30, 1949 (P.L. 152) permitted the executive agencies to accept strategic and critical materials for rent, interest or principal payments under leases and sales of government surplus property; under this authority some contracts were signed providing for acceptance of aluminum pig, but apparently no deliveries were made.

[9] In some of its reports, ECA gives these figures as $26.7 million and, $48.3 million, respectively. It also signed contracts with the approval of the Federal Supply Service obligating the latter's funds for an additional $3.3 million of such materials.

[1] In 1939, Congress passed a similar law, and under its provisions CCC bartered 600,000 bales of cotton to the United Kingdom for 90,000 tons of crude rubber.

By the end of 1949, some 30 percent of the total value of the expanded stockpile program was on hand and an additional 11 percent was under contract (Table XXV). The Munitions Board estimated that by June 30, 1950, with funds already available, nearly 54 percent of the proposed stockpile would be on hand or under contract.

TABLE XXV

Status of Stockpile Program, As of December 31, 1949
(in millions of dollars)

Source	Estimated Total Cost	In Inventory	Programmed for Delivery Jan.–June 1950	Programmed for Delivery after June 30, 1950
Federal Supply Service	606	362		461
War Surplus	452	25		6
ECA	31	19		6
Pre-War Stockpile	60	—		—
	3773	1149	406	473

Source: *Stockpile Report to the Congress,* Munitions Board, Washington, D.C., January 23, 1950, p. 43.
Notes: The figures for War Surplus and Pre-war Stockpile are lower than those shown for the end of 1948, apparently as a result of price changes, deterioration, and the decision that some of the materials did not meet the stockpile specifications and were being reprocessed.
    ECA data exceed by some $5.2 million the figures given in the text for ECA operations. The discrepancy may represent programmed deliveries in repayment of funds advanced by ECA for project development.

Summary

The United States has had an export surplus on current account for every year since the beginning of the first World War, and during 1949 there was a growing conviction in both private and official circles that it was undesirable to maintain this by continued gifts or to have it eliminated entirely by a reduction in exports. Increasing attention was therefore given to expanding United States imports. The problem was attacked on many fronts, but accomplishments were not impressive. The United States actively encouraged dollar exports by ERP nations. The Reciprocal Trade Agreements Act was extended for two years and the restrictive "peril points" clause was eliminated. Minor tariff concessions were granted at Annecy, and a beginning was made on the problem of simplifying customs procedures and tariff administration and making them less restrictive. On the other hand, despite repeated urgings from the Administration for approval, Congress did not even hold hearings on the Havana Charter. Although their original justification no longer existed, several of the war-inspired direct import controls were extended by Congress with the frank purpose of protecting American agriculture. There were no indications that official consideration was given to removing the import quotas on sugar or those instituted to support various domestic programs of the Department of Agriculture.

The prospects of the stockpiling program providing substantial foreign exchange to foreign nations were doomed by pressure from Congress to expand domestic purchases of strategic and critical materials and by the institution of the program for bartering surplus commodities held by the Commodity Credit Corporation for stockpile commodities from abroad.

Note on Export Controls

Direct control over many exports was instituted in July 1940 and extended and broadened during the war until practically every export was subject to rigorous control. In September 1945, the Department of Commerce took over from the Board of Economic Warfare the administration of export controls,[2] but all important policy decisions are taken only after consultation with several other Government agencies, including the State Department.

In response to the widespread pressure for decontrol after the war, most of the emergency economic controls in the United States were quickly abandoned completely or their scope steadily narrowed, but the Second Decontrol Act of July 15, 1947 retained

[2] A few items are controlled by other agencies: fissionable materials by the Atomic Energy Commission, gold and narcotics by the Treasury Department, sugar by the Department of Agriculture, and certain munitions and implements of war (including helium) by the State Department. Of special importance for policy reasons are the controls over tobacco seeds and plants and tinplate scrap which were designed to protect domestic industry. In 1940, a law was passed prohibiting the export of tobacco seeds and plants (except for experimental purposes) to protect the export tobacco industry of the United States. Even earlier, in 1936, licensing of exports of tinplate scrap was introduced to preserve the domestic supply of tin provided by the detinning industry, which would have collapsed but for the maintenance of its domestic supply of scrap.

the export control authority in essentially the same form as during the war years. This law stated that it was the United States policy to eliminate these export controls as soon as possible except to the minimum extent necessary (1) to protect the United States economy from excessive drains of materials in short supply, (2) to promote production in the United States by assisting in the expansion and maintenance of production in foreign countries of materials critically needed in the United States, (3) to allocate exports where most needed for recovery abroad, and (4) to aid in carrying out the foreign policy of the United States. This law was later extended to February 28, 1949 when the Export Control Act of 1949 was approved, extending without substantive changes until June 30, 1950 the President's authority to control exports. The 1949 legislation repeated the first and fourth objectives noted above, dropped the second and third, and added "to exercise the necessary vigilance over exports from the standpoint of their significance to the national security."[3]

Prior to March 1948, export controls, often involving specific quantitative limitations, were exercised over only those scarce goods specifically listed in a so-called "Positive List" and were applied, with a few exceptions, to all foreign destinations except Canada for which no export license has been required for any commodity.[4] On March 1, 1948, the requirement of an export license was extended to shipments of *all* commodities (not just those in "short supply") to European and contiguous destinations. This plan, known as the "R" procedure, was originally designed not only to limit the movement of militarily useful goods to Eastern Europe but also to restrict the export of non-essential commodities and so help foreign nations, especially those destined to receive ERP aid, to conserve their dollar exchange. In practice, the latter consideration was not of great importance, but the controls were apparently used to direct goods to areas where they could contribute the most to European recovery. Two months later a so-called GRO list was established for commodities which were neither in short supply nor of strategic importance and so could be exported to any destination without an export license.

During 1949, as inflation became less a worry than deflation,

[3] Export Control Act of 1949.
[4] It is assumed Canadian authorities cooperate closely with the United States on these matters. Such cooperation would be consistent with the Hyde Park Agreement.

export controls were relaxed or removed altogether for hundreds of items which were regarded as in adequate domestic supply and of little or no military importance. For many of the goods still requiring an export license the previous specific quantitative limitations were, throughout the year, replaced by "open-end quotas," indicating that the emphasis was primarily on security objectives even for those commodities being shipped to other than European and adjacent destinations.[5]

On August 12, 1949, in a move designed to increase the effectiveness of the security controls and keep to a minimum the burden on the United States export trade, the Department of Commerce abolished the previous lists and issued a single master list of all goods requiring an export license whether for reasons of domestic shortages or national security.[6] Commodities on this list were subject to two alternative types of geographic control. One group was under control only to Europe and a few adjacent areas, and the other group required an export license for shipment to any country except Canada. In late October and early November, a further step toward world-wide security control was taken when a large number of goods which previously had required licenses only for shipment to Europe were reclassified so as to require a license for shipment to *any* destination except Canada. This action was aimed at preventing trans-shipments, particularly by Latin American and Far Eastern countries, to Eastern Europe.[7]

[5] The more important items still under quota limitations at the end of 1949 were iron and steel scrap, galvanized sheets, tin metal and tin compounds.

[6] To avoid unnecessary delays and paper work, small shipments of many of the goods on the "Positive List" have been permitted without a validated export license. For details on the administration of the export controls and the specific commodities controlled, see the quarterly reports of the Secretary of Commerce to the President and Congress on *Export Control and Allocation Powers.* See George, J. M., "Export Control: An Appraisal of Significant Recent Developments," *Foreign Commerce Weekly,* March 27, 1950, p. 3 ff., for a detailed discussion of export controls.

[7] The press reported that with United States encouragement ERP nations were also applying restrictions on exports of strategic materials. The Economic Cooperation Act directs ECA to refuse delivery to participating countries of goods which go into the production of a commodity for sale to a European non-participant if that good would be denied an export license by the United States. ECA has gone beyond this and has "tried . . . to get the participating countries to enforce the same sort of restrictions on exports to the Soviet-dominated area that the United States maintains." The results have been disappointing and especially important

At year's end, 401 export commodity classifications required an export license for shipment to all destinations except Canada, and 473 were under control only for shipment to Europe and adjacent areas. Approximately 22 percent of United States exports, by value, during the last quarter of 1949 required a license.

In November, the Department of Commerce also instituted a plan for voluntary controls over the export of technical data which had significance for our national security. Persons desiring to export such information were requested to obtain the opinion of the Department of Commerce before transmitting the information. Some firms reported, however, that voluntarily withholding such information would be a violation of a contract; in late December, the Department of Commerce announced that in exceptional cases its opinion would be legally binding. Since postal censorship was not contemplated, this ban would apply only in cases where the United States firm first sought the opinion of the Government. Exporters were reported to have been very cooperative in this program.

In early 1949, the Secretary of Commerce reported that in restricting exports of goods having potential military significance consideration was given to promoting an adequate flow of essential commodities to the United States and to minimizing interference with East-West trade in Europe, but Russian officials on several occasions during the year blamed the United States export controls for the low level of East-West trade. The effectiveness of the export controls in reducing United States exports to (and imports from) Eastern Europe is shown by the fact that in 1949 direct exports to that area were less than one percent of total United States exports, as compared with an average of around 4 percent during 1936–1938, while imports fell from over 4 percent to less than 2 percent.[3]

---

have been shipments to the embargoed areas from Western Germany. (*Senate Document No. 142*, 81st Cong., 2nd Sess., March 3, 1950, p. 15.)

[3] An exception to American policy toward Eastern Europe was the treatment of Yugoslavia. In addition to the loans extended during the year to Yugoslavia through the International Bank, the International Monetary Fund and the Export-Import Bank, (noted above) permits were granted for the export of oil refining machinery in April, a steel mill in October, airplane fuel and lubricants in November, and commercial aircraft engines and civil aviation equipment in December.

VII · THE BALANCE OF PAYMENTS OF THE UNITED STATES DURING 1949

INTRODUCTION

THE balance of payments of the United States in 1949 reflected the continuing disequilibrium in our international economic transactions, but there was also evidence—especially during the latter part of the year—that some basic adjustments were being made and that perhaps a pattern of more permanent and more balanced relations was beginning to emerge.

Net unilateral transfers and loans of the United States Government reached a peacetime peak of over $5.7 billion in 1949, exceeding 1948 by more than one billion dollars and being slightly in excess of 1947. This was accompanied, however, by declines in the value of both exports and imports of goods and services as compared with 1948, with the fall in exports being, in absolute terms, over a third greater than the decline in imports. As a result, the current account export surplus was at a post-war low. These developments reflected a more than halving, as compared with the previous year, of net private long and short-term capital outflow and dollar disbursements by the International Bank and Fund, plus the fact that in 1949 the rest of the world ceased the large-scale liquidation of its gold and dollar assets, which had characterized the earlier post-war years, and actually increased its holdings slightly.

These changes did not take place uniformly throughout the year. Net Government aid in the first half was at an annual rate of approximately $1.2 billion greater than in the second six months; and, whereas foreign nations in their transactions with the United States were liquidating gold and dollar assets at an annual rate of $0.6 billion in the period January through June, in the next

TABLE XXVI

The International Transactions of the United States, 1946–1949

(in millions of dollars)

Type of Transaction	1946	1947	1948	Total	1949[1]			
					First Quarter	Second Quarter	Third Quarter	Fourth Quarter
Exports of Goods and Services								
Recorded Goods[2]	10186	15230	12615	11953	3286	3356	2682	2629
Other Goods[3]	1688	826	830	448	167	138	100	43
Total Goods	11874	16056	13445	12401	3453	3494	2782	2672
Income on Investment	820	1074	1263	1328	263	350	305	410
Transportation[4]	1375	1709	1233	1196	322	303	308	263
Travel	252	334	307	352	70	99	109	74
Miscellaneous Services[5]	645	568	543	637	158	168	158	153
Total Exports	14966	19741	16791	15914	4266	4414	3662	3572
Imports of Goods and Services								
Recorded Goods	4933	5756	7124	6626	1790	1601	1477	1758
Other Goods[3]	235	315	573	508	173	140	127	68
Total Goods	5168	6071	7697	7134	1963	1741	1604	1826
Income on Investment	216	227	291	296	81	57	63	95
Transportation[4]	534	701	839	972	225	237	271	239
Travel	457	544	601	695	111	171	296	117
Miscellaneous Services[5]	792	920	1053	734	228	216	158	132
Total Imports	7167	8463	10481	9831	2608	2422	2392	2409

174

Surplus of Exports of Goods and Services

Goods	6706	9985	5748	5267	1490	1753	1178	846
Income on Investment	604	847	972	1032	182	293	242	315
Transportation	841	1008	394	224	97	66	37	24
Travel	−205	−210	−294	−343	−41	−72	−187	−43
Miscellaneous Services	−147	−352	−510	−97	−70	−48	0	21
Total Surplus of Exports	7799	11278	6310	6083	1658	1992	1270	1163
Means of Financing Surplus of Exports of Goods and Services (Net)								
Liquidation of gold and dollar assets by foreign countries[6]	1968	4513	857	−47	−28	330	93	−442
Dollar disbursements (net)								
By International Monetary Fund	—	464	196	101	32	18	3	48
By International Bank	—	297	176	38	8	8	11	11
U.S. Government Sources:								
Grants and other unilateral transfers (net)	2279	1812	3761	5085	1273	1490	1268	1054
Long and Short Term Loans (net)[7]	2774	3901	897	656	292	110	184	70
U.S. Private Sources:								
Remittances (net)	598	568	648	538	147	141	108	142
Long and Short Term Capital (net)[8]	335	727	1017	455	115	53	103	184
Total Means of Financing	7954	12282	7552	6826	1839	2150	1770	1067
Errors and Omissions	−155	−1004	−1242	−743	−181	−158	−500	+96

Source: 1946–1948 data, *The Balance of International Payments of the United States 1946–48*, Department of Commerce, Washington, D.C., 1950, pp. 183–4, 206; *The Annual Economic Review* by the Council of Economic Advisors, (included in *The Economic Report of the President*) Washington, D.C., January 1950, p. 183; *Survey of Current Business*, Department of Commerce, Washington, D.C., March 1950, pp. 4–7.

1. Preliminary, subject to considerable change.

(*Notes continued on next page*)

175

2. Includes reexports.

3. Includes goods sold to or bought from other countries that have not been shipped from or into the United States customs areas (e.g., surplus property sales and certain amounts of civilian supplies for occupied countries not included in recorded exports; and military purchases abroad and foreign purchases by other Government agencies not included in recorded imports; plus certain other unidentified adjustments), as well as certain other minor adjustments.

4. The methods of estimating receipts from and payments for transportation services were revised by the Department of Commerce for the last half of 1949 and they report that revisions for earlier periods will later be made. The revision resulted in both receipts and payments being raised with the former by somewhat more than the latter.

5. The Department of Commerce reports it is revising these data insofar as they refer to currencies supplied by the occupied countries to the occupying forces.

6. Excluding the increase in short-term balances and gold holdings of the International Bank and Monetary Fund resulting from payment of United States subscriptions, sales of debentures and notes in the United States, and the reduction in such balances and gold holdings resulting from dollar disbursements to foreign countries.

7. Excluding the United States subscriptions to the International Bank and Monetary Fund.

8. Excluding purchase of debentures sold or guaranteed by the International Bank. (1946, $243 million; 1948, $8 million; 1949, $20 million.)

six months they increased their holdings at an annual rate of $0.7 billion. Total exports of goods and services were at an annual rate of $17.4 billion during the first six months but fell to $14.5 billion during the second half, the lowest level since the end of the war. Total imports fell from an annual rate of $10 billion during the first six months to $9.6 billion in the last half of the year, with the result that our export surplus on current account during the first half of the year was at a rate well in excess of 1948 but was reduced by one-third during the second half of the year to the lowest level since the beginning of the war; the decline continued during the first months of 1950.

Details of the 1949 developments and the record of United States international transactions during the years 1946–49 are given in Table XXVI.

A. CURRENT ACCOUNT
Merchandise Trade[1]

i. EXPORTS

For the entire year 1949 the merchandise exports of the United States were more than one billion dollars less than in 1948 but this was almost entirely a reflection of lower prices, and indeed, it may be the volume was slightly greater than in the previous year. During the first half of 1949 commodity exports of the United States were at an annual rate of nearly $13.9 billion—approximately half a billion dollars above the 1948 rate, despite a fall in prices of about four percent as compared with that year.[2] Under the stimulus of our official aid programs, the increase was primarily in shipments to Europe and the Far East and was largely in raw cotton, iron and steel products, machinery and other goods to be used in production abroad rather than in direct consumption. Exports to Latin America and Africa during this period fell below the 1948 rates due to tighter import restrictions (especially by Argentina and South Africa), devaluation of some currencies, and satisfaction of some of the post-war deferred demand.

[1] Most of the data in this section were taken from the *Survey of Current Business*, Department of Commerce, February 1950, pp. 24 ff., and March 1950, pp. 4 ff.

[2] As measured by the index of unit value of exports of United States merchandise computed by the United States Department of Commerce.

Beginning in July, however, total commodity exports declined to an annual rate of about $10.8 billion and remained near that level for the rest of the year. A slight recovery in December was apparently only temporary and seasonal, for the value of exports in January and February 1950 were the lowest for any months since October 1946 and were only approximately two-thirds of the same period in 1949. The drop in exports during the second half of 1949 extended to every major commodity group and area. A part of the decline was due to a further average fall of about four percent in the prices (unit value) of exports, but most of it was a reduction in quantity shipped. Several factors were responsible for the fall. Of major importance were the tighter import controls imposed in the early summer by the United Kingdom and other countries in the sterling area in the face of heavy drains on their reserves (see page 129) and the further curtailment of imports by several Latin American countries as they sought to reduce their outstanding commercial debts to the United States. Also very important was the diminution during the second half of the year in aid rendered foreign nations by the United States Government. Further, the continued increase in current production in much of the world—especially Europe—not only served to reduce their imports but also permitted many countries to obtain imports from areas other than the United States. It is probable that the September 1949 devaluations will result in still greater ability of foreign goods to compete with American exports in third countries.

The direct effect of the devaluations on United States exports cannot yet be determined. Although they increased the local currency cost of our exports, the Council of Economic Advisers concluded that they probably had little effect on the quantity or prices of our exports. They reported in January 1950 that "Under present conditions . . . our exports are limited mainly by the dollars we make available to other countries through our purchases, gifts, and foreign investment." . . . "It is quite likely . . . that the effect of devaluation . . . will be to lessen the need of these countries for direct restrictions upon imports. If this is the case, our exports are not likely to be any lower than they would have been had devaluation not occurred."[3]

[3] *The Annual Economic Review*, A Report to the President by the Council of Economic Advisers (included in *The Economic Report of the Presi-*

178

ii. IMPORTS

United States merchandise imports declined during the first three quarters of the year, recovered during the last three months, but for the year as a whole were over one half billion dollars below 1948. This decline resulted from a two percent reduction in volume of imports and a five percent fall in prices (unit value). The unit value of our imports fell during the first half of the year but remained practically stationary from July onwards. There was also a small decline in the ratio of imports to gross national product during 1949 as compared with 1948.

The contraction in both quantity and total value during the first nine months was in part the result of the temporary recession in the United States and the increased substitution of domestic for imported goods, but also important were delayed imports, and payments, in anticipation of devaluation. The reduction in imports extended to all areas and to all major commodity groups except coffee, sugar and non-ferrous ores and metals and in large part reflected the desire of United States firms to reduce inventories in the face of the business recession, more ample supplies (both from domestic and foreign sources), and the possibility of lower prices.

After September, the revival of industrial production in the United States, combined with the devaluations, resulted in a substantial increase in both total value and volume of imports. Part of it was due to seasonal factors, but it also reflected the fact that many inventories needed to be replenished. A part of the increase during this quarter represents imports and/or payments which had been deferred in expectation of the devaluations. (It might be noted in passing that some 14 percent of the increase in imports during the fourth quarter was the result of the sharp rise in coffee prices.) It is not yet possible to reach firm conclusions as to the effect of the widespread devaluations on United States imports. Through 1949 they had little effect on the dollar prices of our major import commodities; such prices on some of the goods supplied by Europe did fall, although usually not in full proportion to the devaluations.

---

dent, Washington, D.C., January 1950), pp. 58–9. It should be added that our exports in the immediate future may also be limited by the efforts of foreign nations to restore their gold and dollar balances.

iii. CHANGING PATTERN OF UNITED STATES FOREIGN TRADE

As a consequence of the war, the world's trade pattern was greatly altered. The United States has been no exception. Accompanying a tremendous increase in our exports, a smaller increase in imports and the resulting great expansion in our export surplus, have been large shifts in both the commodity composition and the geographical pattern of our merchandise trade.

The most important change in the commodity composition of our foreign trade has been the steady and large increase in the share of both our exports and imports taken up by crude foodstuffs, as is shown in Table XXVII.

TABLE XXVII
Foreign Trade of the United States, by Commodities, 1936–1949
(in percentages)

Commodity Group	Exports of U.S. Merchandise[a]			Imports for Consumption[b]		
	1936–38 Average	1947–48 Average	1949[p]	1936–38 Average	1947–48 Average	1949[p]
Crude Materials	23	11	15	31	30	28
Crude Foodstuffs	4	9	11	14	18	20
Manufactured Foodstuffs and Beverages	6	11	7	15	11	11
Semi-Manufactures	18	12	12	20	23	22
Finished Manufactures	49	57	55	20	18	19
Total	100	100	100	100	100	100
Total Value[a,b] (in millions)	$2925	$13828	$11884	$2461	$6351	$6598

p. Preliminary.
Sources: *Survey of Current Business, 1949 Statistical Supplement*, Department of Commerce, 1949, pp. 107–113 for pre-war and 1947–48 data. 1949 data are from *Survey of Current Business*, February 1950, and March 1950, pp. S-21, S-22.
a. Differs from exports of following table in that reexports are not included here.
b. "Imports for consumption" differ from "general imports" in that to goods entering consumption channels immediately upon arrival the former adds *withdrawals* from bonded warehouses while the latter adds *entries* into bonded warehouses.
Note: The year 1946 has been excluded in this and the following table since the published data on a commodity and geographical basis for that year do not include estimates of the goods supplied civilians abroad through the United States armed forces. Such supplies are included in the 1947–1949 data and are also included in the world totals given in Table XXVI.

The role of manufactured foodstuffs and beverages in our imports, on the other hand, has been appreciably less important since the war than before. While our exports of these commodities were very high in the years immediately following the end of hostilities, there was a sharp decline in 1949 as relief operations abroad declined; for the year, their relative importance was only slightly higher than it had been in 1936–38. Another important shift in our exports has been the increasing share represented by finished manufactures and the declining relative importance of semi-manufactures. A smaller but reverse change has occurred in our imports of these goods. Finally, crude materials, other than food-

TABLE XXVIII

Foreign Trade of the United States, by Geographic Areas, 1936–1949
(in percentages)

	Exports[a]				General Imports[b]			
	1936–38	1947–48	1949[p]		1936–38	1947–48	1949[p]	
Area	Average	Average	First Half	Second Half	Average	Average	First Half	Second Half
Western Hemisphere	34	41	39	42	37	58	59	62
Canada	15	14	15	17	14	21	22	24
Latin American Republics	17	25	22	23	22	35	34	35
Other	2	2	2	2	1	2	3	3
Europe	42	36	36	33	28	15	14	14
Africa	4	6	5	5	3	6	5	5
Asia and Oceania	20	17	20	20	32	21	22	19
Total	100	100	100	100	100	100	100	100
Total Value (in millions)	$2967	$13977	$6687	$5314	$2489	$6402	$3390	$3236

p. Preliminary.
Sources: Same as Table XXVII.
a. Includes reexports but not goods sold which have not been shipped from United States customs areas. The small discrepancies between the total value of exports in this table and "recorded goods" in Table XXVI are the result of recent revisions which have been published for the total but not yet for the geographic distribution.
b. Includes general imports only. Does not include purchases for offshore use and certain other adjustments. The slight discrepancies between the totals in this table and those for "recorded goods" in Table XXVI are apparently the result of revisions which have been published for the totals but not yet for the geographic distribution.

stuffs, have also declined in relative importance in our total foreign trade, but the decline in exports has been much greater than the decline in imports.

Perhaps the outstanding development in the shift in the geographical pattern of our trade has been the increasing importance of Canada and the Latin American Republics, as both markets for our exports and sources of our imports, as is shown in Table XXVIII. On the other hand, despite the fact that our post-war aid programs have been concentrated in Europe, the share of our total exports going to this area has been appreciably less than it was before, and the percentage of our imports from Europe has been only about one half as large as in the pre-war years. The relative importance of Africa in our trade has increased slightly, and while the percentage of our exports going to Asia and Oceania has been fairly stable there has been a big decline in the relative importance of the area as a source of imports.

Prior to the war, 1936–38, the United States had an import surplus on merchandise account with the Latin American Republics and with Asia. This was a significant factor in the functioning of the multilateral trade system. As our exports increased much more than our imports following the war, the United States developed an export surplus with every major geographic area. In 1949, however, there was some evidence that something like the pre-war pattern might be emerging. As the total value of our export surplus declined, the percentage of it arising from trade with the Western Hemisphere was declining rapidly, while that with Europe and Asia and Oceania was increasing, as is seen in Table XXIX.

When one breaks down the data for Asia and Oceania, however, it is seen that a large part of the export surplus resulted from our trade with Japan, the Philippines and Korea—all recipients of extensive official United States aid. Before the war a large part of our import surplus with Asia rose from our trade with British Malaya, and although this has continued each year since the war it was smaller in 1949 than it was in 1947 and 1948. During the last half of 1949, however, there were, for the first time since the end of the war, small import surpluses on commodity account with the Netherlands Indies and India and Pakistan, thus suggesting a possible return to the pre-war relationships.

TABLE XXIX
Geographic Distribution of Surplus of Recorded
Exports over General Imports, 1936–1949
(in percentages)

| | | | | 1949p | |
| | 1936–38 | | | First | Second |
Area	Average	1947	1948	Half	Half
Western Hemisphere	17	29	22	18	12
Canada	23	10	6	9	7
Latin America	−12	18	15	9	5
Other	6	1	1	*	*
Europe	112	51	57	58	62
Africa	13	5	7	5	5
Asia and Oceania	−42	15	14	18	21
Total	100	100	100	100	100
Total Value (in millions)	$478	$9607	$5544	$3297	$2078

p. Preliminary.
* Less than one half percent.
Source: Same as Table XXVII.

A perhaps more important change, although seasonal factors may have been partly responsible, occurred during the last three months of 1949 when, again for the first time since the war, the United States had a small import surplus in its total merchandise trade with Canada and Latin America. At the same time there was some evidence that Europe was reducing its deficits with these areas, in part by displacing the United States as a source of imports, thus holding out a possibility that a pattern might again be developing whereby a European deficit with the United States could be partly paid for out of the proceeds of the United States import surplus with other countries of the Western Hemisphere and with southern Asia.

Income on Investments

There were no large changes in income on investments during the year and receipts exceeded payments by over one billion dollars, strikingly reflecting the international creditor position of the United States. Since various aspects of investments and income on investments have been discussed previously in this report, only a few words need be added here.

United States receipts from this source in 1949 were $65 million greater than in the previous year, with all the increase being received by private investors. Although detailed data for 1949 are not yet available, in 1948 nearly 80 percent of the total was paid to private direct investors, some 12 percent to private portfolio investors, about one percent to private persons having short-term investments abroad, and 8 percent to the United States Government. Payments from this country to foreign persons during 1949 were only $5 million in excess of 1948. In 1948, 40 percent of the total represented dividend payments by foreign direct investment companies in the United States and profits of United States branches of foreign companies (largely insurance companies); 55 percent represented dividends and interest payments on foreign-held American corporate, state and municipal stocks and bonds; and the remaining 5 percent represented interest payments by the United States Government on its securities held by foreigners and on foreign deposits with the Treasury. These percentages were probably not significantly altered during 1949.

Transportation[2]

Prior to the war (1936–1938) United States payments for transportation services exceeded receipts by a yearly average of approximately $85 million, but this position was sharply reversed during the war years as a result of the tremendous shipbuilding program in the United States, the sinking of foreign vessels, and the large merchandise export surplus of the United States.[3]

The United States surplus on transportation account reached an all-time peak of over one billion dollars in 1947 but declined

---

[2] The reader is referred to the *Balance of International Payments of the United States 1946–48, op. cit.*, pp. 62–69, for more detailed discussion of the transportation account. This document is the source of most of the information included here.

[3] The net shipping balance tends to vary directly with the net export balance since the United States receives payments on international account by carrying goods between foreign countries and its own exports and pays on international account only for foreign vessels carrying our imports.

It should be recognized that United States balance of payments statistics on shipping receipts are not the same as the earnings by American ships in foreign trade since carriage payments for imports transported in United States bottoms are not included in the former.

by over 60 percent in 1948 and another 42 percent in 1949 to $224 million. This rapid decline has been primarily the result of (a) foreign nations' rebuilding their fleets (including purchases of war surplus vessels from the United States) and thus increasing their participation, (b) the reduction in the total volume of United States trade, (c) the fall in freight rates, and (d) the decline in the United States commodity export surplus. The decline in participation by United States bottoms led, as noted on pages 12 f and 38, to the insertion of a clause in both the European recovery and the military assistance legislation requiring that at least half the cargoes from the United States financed under these programs be carried by American flag vessels. As the Marshall Plan tapers off it is probable that the percentage of our foreign trade carried in American bottoms will decline even more. This would seem to be certain unless the rate differentials between foreign flag and American flag vessels for some major bulk cargoes, especially coal and grain, are eliminated.

While ocean freight constitutes the biggest item in the transportation account, also included are ocean passenger fares, air, rail and lake traffic and port charges. Details on ocean passenger fares for 1949 are not yet available, but during the period 1946-48 receipts were in excess of payments by an average of some $14 million per year. With an increasing number of foreign ships engaged in passenger carriage it is possible these accounts were more nearly balanced in 1949.

Air transportation has been of increasing importance since the war, and the share of American companies in both passenger and cargo trade is much higher than in steamship lines although the sums involved are much smaller. For the three years 1946-48, United States receipts on passenger account averaged $31 million per year and on cargo account nearly $30 million, while payments averaged only $9 and $2 million respectively.

Rail traffic payments and receipts (representing American railroad receipts and expenditures in Canada and in-transit traffic) have approximately balanced since the war at around $40 to $45 million per year, while Great Lakes traffic has also balanced at approximately $5 million per year.

Finally, the transportation account also includes expenses of foreign carriers in United States ports and American carriers in foreign ports. Again details for 1949 are not yet available, but for the three previous years these accounts were approximately in balance, with payments and receipts averaging around $280 million a year. It may be that payments would have been much higher had it not been for the fact that repairs to American ships made in foreign yards are taxed at a rate of 50 percent unless it can be proved that the ship could not have returned to the United States without such repairs.

Travel[4]

Travel expenditures are an important source of dollars for the rest of the world. Net payments on this account (excluding transportation costs between the United States and foreign areas) have increased steadily since the end of the war, reaching an all time high of $343 million in 1949. Total travel expenditures by American residents in 1949 were $695 million, as compared with $601 million in 1948. Over 60 percent of the *increase* represented expanded travel in Europe and the Mediterranean area, and another 22 percent reflected the sharp rise in travel to Mexico resulting in large part from the peso devaluation. Of total expenditures during 1949, over 40 percent were in Canada; nearly 28 percent were in Mexico, the West Indies and Central America; and only some 25 percent were in Europe and the Mediterranean countries. There has been a steady growth since 1946 in the travel expenditures in Europe and the Mediterranean area as more transportation facilities became available and internal living conditions improved, but the proportion of total expenditures in this area still falls far short of the 54 percent recorded in 1920 or the 44 percent in 1929.

This concentration of travel to nearby areas in 1949 reflects a trend evident in the thirties and appears to be the result of many

[4] The reader is referred to Sasscer, F. P., "American Expenditures for Foreign Travel in 1949," *Survey of Current Business*, March 1950, pp. 16–19, and the *Balance of International Payments of the United States 1946–48, op. cit.*, pp. 69–79, for a description and analysis of the travel account since the war. These are the sources for most of the information presented here. See also Longmore, K. M., "American Tourist Expenditure and the European Balance of Payments," *Bulletin of Oxford University Institute of Statistics*, March, 1950, pp. 65–73.

factors, of which the more important are (1) the gradual decrease in our European-born population, (2) steady improvement of highways in Mexico and Canada, (3) increase in paid vacations which has stimulated short trips abroad, (4) expansion of air travel facilities to the Caribbean area, and (5) popularization during the depression of nearby countries.[5]

Although exchange control authorities abroad have placed severe restrictions on the use of dollars for travel purposes, such expenditures in the United States by foreign residents have averaged more than twice the amounts spent in the years immediately preceding the war and have been relatively stable since 1946. No detailed data for 1949 are available, but for 1946–48, 43 percent of total receipts on travel account were from residents of Canada, 30 percent from the Latin American Republics, and 16 percent from ERP countries.

Expanded travel abroad by Americans has been urged by many persons as an especially desirable method of providing dollars to the rest of the world. The United States Government encouraged this in June 1948 when the liberalized customs exemptions were instituted, and, previously, when it removed the 15 percent tax on transportation to points outside North America and adjacent islands. The programs sponsored by the Government for the large exchange of students and teachers between the United States and various foreign countries may also serve to stimulate foreign travel. On their part, several European countries have recently waived visa requirements for United States travelers, certain other formalities have been eased or eliminated, and promotional campaigns are being increased. The many currency devaluations in 1949 may also stimulate travel, as should a gradual improvement in tourist accommodations in many foreign lands. "Still," the Department of Commerce concludes, " . . . it is highly possible in view of significant changes in basic economic and political conditions brought about by the war that United States travel expenditures will not reach the 'calculated' volume as determined by the prewar relationship."[6]

[5] With respect to Canada and Mexico a large percentage of the expenditures (in 1949, 22 percent in the case of Canada and 48 percent in the case of Mexico) were made by persons living or visiting adjacent to the frontier.

[6] "American Expenditures for Foreign Travel in 1949," *op. cit.*, p. 16.

Miscellaneous Services

In 1949 net dollar payments by the United States on miscellaneous services totalled only $97 million, as compared with over one half billion dollars in 1948, as shown in Table XXX. This reduction was due in large part to a sharp fall in payments abroad by United States military agencies, especially net payments to troops, and the Department of Commerce warns that statistical revisions to be made may reduce these payments still more.

TABLE XXX
Miscellaneous Services, 1946–1949
(in millions of dollars)

					1949[p]			
					First	Second	Third	Fourth
	1946	1947	1948	Total	Quarter	Quarter	Quarter	Quarter
Receipts								
Private	483	504	433	475	112	119	125	119
Government	162	64	110	162	46	49	33	34
Total	645	568	543	637	158	168	158	153
Payments								
Private	185	255	197	194	49	51	51	43
Government	607	665	856	540	179	165	107[a]	89[a]
Total	792	920	1053	734	228	216	158	132

p. Preliminary.
a. These two quarters have been revised downward by about $60 million per quarter on the basis of new information regarding troop pay. The Department of Commerce reports that substantial reductions may later be made in the first two quarters of 1949.
Sources: 1946–1948 data: *The Balance of International Payments of the United States, 1946–48,* Department of Commerce 1950, pp. 79–86, 255; 1949 data: *Survey of Current Business,* March 1950, p. 6. The reader desiring more details again is referred to the first cited source from which most of the information in this section came.

On private account alone net receipts by the United States have been large since the war and rose from approximately $250 million in 1947 and 1948 to slightly over $280 million in 1949. Motion picture rentals have accounted for approximately half of the net receipts in each of the post-war years. Most of the rest represents the expenditures in the United States of the various international organizations and foreign governments and the management fees, etc., which United States companies charge their foreign branches and subsidiaries. Payments and receipts for communication services and insurance transactions have largely offset each other.

The net receipts on private account for miscellaneous services have, however, been overbalanced by net payments on Government account. In the three pre-war years 1938–1940, total net payments by the Government on this account averaged only about $50 million a year, while the average for the first four post-war years was nearly $550 million. As compared with 1948, Government payments in 1949 decreased by $316 million and Government receipts increased by $52 million, thus reducing the net payments from $746 million to $378 million.

Since the war, military agency payments have dominated this account with such disbursements divided approximately evenly between payments to personnel and payments for the maintenance and operation of military facilities and installations for the period as a whole although the percentage has varied from year to year.[7] The large increase in Government payments in 1948 was almost entirely the result of increases in net troop pay as extra-legal transactions between American personnel and the local populace declined. The reason for the very large decline in Government payments in 1949 was probably the result of reductions in both the number of troops stationed abroad and in the costs of operating and maintaining military installations and facilities, including the Berlin airlift.

In addition to payments by United States military agencies, various civilian branches of the Government also make payments abroad on service account. Most important here are the expenses of the diplomatic establishments, the foreign cost of United States participation in various international organizations and service payments by the Veterans Administration, the Philippine War Damage Commission, and the Agriculture Department.

Services rendered (receipts) by the Government since the war may be divided into two broad categories: those associated with the regular operations of the Government and those associated with the special foreign aid programs. In 1947 the former

[7] Not all costs of maintaining United States forces abroad affected the balance of payments. The largest portion took place in the United States or were paid directly by the occupied countries themselves.

(largely receipts by the Treasury Department to cover handling charges on gold transactions for account of foreign nations and receipts by the Post Office Department, Panama Canal and Panama Railroad) exceeded the latter. But in 1948 and 1949 there were large increases in services rendered under the many foreign aid programs, and much of the increase in 1949 represents the expanded activities of ECA.

B. CAPITAL ACCOUNT

Foreign Dollar and Gold Assets

A striking development in the international transactions of the United States during 1949 was that the rest of the world ceased liquidating its gold and dollar assets and actually increased such holdings by a slight amount. The Department of Commerce estimates that, in their transactions with the United States, foreign sources (excluding the International Bank and Fund) increased their gold and dollar assets by $47 million,[8] as compared with liquidations of roughly $2 billion in 1946, $4.5 billion in 1947, and $0.8 billion in 1948.[9] This reversal was the result of many factors; the more important were (1) the expanded flow of United States aid for the year as a whole, (2) recovery of both production and trade in the rest of the world, (3) further tightening of exchange and import restrictions in many countries as reserves reached what were regarded as at or below safe minimum working balances, and (4) the devaluations of the year

[8] Both long and short-term dollar assets are included, but this figure excludes the net dollar disbursements of $139 million during the year by the International Bank and Monetary Fund. Were these international institutions included in "foreign sources" there would have been a small net liquidation of gold and dollar assets in their transactions with the United States.

[9] These figures are not the same as total changes in foreign-held gold and dollar assets since foreign gold production also affects the latter. Thus, the Federal Reserve Board has estimated that total foreign holdings of gold and short-term dollar balances increased by approximately $300 million in 1949 and totalled $15.2 billion at year's end. (See *Federal Reserve Bulletin*, Board of Governors of the Federal Reserve System, Washington, D.C., March 1950, pp. 269–278; *The Balance of International Payments of the United States 1946–48, op. cit.*, pp. 149–161; and *Survey of Current Business*, March 1950, pp. 4–7, for detailed discussions of foreign gold and dollar transactions since the war. These documents are the source of most of the information included here.)

which, in addition to their effect on commercial transactions, resulted in an appreciable flow of speculative capital. In general, foreign countries were able to increase their reserves primarily as a result of reduced imports from the United States after July.

These developments were neither uniform for all countries nor were they continuous throughout the year. As a result of their transactions with the United States the United Kingdom suffered a liquidation of gold and dollar reserves[1] of nearly $400 million, and the rest of the sterling area liquidated approximately another $150 million. On the other hand, the Marshall Plan countries, other than the United Kingdom, built up their reserves by more than $200 million, with most of the increase going to Belgium, Italy, the Netherlands and Switzerland. In its transactions with the United States, Canada accumulated gold and dollar reserves of about $70 million, while the Latin American Republics gained approximately $360 million, with Argentina, Brazil, Peru, and Venezuela being large gainers. The Far Eastern area drew heavily on their reserves to finance purchases from the United States, primarily as the result of large liquidations by the Philippines and China. These figures highlight, as has been pointed out in several places in this survey, the importance and difficulties of the financial relations between the sterling area and the United States.

During the first quarter of the year there was a small ($28 million) accumulation of gold and dollar assets by foreign countries as a result of their United States transactions in continuation of a similar development during the last quarter of 1948; but during the second quarter of 1949, as imports by the United States fell in response to the business recession here, net liquidations totalled $330 million. A tightening of import and exchange restrictions by many countries—especially those in the sterling area—resulted in a sharp fall in purchases from the United States, aggravated by a decline in United States aid, and net liquida-

[1] It may be noted that monetary authorities commonly attempt to maintain short-term dollar balances at some customary level by buying and selling gold as their dollar balances exceed or fall short of these levels. In this paragraph "dollar reserves" refers only to short-term dollar balances and gold while in the previous and the following paragraphs "dollar assets" refers to gold plus short-term *and* long-term dollar assets. Changes in long-term dollar assets in this geographic break-down are not taken into account, but the general picture given would not likely be altered by their inclusion.

tions were only $93 million during the third quarter despite a continued fall in imports by the United States. Following the devaluations in September, United States exports continued to fall (though less than the decline in United States aid); imports increased, and the liquidations were replaced by large accumulations so that for the final quarter of the year the rest of the world, in its transactions with the United States, increased its gold and dollar holdings by some $442 million. These sharp shifts in the gold and dollar holdings of foreign nations during the last half of the year appear to have been heavily influenced by speculative action. In anticipation of the devaluation, many United States importers postponed purchases and payments during the summer and then increased them after September 18, thus tending to increase liquidations in the third quarter and accumulations in the fourth. More important perhaps, though specific data are not available, was a large movement of speculative capital to the United States prior to the devaluation and its repatriation afterwards. It would appear, therefore, that the impressive record of the last quarter of 1949 over-states the degree of basic adjustment between the United States and the rest of the world.

Taking newly mined gold into account, as well as their transactions with the United States, foreign nations, excluding Russia and the international institutions, were able during 1949 to increase their gold and short-term dollar balances by approximately $300 million. Although this was a welcome change from the large reductions in the three previous years ($1.2 billion in 1946, $4.2 billion in 1947, and $0.3 billion in 1948),[1a] the total at the end of 1949 ($15.2 billion) was still only slightly above prewar holdings, while wholesale prices in the United States had doubled and the dollar value of world trade had risen between two and three times pre-war. It would thus appear probable that the reserves of foreign nations would have to be vastly increased before there would be any general movement abroad to abandon extensive currency and trade controls in favor of a system of currency convertibility and multilateral trade, which

[1a] These data are less than the figures for gold and dollar asset liquidations given in the first paragraph of this section since newly mined gold is included here and net liquidations of long-term dollar assets are excluded.

is such an important element in United States international financial policy.[2]

Other Items

The other means of financing the surplus of United States exports of goods and services—dollar disbursements by the International Monetary Fund and International Bank, official Government gifts and loans and private gifts and loans—have been discussed in some detail elsewhere in this survey and need not be reviewed here.

C. ERRORS AND OMISSIONS

A word regarding "errors and omissions," will complete this review of the 1949 balance of payments of the United States.[3] Some errors and omissions are unavoidable since nearly all the figures in the balance of payments, except Government aid, are estimates. For every year since the war this item has been consistently both large and in the same direction (negative), indicating either a serious over-estimation of payments or under-estimation of receipts, or both. It is probable that a large part has been due to unrecorded flows of foreign capital to the United States. The item has, both before and after the war, been large and negative during periods of serious political and economic tension abroad. This explanation is given support by the very large negative errors and omissions figure in the third quarter of 1949 and the positive item for the fourth quarter. It is also probable, however, that a part of it since the war represents an undervaluation of exports growing out of, among other things, inadvertent omission of inland freight and certain other charges, under-estimation in reporting by the United States exporters of so-called "gray market" goods and perhaps more or less arbitrary under-valuations set on some exports by American companies to their

[2] This is not to suggest that adequate reserves alone would lead to the dropping of many controls on payments but only that it is one prerequisite. It may well be, for example, that a nation following a policy of direct controls over its internal economy would not regard it desirable to leave its international financial affairs uncontrolled no matter what the state of its international reserves.

[3] For further discussion of this problem see *The Balance of International Payments of the United States 1946–48, op. cit.*, pp. 35–7, 166, from which the summary analysis below was taken.

branches and subsidiaries abroad. The official data on imports since the war may also have over-estimated actual payments since the rate of exchange used by the authorities in valuations may in many cases have been less favorable to the dollar than the actual rates obtained by the importer. Also important here may have been the inclusion of ocean freight and insurance in the declared value of imports which are duty-free or subject to specific rates and the requirement that "foreign value" be used for customs purposes whenever it is higher than the "export value," even though the actual price paid may have been less than "foreign value."

VIII · CONCLUSIONS

THE United States has repeatedly announced that its foreign economic policy is one of fostering free convertibility of all currencies and a single, non-discriminatory trading system in the world so that the movements of goods, services, and capital among nations may once again be directed by individuals. Further, the policy is one of encouraging a progressive reduction of barriers to trade and of eliminating the necessity for continued unilateral transfers from the United States. For present purposes we accept this broad policy as given—it was reiterated during the September sterling discussions. After the foregoing survey of United States international financial policies and affairs in 1949, it does seem desirable, however, to analyze briefly the extent to which the specific policies and activities of that period have advanced the world toward this long-term goal.

Probably the most important immediate obstacle to multilateralism is the continued pressure on the international reserves of most of the rest of the world. This strain, in turn, has been blamed on: the war; inflation; changes in tastes and sources of supply of internationally traded goods resulting in widespread misallocations of productive resources (accentuated by nearly two decades of relative isolation from overseas competition); economic controls and central planning; over-valued exchange rates; excessive investment and/or consumption; full employment policies; and, increasingly, on the "free enterprise" economy of the United States which has ascended to primacy in world economic affairs, which is stated to be unstable in the short-run, which has a long-run tendency to outpace the rest of the world in productivity, and which is relatively self-sufficient. The mere listing of these factors shows that the economic and financial policies of foreign countries, not subject to direct influence from the United States, must carry a full share of the responsibility for creating conditions necessary for multilateralism.[1] Admittedly, however, their policies may be affected indirectly by American policy. The question before us, therefore, is to what extent United States policy in 1949 attacked and eliminated or alleviated those factors within its sphere of influence.

A. GOVERNMENT AID PROGRAMS

In the immediate post-war years, large-scale aid from the United States appears to have been a necessary, though not a sufficient, condition for achieving multilateralism in a reasonably short time. It is clear that most countries today are not prepared to leave to the open market the decision of what and where to import and export so long as there exists what the authorities regard as acute shortages of certain goods deemed essential to the welfare of their people and necessary for internal political stability.[2] Therefore, the United States policy of extending substantial economic aid to many foreign nations—entirely apart from political and humanitarian considerations—was justifiable to the extent that it contributed importantly—as it has—to increasing production and productivity abroad. But this is not enough. To obtain the maximum possible advantages from non-discriminatory multilateral trade and free exchange markets, it is also necessary that the expansion of productive facilities be along lines of comparative advantage. American aid must be given in such a way as to result in an alteration of production structures to take account of the many shifts in demand and supply conditions

---

[1] See Lutz, F. A., "The Marshall Plan and European Economic Policy," *Essays in International Finance* No. 9, Spring 1948, for a cogent argument that the return of Western Europe to a system of multilateral trade depends primarily on the general economic policy of the European countries rather than on the amount of aid they receive from the United States.

[2] In this connection, it must be recognized that the amount of supplies needed to satisfy these shortages is not only subjective and so exceedingly difficult to assess but also, and perhaps more important, the very act of extending extraordinary aid on this basis may serve to create socially and politically acceptable minimum standards of living above those which can be maintained in the foreseeable future from the efforts of the countries receiving aid. If this should occur, the United States would have helped create a situation in which continued aid may be necessary as a condition for restoration of convertibility and non-discriminatory multilateral trade.

in the past two decades. Otherwise, the nations receiving aid may not deem themselves capable of removing controls on their trade; that is, unless such alterations are accomplished, various forms of protection, possibly including bilateral agreements to insure foreign markets, will be needed if their resources are to be fully utilized. The pressure for such adjustments is not ⌐ strong so long as aid is being received, but it is much easier to make them during such a period. These considerations dictate a policy of gradual reduction, and the setting of a firm date for the termination, of United States assistance, as is the present ⌡ policy of ECA at least. There is little evidence yet available to indicate whether such structural changes have been made, and that convincing evidence can be given so long as controls exist is doubtful.

An important and positive part of United States aid programs ⌐ also has been the elimination of inflationary pressures abroad. This has been pursued not only by increasing the amounts of goods and services available to foreign countries but also via advice as to internal monetary and fiscal policies, the use of counterpart funds, and, at least in the occupied countries, by ⌡ more direct measures. This again was a consistent policy since the suppression of inflation is a necessary condition for adoption of liberal trade and payments practices. On the other hand, the United States has not seen fit to, nor is it here suggested that it should, make its aid conditional on the return of recipient countries to internal free-market economies (in fact, the American aid programs have been accompanied by greater internal economic controls in some areas), although the maintenance of comprehensive domestic controls is in practice incompatible with free exchange markets and non-discriminatory multilateral trade.

Again consistent with its long-term objectives, the policy of ⌐ the United States Government in 1949 was to substitute outright grants for aid in the form of loans and credits. Heavy fixed dollar obligations increase the drain on the debtors' reserves, thus delaying the possibility of adopting more liberal commercial and financial policies. Indeed, the burden of servicing existing Government loans and credits will be so large by 1952 that it has been ⌡ suggested that, if continued aid by the United States at the termination of the Marshall Plan is for any reason desirable, such aid might in part at least take the form of cancelling or postponing the servicing of these obligations to the United States.

Throughout the official aid programs—prefaced as they have been by the intent of supporting multilateralism—there runs, however, a serious contradiction in the form of tying nearly all loans, and a large share of all gifts, directly to purchases of United States goods and services. During the first few years after the war, this country was the only possible source for many of the goods needed by foreign nations. But, as noted in the text, the percentage of purchases from aid-supplied funds required to be made in the United States increased substantially in 1949 in the face of increases in competitive sources of supply in the rest ⌐of the world. Restricting the use of aid funds to purchases in this country—to the extent it forced countries to purchase goods here which might have been obtained for the dollars on more favorable terms elsewhere—is equivalent to making these dollars inconvertible and denies the very essence of multilateral trade, ∟according to which purchases are made in the cheapest market. This distortion of trade is more than a temporary phenomenon and will tend to persist after the termination of our aid. Its continuance may result from, for example, conditioning of tastes (one is reminded of tobacco and branded consumer goods), development of commercial ties through familiarity with the market, and, of great importance, the necessity of buying replacement parts for durable goods from the original supplier. The grant of assistance with no restrictions as to the areas in which the funds may be spent probably would not result in a large decline in the total value of United States exports because most of the dollars would be ultimately spent in the United States.[3] It probably would, however, result in important changes in their composition and direction and so require adjustments in the American economy. These changes in United States production and trade patterns may not be a pleasant prospect, but they are implicit in the non-discriminatory trading world which the United States, above all other countries, encourages.

⌐   If recipients of United States aid were free to spend the dollars

---

[3] Such freedom on the use of dollar aid would probably result in some of it being used to build up international reserves, but, as argued below, this also is a prerequisite of multilateralism.

anywhere, the effect, as compared with tying such aid to purchases in the United States, would be to increase the volume of
world trade, to make the additional trade more multilateral,
and to decrease the dependence of the rest of the world on continued assistance from the United States—all United States objectives.   There is now an appreciable amount of potential trade ⌋
among the other nations which is effectively blocked by the inconvertibility of their currencies. If our dollar aid could be
freely spent, much of this trade might be unblocked, and in multi-
ples of the amount of our aid. Thus, for example, the tying of
aid extended to nation B, which has an inconvertible currency,
might perpetuate a condition under which it is unable to purchase
goods available in nation A if the latter does not at that particular
time wish to buy in B. If, on the other hand, B could offer to
pay, at the seller's option, dollars or its own currency, the trade
might well take place and might ultimately be financed in either
dollars or local currency. If the former, then A has dollars to
carry out the same sort of operation with C (or later with B), etc.
If the latter, then B can repeat the operation. Further, if aid ⌐
dollars could be spent freely, those nations having persistent deficits with the United States would be encouraged to compete
in third markets for dollars with which to finance their deficits ⌐
with the United States.

The expanded United States programs of military assistance ⌐
to foreign countries in 1949 also may operate as an obstacle to
the abandonment of restrictive trade and payments practices
abroad. In their presentation to the Congressional committees, ⌐
spokesmen for the Executive branch argued such assistance would
contribute to, rather than retard, economic recovery in the recipient countries. Some European officials, however, have raised
serious questions on this score, and their concern is well founded.
The diversion from the production of consumers goods and exports of the large amounts of local resources necessary to utilize
effectively the military supplies given, and to implement the
military programs encouraged, by the United States would seem
likely to increase seriously the pressure on the recipients' balances
of payments. Thus, it is possible that a program designed to
promote military and political security will become a serious
deterrent to the establishment of a liberalized trading world.

This possibility represents a real and most serious dilemma for American foreign policy. While it is commonly recognized that political and military security are prerequisites to a successful multilateral economic and financial policy, in the present world conditions, the very techniques chosen (required?) to accomplish the former may militate strongly against the latter.

B. PRIVATE INVESTMENT

In the past, long-term private capital movements have been an important factor in meeting the problem of unbalanced trade and productivity and facilitating the development of trade along the multilateral lines of comparative advantage. In 1949, the United States Government indicated that increased reliance should again be placed on expanded private capital outflows. The Point Four Program and the increased emphasis on investment treaties and tax conventions were the more important specific reflections of this policy.

There are difficult and complex problems as to the possible and proper role of large-scale private international investment by the United States at this time. Analogies with British and Western European activities in the last century are misleading. There are several major difficulties, apart from the unstable political and uncertain military outlook, in the path of American assumption of the role of an increasing creditor nation: (a) Productive private capital flows are not likely to be large at a time when international disequilibrium is intense. Private investors are reluctant to engage in long-term foreign investments precisely because there is already a huge imbalance in the current account between the United States and the rest of the world. (b) The existence in many countries of exchange controls, combined with the assumption by the authorities in most countries of responsibility for insuring a minimum level of imports for maintaining domestic consumption, creates serious uncertainties for the investors. (c) As compared with the nineteenth century, the political influence of the investor's government is much less strong in assuring "favorable treatment" in the recipient countries. (d) The existence of very heavy fixed-payment obligations to the United States Government on outstanding foreign credits constitutes a serious restraint on private equity investments.

(e) Frequently the investments encouraged by the governments of the receiving countries are not of the type which will quickly or importantly improve their balance of payments position.

Entirely apart from the above considerations, the rates of return on investment in the United States are frequently more attractive; thus, a volume of private investment sufficient to finance anything like the 1949 export surplus would, due to the very high returns necessary to cause American capital to move, impose in a short time on both the United States and foreign countries a substantial reversal in present trade flows. At best, therefore, a greatly expanded flow of private long-term capital from the United States can only postpone the fundamental structural adjustments which seem to be required both in the American economy—long oriented to an export surplus—and abroad, if a balanced structure of world trade and finance is to be achieved.

In spite of the above considerations, the misallocation and underdevelopment of resources in much of the world indicates that avenues should be opened for larger private capital flows from the United States than were recorded during 1949 and that the Administration's proposals for investment guaranties, to supplement its expanded efforts to conclude more investment treaties and tax conventions, constituted a step in the right direction.[4] However, the investment guarantee device would

---

[4] The view of much of the business community was that intervention by the United States Government should, by and large, be restricted to encourging foreign countries to produce a "favorable climate" for private foreign investment. The conditions outlined as a "favorable climate" seem prohibitively exacting. Suspicion of private foreign investment is deeprooted in many of the undeveloped areas and tends to increase with growing nationalism. It appears most unlikely, therefore, that many nations will abdicate their internal controls over fiscal policies and over the direction and volume of investment to the degree involved, in the business-inspired codes of fair treatment for foreign investment. Nor does it seem likely that most foreign nations will agree to invite future exchange crises by agreeing in advance not to restrict conversion of local currencies arising out of foreign investments. This is not to argue against attempting earnestly to negotiate investment treaties, but it is to suggest that little more than non-discriminatory treatment and the limitation of exchange restrictions to those approved by the International Monetary Fund can be hoped for. Large amounts of private capital outflows cannot be expected if, for example, the United States insists on binding priority commitments regarding convertibility, or on the degree of local participation in management and operations being left entirely to the American investor.

remove only one of the deterrents mentioned above and so probably would not greatly stimulate private capital movements. And investment guaranties themselves face difficulties over and above the problems of defining the terms and conditions on which guaranties will be given. Their successful administration will require that investors give the Government extensive information on their operations abroad, possibly making the guaranties unattractive. Delicate international political problems may result if the Government refuses guaranties on investment projects in one country while approving some in another; such a selection may be economically justifiable but at the same time appear "discriminatory" to a sensitive foreign government. Serious political disputes may also arise in the event an agency of the United States Government accumulates, or is threatened with accumulating, large amounts of local currency in any country and so is tempted to impose conditions on that country to provide for convertibility.[5] In the not unlikely event that both the United States Government and private United States persons held the same non-convertible currencies, unpleasant controversies may arise within the United States as to priorities of conversion. Further, no existing Government agency seems to be an ideal one for administering the program. While the Export-Import Bank has been proposed and has considerable experience in foreign lending, the statements of the Bank's officials and the past record of the Bank affirm that it is first a *bank*, which operates on a traditionally conservative basis, which is interested in maintaining a record for "sound" loans, and whose first interest and task has been aiding United States exporters. This may be quite proper behavior for its normal duties, but it is scarcely the attitude needed to inaugurate a "bold new program" of encouraging large-scale private foreign investment.[6]

[5] See Wu, Y. L., "Government Guarantees and Private Foreign Investment," *American Economic Review*, March 1950, for a recent critical study of some of the implications of investment guaranties.

[6] Since nearly all the discussions to date have centered around *direct* investment in underdeveloped areas, it appears that this program will not in any case provide appreciable immediate relief for Europe's dollar difficulties. Indeed, it may actually serve to strengthen commercial relations between the underdeveloped areas and the United States at the expense of Europe. Some British sources have suggested that the Point Four Program might best be tied in with investments by European countries and chan-

The problems with respect to the technical assistance under the Point Four Program seem less difficult and the concept less debatable. This type of aid could help materially to increase productivity abroad. But it must not be forgotten that, while such assistance may in some cases be a necessary prelude to investment, much of it can have only very limited effects unless it is in fact accompanied or quickly followed by capital flow. The Administration is, however, taking the right approach in urging that technical assistance be on a cooperative basis and that at least part of the American help be extended through the international organizations. Such a procedure should lessen the charges that the United States is acting in an imperialistic fashion; in addition, other nations have much to contribute on such problems. Even though successful, the Government technical assistance program is limited in scope, for that which can be offered through these channels is by and large restricted to health and welfare, government administration, public utilities, and agricultural undertakings. Technical assistance in the industrial field is, apparently, not for government institutions to give.

Finally, some of the public statements as to plans under the Point Four Program give cause for fear that it may misdirect economic efforts in foreign countries, especially if it unduly encourages industrial development rather than increased efficiency in areas of comparative advantage held by the borrowing country. The major difficulties here lie in the feeling by many would-be borrowers that strategic considerations require industrialization and in the emotional affinity for urbanization and smoking chimneys.

C. EXCHANGE RATES, INTERNATIONAL RESERVES, AND IMPORT POLICY

Pressure on a nation's reserves is often the result of a multitude of factors, but it is immediately the consequence of an overvalued

---

neled through the "merchant bankers and issuing houses" of Europe (and the United States) who have extensive knowledge of and experience in underdeveloped countries. (See, for example, *The Economist,* March 11, 1950, pp. 546–7. See also, Mendershausen, H., "Future Foreign Financing," *The Review of Economics and Statistics,* November, 1949, for an analysis of this aspect, as well as others, of large scale American foreign investment.)

⌐exchange rate. To the extent that the United States pressed other nations to devalue in 1949, it was a move toward creating conditions which would permit a restoration of currency convertibility.⌐ There was also involved here an important change in United States post-war policy in that an attempt was made to restore to exchange rates something of their proper function under a multilateral system. It is to be remembered, however, that the 1949 devaluations, though large and extensive, were not alone sufficient to restore convertibility. They did not permit a removal of exchange controls and in most cases were based on the assumption of the continuance for at least two years of large financial aid from the United States. However, during the first two years of ERP, the deficits resulting from Europe's planned recovery programs (made in conjunction with ECA) in large measure dictated the amount of aid, while in preparing for the third year there was more of an attempt by ECA to set the amount of aid first and force a balance at that level through—among other things—exchange rate changes.

⌐   One of the very serious immediate deterrents to any wide-spread movement in the rest of the world toward freer trade and Lpayments policies is the low level of their international reserves. For the rest of the world, excluding Russia, these reserves at the end of 1949 were approximately the same as in 1938, but, in view of the very substantial rise in prices and in the value of world trade, most nations regarded their reserves as at a level which would not permit them to meet, without rigorous controls, even temporary disturbances in their balances of payments. The effect of inadequate *fonds de manoeuvre* is to reduce the volume of world trade, to make it more bilateral, and to warp its pattern.

⁷ It is a truism that any country *can* balance its international accounts and achieve currency convertibility if it leaves the determination of the exchange rate to free market forces. Such a balance may not, however, be "optimum" or desirable from one nation's viewpoint, especially if it can otherwise obtain grants from abroad. Nor is it necessarily a desirable condition if free market forces include the effects of speculation or fear of war and political instability. Finally, it is not a desirable balance if it forces structural adjustments on a nation at so rapid a rate as to cause widespread—rather than localized—unemployment and extreme deflation. This is only to say that the achievement of currency convertibility by exchange rate fluctuations alone is not desirable under present conditions and that many additional and supporting measures should be employed.

Although there were no indications during 1949 that the United States Government was prepared to regard this as a major policy problem,[8] some minor actions were taken which served to improve the reserve position of some countries.   For example, Belgium was given ECA aid in excess of its planned dollar deficit, and several other European countries were able to increase their reserves, in effect out of ECA aid.   The announced decision of Mr. Hoffman to distribute ECA assistance according to merit rather than need after the end of 1949 should, if carried out, also serve this end.   But the fact remains that, for the most part, the basis of United States assistance remained expansion of the assisted countries' imports and not an improvement in their reserve position.   It would no doubt be hard to obtain Congressional approval for using American aid to build up reserves abroad, but the strengthening of such reserves is a prerequisite to the adoption of the commercial and financial policies urged by the United States.

It is probably impossible to have a system of full multilateral trade so long as the pound sterling is inconvertible, and it is not likely that sterling will again be freely convertible so long as sterling balances of their 1949 size and distribution exist.   The United States did become increasingly concerned over these balances during the year.   In the September sterling-dollar area discussions, it was agreed that this was a subject requiring further study, but in the following months the United States Government officials reached no definite decisions and made no definite proposals—a lack of action which is a serious obstacle to the restoration of convertibility and multilateralism.[9]

[8] In early 1948, Secretary Snyder, in testifying on behalf of the NAC in support of the Marshall Plan, had foreseen a time when United States loans to replenish reserves might be desirable.

[9] It may be easy to overestimate the extent to which these balances are currently putting pressure on the United Kingdom balance of payments and hard currency reserves.   For example, as production increases in the countries holding such balances, protectionist considerations may militate against continued large withdrawals.   As these balances are shifted from nations such as India and Pakistan to countries such as Australia, the United Kingdom will probably find it at least much easier to delay liquidations.   Further, if, as seems likely, the United States assumes greater financial responsibility in Asia, the political necessity of the United Kingdom's supplying unrequited exports (made financially convenient by the existence of sterling balances) will be lessened.   Also, the September devaluations

Several other aspects of the particular problems of the sterling area were examined in the July and September meetings, but the specific measures agreed to were not of great quantitative importance. While there was at least tacit acceptance by the United States of sterling area administrative discrimination against United States exports, and in subsequent discussions regarding petroleum there was evidence that the American Government might be urging special treatment for a particular export, it appears that these deviations from our long-term policies were regarded as *temporary* or special exceptions. Against these contradictions in our foreign economic policy must be placed three major decisions arising from the discussions: First, the United States made it clear that other than purely temporary solutions for the sterling area problems must be found which would enable international trade and payments to develop on a multi-lateral basis. Second, additional unilateral financial aid was not regarded as the appropriate answer to a serious British crisis. And third, the United States recognized its responsibilities to expand imports.

Free convertibility of foreign currencies into dollars requires that the supply of dollars abroad be relatively large and that they be obtainable on other than especially onerous terms of trade. High United States tariffs, import embargoes, and burdensome customs formalities contributed importantly to the "dollar shortage" and to the resulting preference of individual foreign countries for bilateral arrangements and insistence on inconvertibility of their own currencies as a defense against depletion of their gold and dollar reserves. The general desirability of larger imports by the United States was widely acclaimed in both official and unofficial circles during 1949, and certain small steps were taken: the tariff reductions at Annecy, the extension and liberalization of the Trade Agreements Act, the encouragement by ECA of European exports to the United States, and minor reforms in customs administration. None of these represented major concessions, however, and the practice followed during the year of severely restricting by direct controls the imports of many agri-

---

made the conversion of the balances into hard currencies less desirable. Nonetheless, permitting unrestricted convertibility of these balances under present conditions would probably put intolerable pressure on the area's hard currency reserves.

cultural products, as well as shipping services, flew in the face of our overall policy. A program which seemed to promise much in the way of increasing current dollar earnings of the rest of the world was the stockpiling of strategic and critical materials by this country. Here again, however, a conflict developed be-tween certain domestic industries and the United States external economic policy, with the issue being resolved in favor of the former. On balance, it would appear that this country probably did follow policies in 1949 destined to increase imports, but the many protective measures adopted or continued (including very high tariff rates of many goods which might otherwise be imported and the "Buy American" regulations), the narrow margin by which the "peril points" were removed from the Reciprocal Trade Agreements Act in the Senate, the failure of Congress to consider the ITO Charter, and the subsidies on some agricultural exports plus the statutory requirements covering purchases of surplus agricultural products by ECA, indicated that the forces operating to prevent an adjustment of America to her international creditor position via increased imports were very potent indeed, despite repeated high-level policy proclamations to the contrary.

D. INTEGRATION

The major new American policy in 1949 was the urging by ECA of the formation *within Europe* " . . . of a single large market within which quantitative restrictions on the movement of goods, monetary barriers to the flow of payments and, eventually, all tariffs are permanently swept away."[1] This policy should be examined from several viewpoints. First, given existing military considerations, full employment policies, and the sharp differences in view as to the role of the state in the economic process, is the project politically feasible in the limited period of time which seems to be called for in the official ECA pronouncements? Second, is it desirable, from the viewpoint of Western Europe alone, as a movement toward international specialization in accordance with comparative costs thus raising productivity and closing the "dollar gap" without reducing standards of living?

[1] Address by Mr. Hoffman on October 31 to the OEEC Council, Paris (*New York Times*, November 1, 1949).

Third, is it compatible with the long-term foreign economic policy of the United States?

No attempt can be made here to assess the first of these, but that the obstacles are very great is obvious. With reference to the second, some questions can only be raised and no answers attempted since detailed and thorough studies of the European economies are required. In view of United States pressure for this policy, however, and the costs of implementing it, it is imperative that more adequate answers, than have yet been made public at least, be found to the following questions and that, in some overall measure, the replies be affirmative.[2]

First, are the various European economies, in important respects and degrees, now competitive *as a consequence of existing barriers*, so that the removal of restrictions will force a reallocation of resources toward complementarity, resulting in an increase in real income? (To the degree and extent that the economies are complementary, even with existing barriers, the removal of such restrictions may also result in some reallocation of resources and an increase in real income within Europe, but the more important effect of integration in this case would seem to be to extend the area of protection against outside competition.)

Second, are there large differences in unit costs of production as among similar protected industries in the various European countries so that great economies may be derived from unification?

[2] This is not intended to be an inclusive list of queries, but only those which seem most important and difficult. See Viner J., *The Customs Union Issue*, Carnegie Endowment for International Peace, New York, 1950, pp. 41–82. Although not directed to the specific problem of European integration, these pages include a rigorous analysis of many of the economic issues involved in such an integration. For recent critical discussions of several specific aspects of the question of integrating the European economies, see Williams, J. H., "The Marshall Plan Halfway," *Foreign Affairs*, April 1950; Haberler, G., "Economic Aspects of a European Union," *World Politics*, July 1949; Hawtrey, R. G., *Western European Union*, Royal Institute of International Affairs, London, 1949; Harrod, R. F., "European Union," *Lloyds Bank Review*, July 1948; Robertson, D. H., "Britain and European Recovery," *Lloyds Bank Review*, July 1949; Wallich, H. C. and Loud, F. V., "Intra-European Trade and European Integration," *Columbia Journal of International Affairs*, Winter 1950; and *European Recovery Programme, Second Report*, Organization for European Economic Cooperation, Paris, February 1950, pp. 217–46.

Third, will the "average" barriers on imports from the rest of the world be lower after integration than at present?

Fourth, will an expansion in European markets for individual plants, firms, and industries permit appreciable economies of large-scale production?

Fifth, with respect to Western Europe's position *vis a vis* the rest of the world, does its comparative advantage lie more in mass-produced goods than in those of "special quality, variety, and distinction of design"?

Sixth, given the full employment policies of many European countries, are they prepared to sacrifice security and stability of income for the larger real income resulting from greater international specialization?

Seventh, will a lowering of barriers within Europe alone result in structural readjustments bringing about a new *composition* of trade, thereby improving the overall balance of payments position of the European countries—instead of merely a shift to other European countries of the same export goods now going to extra-European markets, and so perhaps intensifying the "dollar shortage?"

Eighth, on a somewhat different level, will unification result in an invigoration of the spirit of competition, entrepreneurial initiative, and morale within Europe?

Ninth, if unification does tend toward increased competition and reallocation of resources, will facilities be at hand to prevent cartels from blocking such developments?

Finally, is integration *within Europe* the only, or even the most desirable, alternative to the continuance of the protection and compartmentalization of recent decades?

Lack of compatibility of the policy of European integration with the long-run foreign economic policy of the United States was suggested in January 1950[3] when the National Advisory Council entered reservations against the European payments union which was being pressed by ECA as an essential step in the

---

[3] There was an obvious inconsistency between the repeated United States objections to British imperial preferences and its urging the United Kingdom to grant preferential treatment to imports from Europe. This is not new, however, for the United States has often disapproved of preferential reductions of tariffs but approved of customs unions.

direction of economic unification. Objections on the policy level should, however, logically be directed against overall unification and not merely against the technique of the payments union. The main questions here are whether unification (erecting a large protected free-trade *area*) would involve discrimination against outside areas, and, if so, in such a way as to thwart future movements toward world non-discriminatory multilateral trade. Examination of this question is especially important since, if a regional integration is accomplished, it cannot be reversed readily; therefore it cannot be stated that, though there exists a contradiction in policy, integration is a "temporary but necessary expedient."[4]

There is no *a priori* basis on which to determine whether—or the extent to which—the unification of Europe will involve discrimination against the rest of the world, but it seems almost certain that some discrimination will result.[5] Thus, if, under a system of non-discriminatory protection or world free-trade, the direction of trade for a given commodity is the same as under a restricted free-trade area, then no discrimination is involved in a preferential lowering of barriers, and there may be a gain from larger trade. But there is nothing gained or lost as compared with a multilateral reduction of barriers. If the regional reduction of barriers results in a shift of source of supply for any given commodity from a domestic industry to another within the region, which would be a source of supply under universal free-trade or a multilateral reduction of restrictions, then again no discrimination is involved, and there is a gain resulting from international specialization. But the same trade-creating result could be obtained at no additional cost by a world-wide lowering of the walls against this commodity. If, however, the integration of Europe causes the source of supply of a given commodity to be diverted from a third country to one of the members, then discrimination is

[4] Discrimination which was probably of the nature of a temporary expedient was that given tacit approval by the United States against its imports when in July 1949 the sterling area reduced its dollar imports by 25 percent. Such transitional discrimination against United States exports to meet pressing current problems seems to be inevitable and does not, therefore, necessarily represent a basic conflict in United States policy.

[5] Indeed, unless it does there would seem to be little incentive for the European countries to welcome it.

involved. And, while the exporting country gains on this commodity, as compared with either non-discriminatory protection or universal free-trade, the importing country loses, as does the rest of the world.[6] The overall discriminatory effect of European integration will depend on how important the trade-diverting tendencies are, and no conclusions are possible without a careful examination and weighing of each case. In any event, the establishment of such discrimination may be considered appropriate by the European countries at present if it will help adjust the deficit *vis a vis* the United States, especially if they are not prepared to undertake the internal monetary and structural reforms necessary to eliminate this deficit. But by the same token it may perpetuate Europe as a high-cost area, effectively isolated from outside competition.

Even if European union did not involve discrimination against third countries, there still remains the question of whether such an integration advances the world to a position from which a more extensive reduction of barriers may be made easier. If integration increases the ability of Europe to compete in world markets and so relieves the pressure of the "dollar shortage," then it may make easier the subsequent adoption by that area of more liberal commercial and payments policies. But there are other considerations which operate to make an extension very difficult. First, vested interests are created within an area just as they are within the national economies, and the inclusion of more countries in the area later (eventually to encompass the world?) is likely to be just as difficult as obtaining the first agreement (especially if new entrants are economically important), since rather painful readjustments would be required. Second, prospective new entrants are not likely to find it as advantageous to join an existing union as one in the formative stage, for some of the opportunities which the union might have offered at the outset have already been filled by producers within the original union. Finally, it is not impossible that retaliation against the discriminatory effects, if there be any, of a restricted free-trade

[6] This conclusion with respect to gains and losses is not correct for the case (rare?) where the additional market given a member of a preferential trading area results, because of conditions of decreasing costs, in a unit cost below that at which the good could be produced abroad before the preferential area was established. See, Viner, *op. cit.*, p. 45.

area will induce the growth of new barriers to trade between a unified Europe and the rest of the world. It would seem necessary, therefore, that if the United States deems it desirable at this time to urge a European integration, that it at least make it clear, from the very beginning, that such unification is regarded as only a stepping stone to an economically unified world.

All this adds up to suggesting that in 1949 the United States preoccupation with the problems of Western Europe had the effect of diverting attention from the fact that the imbalance of trade was a world-wide problem, that it was not limited to Europe and the United States, and that even Europe's difficulties would be more adequately resolved for the long-run if the United States broadened and intensified its attack on the factors making for imbalance in the whole world, including those originating in the United States.

E. SUMMARY

A balance of the specific policies and activities during 1949 which advanced the general foreign economic policy of the United States of currency convertibility and non-discriminatory multilateral trade, as against those which obstructed the reaching of this goal, indicates that the balance tips toward the former. But the record is very mixed, and, if inaction in relevant areas is added to adverse action, the net effect of our policies was perhaps neutral or even unfavorable.

Important in the area of favorable activities were: the granting of aid so as to raise foreign productivities; using the aid directly and indirectly to reduce inflationary tendencies abroad; shifting of most aid from a credit to a grant basis; urging the rest of the world to devalue; reducing tariffs at Annecy; continuing the stockpiling of strategic and critical materials; actively encouraging European exports; starting to simplify customs procedures; making plans for expanded technical assistance; and encouraging private foreign investment by increased attention on investment treaties, tax conventions, and plans for investment guaranties. Mention should also be made of the efforts (not completely successful) to maintain a high level of employment and income within the United States. This was more important than any of the above factors, but it has not been discussed since it was deemed outside the scope of this survey.

VIII. CONCLUSIONS

Important aspects of our policies which were unfavorable to the achievement of the long-term economic goals included: the tying of loans and gifts to purchases in the United States; sponsoring and encouraging larger military programs abroad; expanding protection of United States agriculture and shipping; and increasing the reliance on domestic sources for stockpiling. An apparent tendency to focus attention on specific areas, with a failure, in some cases perhaps, to appreciate the world-wide nature of the problem, must also be listed in this adverse column, but the record was better in this connection in 1949 than in previous years. The favorable or unfavorable effects of American policy with respect to the economic unification of Europe cannot yet be determined, but there are grounds for suspecting that the outcome may not be favorable.

The major fields in which action by the United States seems called for but in which little or nothing was done included the high tariffs on many of those goods which might otherwise be imported, the sterling balances, and the international reserve position of the rest of the world.

INDEX

Lightning Source UK Ltd.
Milton Keynes UK
UKOW01f1043311017
311936UK00004B/273/P